Financial Services Marketing

Proven Techniques for Advertising Direct Mail and Telemarketing

Hartford Beitman

LIBERTY HALL
PRESS™

LIBERTY HALL PRESS books are published by LIBERTY HALL PRESS, an imprint of TAB BOOKS. Its trademark, consisting of the words "LIBERTY HALL PRESS" and the portrayal of Benjamin Franklin, is registered in the United States Patent and Trademark Office.

First Edition
First Printing

©1990 by TAB BOOKS
Printed in the United States of America

Library of Congress Cataloging-in-Publication Data

Beitman, Hartford.
    Financial services marketing : proven techniques for advertising, direct mail & telemarketing / by Hartford Beitman.
        p.   cm.
    Includes bibliographical references.
    ISBN 0-8306-8062-4
    1. Advertising—Financial services industry—United States.
I. Title.
HF6161.F46B45 1990
332.1'068'8—dc20   89-77257
                                                              CIP

TAB BOOKS offers software for sale.
For information and a catalog, please contact:
TAB Software Department
Blue Ridge Summit, PA 17294-0850

Questions regarding the content of this book
should be addressed to:
Reader Inquiry Branch
TAB BOOKS
Blue Ridge Summit, PA 17294-0214

Acquisitions Editor: David J. Conti
Book Editor: Shelley Chevalier
Production: Katherine Brown

Contents

Part III
Advertising

Part IV
Telemarketing

Part V
Combination Programs

Introduction

The late 1980s were not easy times for those selling financial services and products. The order and simplicity of earlier days were replaced by myriad markets, products, and packages. Competitive commission rates, slimmer payouts, roller coaster markets, and a proliferation of investment alternatives were the hallmarks of the day. Key events such as the market crash in 1987 and the dishonesty of some major investors and dealers tainted the public's perception of financial services and made the environment for marketing investments even more challenging.

The public's confusion over constantly changing tax rules governing their investments, the market's wild swings, and even the savings and loan crisis have made many investors turn away from the markets as investing decisions have become more difficult and often less profitable. One result is that people have sought alternative "safer" products and shied away from traditional investments such as stocks and bonds.

In addition, as their profitability shrank, many financial services firms have demanded ever-increasing performance from their salespeople, raising the threshold of expected sales while maintaining (or even reducing) payout rates. These forces have combined to put severe pressure on salespeople's income and have made it much more difficult to succeed at marketing financial products.

While some financial salespeople have been highly successful—one often hears about investment bankers making millions—the majority must work hard just to earn a decent living. So what can be done to build and maintain business in this difficult and highly competitive environment?

To compete effectively in the modern securities industry, financial services salespeople must become more aggressive. The techniques described in this book have been proven effective not only in the financial services business, but in most other industries as well. They work for products and for services—for nearly anything that can be sold.

The objective of this book is to help you gain a basic understanding of the business of marketing financial products and services. Special emphasis is focused on advertising, direct mail, and telephone sales and how you can make these devices work more effectively for you. These are the areas in which your skills development can be most rewarding, and these are the strategies you are most likely to use as direct mail, telemarketing, and advertising can effectively boost your customer base and sales volume. By reading and using the information contained in this book, you may help yourself survive, perhaps even prosper, in the competitive financial services industry.

This book has been designed for the smaller financial marketer. There are a wealth of textbooks that can help you sell if you have a $1 million ad budget and a staff of 60. For the individual salesperson, local office, or even small firm, however, available funding is often very limited and manpower scarce. In this book I have endeavored to present techniques and concepts useful on this level. While most of the information can be applied to nearly any marketing program, it is those with budgets measured in the thousands and tens of thousands of dollars that can most benefit from this manual.

Like any other skills, effective marketing methods must be learned. There are no "right ways" and there are no "wrong ways" to market and promote. No one can tell you exactly what to write or mail, which ad to run and where it should be placed, or what to say next that will produce specific results. But certain techniques and pointers should steer you toward more successful campaigns.

Marketing, whatever the form, is an imprecise science. Talk to three professional advertising people about your plan and they are sure to suggest at least three different "right" ways to accomplish your goals—and bill you accordingly! Nevertheless, there are some basic concepts that will help you avoid obvious, but often-made mistakes, like placing an ad in the national edition of a prominent business publication when you are registered to sell securities in only two states.

Industry averages, where quoted, are a reflection of much field experience. However, particular firms, products, and policies may deviate from these figures significantly. Payout rates, for example, are set by individual firms.

While every effort has been made to provide accurate information on the pricing and cost structure of various components of marketing, these figures are necessarily only guides and will vary from region to region, supplier to supplier, and even from job to job. Costs are also subject to inflationary pressures and other forces. Therefore, no guarantee can be made that they will accurately reflect the prices or costs in a specific marketing program.

You will want to do your own local research to determine how closely the examples cited herein accurately reflect your situation. Your own experiences will also be your best guide as to the true cost of leads and sales for the type of business you conduct and the marketing methods you choose to use.

While this is certainly a serious book about very serious subjects (marketing and finance), a little levity can go a long way to helping the materials hold, and even stimulate, the reader's interest. You will find, therefore, a number of humorous examples and illustrations throughout the text. Although primarily intended to demonstrate a technique, concept, or procedure, it is hoped that the humor will also produce a smile. The examples cited are based on real life situations. However, any resemblances to actual firms, products or individuals is purely coincidental and unintentional.

Advertising and direct marketing are by nature inexact. The most excellent plans and careful execution can go awry because of special circumstances or unknown events. While no assurances can be made that specific results or improvements will be achieved using the techniques or methods outlined in this book, experience has demonstrated that these concepts can significantly improve marketing results.

In the Beginning

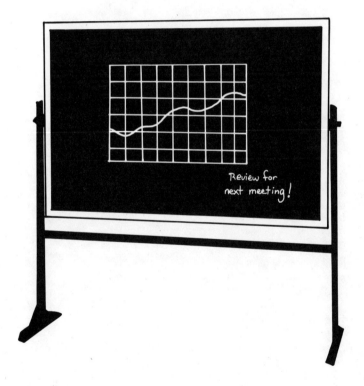

1

How Marketing Can Help You Produce More Business

TRADITIONALLY, INVESTMENTS AND FINANCIAL services such as insurance, accounting, retirement planning, and even banking have been sold on a personal basis. Salespeople cultivated a professional image and developed close relationships with their clients. Subtle marketing by entertaining a potential customer was the norm, while active promotions such as advertising and direct-mail marketing were not considered in keeping with the proper "professional" image. Much of this changed during the 1980s in the financial services industry, as well as in most other professions, particularly medicine and law.

Many services that were formerly viewed as specialized and requiring great skill are now often considered utilitarian commodities, purchased more on the basis of quality and cost, rather than loyalty or image. The rules of the game have been revised, creating opportunities for those who are willing to take advantage of them.

Not long ago a financial "advertisement" was typically just a tombstone ad announcing some deal that had been consummated (Fig. 1-1). Competitive pressures have now pushed most financial organizations into becoming active marketers of their products and services.

Effective marketing makes it possible to yield greater profits. Marketing is simply the means by which you inform potential customers of the product or service you offer. It is relatively easy to market financial services. You are doing it all the time. Each time you cold-call a prospect, mail to a list, ask for a referral, or just talk to someone about investments, you are marketing your services. There are many ways to do it—some effective, some not so effective.

For example, you could stand at a corner and yell "Securities available here!" You might also rent an airplane and sky-write "Best Brokers 555-1212," over the city.

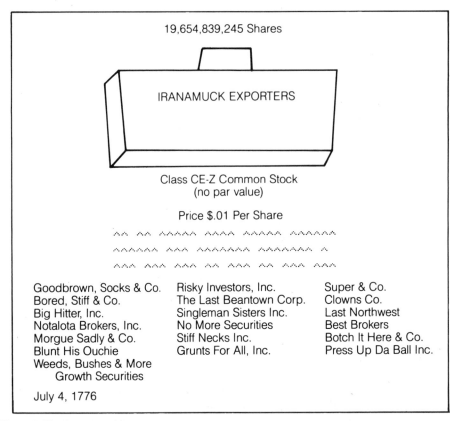

19,654,839,245 Shares

IRANAMUCK EXPORTERS

Class CE-Z Common Stock
(no par value)

Price $.01 Per Share

Goodbrown, Socks & Co.	Risky Investors, Inc.	Super & Co.
Bored, Stiff & Co.	The Last Beantown Corp.	Clowns Co.
Big Hitter, Inc.	Singleman Sisters Inc.	Last Northwest
Notalota Brokers, Inc.	No More Securities	Best Brokers
Morgue Sadly & Co.	Stiff Necks Inc.	Botch It Here & Co.
Blunt His Ouchie	Grunts For All, Inc.	Press Up Da Ball Inc.
Weeds, Bushes & More		
Growth Securities		

July 4, 1776

Fig. 1-1. Tombstone ad.

Throwing leaflets off your tenth-story balcony might also bring in an account or two! But few would claim that these techniques could build your client list effectively. Marketing is one thing; doing it effectively and nonoffensively is quite another.

Over the years, six primary techniques for marketing financial services have become popular in the financial community. These methods are listed in the order in which they are commonly used by individuals and small firms—one being the one used most often and six being the one least often used.

1. Cold-Calling and Telemarketing
2. Client Referrals
3. Direct-Mail Marketing
4. Advertising
5. Premiums and Specialties
6. Promotion

Although there are many variations to each of these types of activities, they represent the vast majority of marketing efforts. Each of these methods has benefits and drawbacks.

Cold-Calling and Telemarketing. Cold-calling develops an immediate line of communication, a two-way street, for those prospects who you reach successfully and who do not hang up. Therein lies the primary problem with cold-calling: to reach the viable prospects requires hours of dialing and potential frustration. And you must do the majority of the work yourself. Although some salespeople have tried using an assistant to make the initial call and screen the client, intending a follow-up call by the actual salesperson, most find that this process is no more productive than calling on their own and may even offend potential clients. The efforts needed to generate a solid lead and ultimately a new client can be enormous. So although cold-calling will produce positive results, the price is often higher than the salesperson wants to pay.

Marketing concepts can be applied to telephone solicitation activity, hence the term *telemarketing*. There are techniques that can enable you to select the right names to call, the correct time and place and the right words—all making the closing of sales and the adding of new clients to your files more likely.

Client Referrals. Referrals are an excellent way to obtain new customers. The chance of obtaining a sale on a referral is very high. However, very few salespeople can ever find enough of them. There always seems to be a limited number of happy customers willing to give referrals, and many of the potential referrals are often committed to another firm or salesperson. If you are able to find referrals, by all means take all you can get, but it is unlikely that you will be able to build your client base solely on the basis of referrals.

Direct-Mail Marketing. Direct mail is strictly a numbers game. If you tell enough people about your products and services, some are bound to buy. The key to direct-mail marketing, like cold-calling, is to reach the real customers before your sanity and funds are exhausted. Direct mail is a desirable method of prospecting for several reasons.

First, it is relatively inexpensive—you can often reach potential clients for half a dollar or so.

Second, you can easily get someone else to do the majority of the work for you. It is possible to hire other people or firms to prepare, mail and even fulfill requests from a direct-mail program.

Third, to a large degree you can select the audience you wish to reach. You also determine how large, or small, your mailing will be, thereby controlling its costs.

However, direct mail must be approached correctly to be effective. The prospectus on a zero coupon bond mailed to the graduating seniors at your state university might get you a couple of funny replies, but it probably will not help pay your next car installment.

Advertising. You play the probabilities when using advertising, just as you do using direct mail. You are betting that the investment you make in an ad campaign will pay off in new clients and sales.

Advertising does have a number of factors to recommend it. First, it is quite inexpensive to reach each member of the audience, very often you might pay just a few pennies. Smaller ads can be relatively inexpensive as well.

Second, you have very little work to do in placing an ad. The production of an ad and its placement are fairly straightforward and do not require an inordinate amount of your time.

Third, you do have some control over what audience sees or hears your ad, primarily through the selection of the particular media in which your ad will run.

However, the ability to choose your target audience is not as precise as with direct mail (everyone reading the publication could see it, everyone listening to the radio will hear it). Thus, with advertising, there will certainly be a lot of wasted coverage on unlikely prospects.

In addition, for a given expense level, an advertisement typically cannot include as much information about your offer as a direct-mail piece would be able to present. Since ads usually give fewer facts, they often offer added incentives or information brochures. These offers, hopefully, get the readers, listeners or viewers sufficiently motivated to inquire further (since they do not know most of the story). Advertising leads do tend to be more likely buyers however. And for sheer exposure to the most people, on a fixed budget, it is hard to beat advertising.

Premiums and Specialties. Specialty items and premiums are useful marketing devices used either on their own or in conjunction with one of the other promotional methods. Specialty items include pens imprinted with your name and phone number, imprinted coffee mugs, key rings, etc. They might also include special reports on emerging growth companies, research data on commodities, annuity calculator tables, and similar items.

Specialties are essentially *giveaways* that endear you to a potential customer. Every time the prospect uses your imprinted pen, they will be reminded of you. A premium is often a reward for actually doing business with you rather than an attempt to induce business. Premiums are generally more expensive "gifts" and are often tightly regulated as to their value and under what circumstances they may be used.

Specialties and, to some extent premiums, can be effective prospecting tools. The trick is to know what will appeal to your potential customers and not to end up being the supplier of pens to your office!

Promotions. Sponsorship of events such as a traveling museum exhibits, concerts, or sports like a baseball game can be very effective forms of promotion. These activities, however, tend to be relatively expensive and are rarely undertaken by an individual salesperson, or even a small firm. It may be possible to participate in some small way in programs like these, perhaps supplying the tickets or baseball caps with some sort of imprint on them.

We know the customers are out there. The problem is finding them. Obviously, the more potential clients you contact the more likely you are to find some that will deal with you. However, as we have seen, the effort you must expend to locate those new customers should not be greater than the benefits of adding them to your client list. Advertising, direct mail and telemarketing are popular means of contacting prospects because they have proven economical in generating new customers.

PLAYING THE ODDS

All marketing, including direct mail, advertising, and telephone sales is essentially an exercise in probabilities and risk. Spending money and effort exposing your products and services to more prospects should produce more inquiries and, hopefully, more sales. This concept can be represented by the following formula:

increased exposure = greater number of inquiries and sales

The key issue, as so often is the case, is striking a balance between the *cost* of these promotional programs and the potential *benefits* of the additional business that may result. Clearly, if you were to execute a marketing campaign involving the mailing of 100,000 letters to a list consisting of people who live in or near your metropolitan area, you would be bound to get at least a few new customers. But unless those were incredibly major new accounts, the payoff is unlikely to come anywhere close to the costs involved, and you would have wasted a lot of money and effort on that program. What you need is a cost-effective marketing system.

There are two elements to keep in mind when considering marketing programs, whatever form they may take (direct mail, advertising, telemarketing, etc.):

1. How many people will you be reaching?
2. How many might respond to your offer?

The ideal arrangement is to reach the *fewest* people (since it costs money and takes effort to reach people) and to achieve the *most* inquiries (since only inquiries can ultimately result in sales). The inescapable fact is that not every prospect you reach will reply and certainly no one you do not reach can respond no matter how much they might have been interested in your offer! Since you must contact some potential prospects in order to generate inquiries, you might as well target those with the most reasonable likelihood of being interested in your services. Selecting the right target audience should help produce sufficient responses and enough new business to more than cover the cost of the entire campaign—the cost to reach both those who do respond and those who do not.

You can quickly see that if you spend one dollar each to contact 100 potential clients, say by mailing them a nice brochure and letter, you will have a net outlay of $100. Since only a portion of those are likely to give you any business, you must recoup the expense of the program from those that end up buying. If you receive one order from the group, you need to make a profit of the full $100 on that individual in order to at least break even. If two people order, you need only make $50 on each to break even. If you were able to sell to five prospects, you would require a profit of just $20 each to offset the marketing costs. Clearly, the more customers you can obtain from a given promotional effort, the easier it will be to recoup and profit from the program.

While it would be nice if every program produced a huge profit by generating a large amount of immediate new business, this will rarely be the case. A promotional program need not be a big profit-maker from day one. If you open an account with an order, that is often only the beginning of an ongoing relationship. Every transaction thereafter from that new account will also be a benefit of your initial promotional campaign (Fig. 1-2).

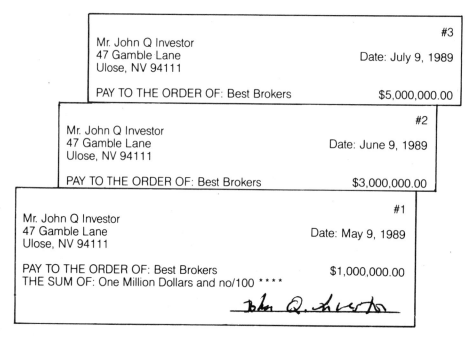

Your first order is likely to be just the beginning of a long series of activity from each new client!

Fig. 1-2. Subsequent business after the initial order.

Even if a program actually loses money initially, it can still be considered a success since you will have opened new accounts, which are likely to produce substantial future business.

ANALYZING MARKET RESULTS

To determine how well a marketing program performed, you need some benchmarks by which to measure it. It is valuable to evaluate your campaigns based upon certain criteria. Two very useful measurements in marketing analysis are: cost per lead, and cost per sale.

Cost per lead is the actual expense you paid to obtain the reply or the lead. It is calculated by dividing the cost of the mailing by the number of replies (leads). While it would be appropriate to include all costs used to produce the lead—postage, materials, labor, etc., adjustments should be made for your initial production expenses that will not be incurred again, such as artwork costs.

Assume, for example, that you include the full cost of artwork and any other one-time (fixed) payments in the total expenses of the first mailing you make. Subsequently you use the same artwork for mailing number two and perhaps for mailing number three. Although the second and third mailings create other additional (variable) costs such as more envelopes and postage, they probably do not require any new artwork expenses since you are reusing the same materials already prepared for the first mailing.

Thus, if you compared the cost per lead of mailing number one, which included those fixed artwork costs, with the cost per lead of the other two mailings which do not include the fixed expenses, you would most likely find that the costs of mailing number one were overstated and the costs of the other mailings were understated. This would provide a false basis for comparing the results and give misleading conclusions as to the relative success of the various efforts.

While this may seem like a minor point, the error can be quite significant. Often, the relative comparisons between marketing programs will be quite close, varying by perhaps just a few cents to a dime or so per inquiry or per sale, and the error created by including nonrecurring costs can often be larger than that.

Ideally, if you knew exactly how many times the artwork in this example would be used, you could prorate the costs among the various mailings. Since it is hard to predict the usage, a practical solution is to calculate the cost per lead (and as you will see, cost per sale as well) by not including those nonrecurring costs. While this will tend to understate the true cost per lead slightly, at least it will provide a fair comparison among programs.

Comparing the performance of various programs is the basis of perfecting marketing skills. It is only through the trial and error of different approaches that you will be able to tell what works for you and what does not. So fair and objective comparisons are essential to successful marketing.

Cost per sale is a concept similar to cost per lead. It is calculated by dividing the total expense figure, as determined in the previous calculation, by the number of sales obtained. The same discussion about including only variable costs in the expense side of the cost per lead calculation applies to the formula for cost per sale as well. Since not every lead will convert into a sale, cost per sale will always be higher than cost per lead, usually by a very large amount (Fig. 1-3).

\$20 on average

Cost Per Lead

\$285 on average

Cost Per Sale

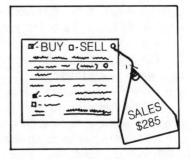

Cost per sale will always exceed cost per lead since not every prospect will become a customer. The cost differential will typically be quite large.

Fig. 1-3. Costs per sale will always be higher than cost per lead.

The calculations for cost per lead, cost per sale, and their relationship can be summarized in the following formulas:

$$cost\ per\ lead\ =\ variable\ expenses/total\ number\ of\ leads\ received$$

$$cost\ per\ sale\ =\ variable\ expenses/total\ number\ of\ sales\ received$$

$$cost\ per\ sale\ >\ cost\ per\ lead$$

Suppose your marketing campaign consists of two 1000 count mailings. The typesetting and artwork cost you $100 and your printing, folding, and stuffing add another $400 in expenses. Thus your mailing pieces cost $.25 each ($500/2000 pieces). If you mail first class, you will probably spend another $.25 per piece, unless your package is very heavy or you use a discounted mailing rate. So your cost per piece would be $.50 and your cost for the entire mailing would come to $1000.

Assume you receive 21 replies from the first mailing and 19 replies from the second mailing. The first one would yield a 2.1% response rate, (21 replies divided by 1000 mailed), while the second would give you a 1.9% response rate.

Your cost per lead for the first mailing should be calculated as follows: $1000 total less $100 for artwork, divided by the two mailings results in $450 being spent on each mailing, not including fixed costs. Now take the $450 and divide by the 21 replies from the first mailing to get a cost per lead of $21.43.

In the second mailing you had the same variable costs divided by just 19 leads, yielding a cost per lead of $23.68. It makes sense that mailing number two should have a higher cost per lead since it was not as successful in generating leads as mailing number one (19 leads versus 21 leads).

If you had included the artwork costs, the first mailing would have "cost" a total of $550 ($450 plus the $100 artwork expense) and given you a cost per lead of about $26, which would have compared very unfavorably with the second mailing's cost of about $24 per lead.

The true cost per lead, knowing that the artwork will be used in exactly two mailings, would be the total costs of the two programs, $1000, divided by the 40 total leads you received, or a cost per lead of $25. While disregarding the artwork costs does slightly understate the true cost per lead, the alternative, when more than one campaign is contemplated, is to unfairly compare the efforts. Additional mailings using the same artwork would again be misleading if the artwork costs were not excluded.

If you successfully open accounts for four of the 40 total leads (two sales from each mailing) by selling them some securities, you would have closed 10% of the inquiries (a rather high rate, but convenient for this example). Your cost per sale would be $225 ($900 variable costs divided by the four sales). Cost per sale for each mailing would also be $225, calculated by dividing the variable costs of $450 per mailing by the two sales produced by each of the mailings. Notice that the cost per sale of mailing number two was the same as for mailing number one, despite the fact that cost per lead for mailing number two was actually more! Apparently, while the leads from the second mailing were more expensive, they were more likely to convert into a sale, resulting in two sales from just 19 leads as opposed to two sales from the 21 leads in the first mailing.

Tip: Remember, the true measure of a successful campaign will be your cost per sale and, as you will see, profitability. It does not matter how cheap leads may be, if they do not end up buying, they are worthless. Conversely, do not be overly concerned how expensive leads might be if they are of high enough quality to make your cost per sale profitable. While cost per lead is a useful measuring tool, cost per sale really makes the difference.

Profitability Analysis

To determine the benefits of any marketing effort, you must first calculate what was spent and then what was, or is expected to be, earned from the campaign.

As you have seen, with some adjustment, the cost side of the analysis is fairly straightforward. Since the income stream from a marketing program can come in over a long period of time, indeed even the linkage between a program and its benefits can be unclear, the income from a program can be a little harder to measure.

While the cost per lead for financial services and products varies significantly, a fair estimate for average quality leads would be in the $20 range. Some leads might cost as little as one dollar or as much as $100, but by and large your typical campaign should end up costing around $20 per lead generated. With practice, you might be able to lower the cost per lead figure by a few dollars, but that will take time.

Experienced financial services salespeople say they can close approximately 7% of decent leads. Which implies that the average cost per sale is about $285 ($20 estimated cost per lead divided by the 7% average closing rate). You would, therefore, need to pay for about 14 leads at $20 each to get one sale on average.

To at least break even on the efforts, you would need to generate at least the cost of the sale in net commissions, assuming you are personally paying the marketing costs to generate the sale. Assuming your experience with marketing programs will be fairly typical, your costs to generate a sale should run about $285. This implies that you need to generate about $28,500 in trade volume, assuming a 1% average payout to you, to cover the sale's cost (1% × $28,500 = $285). Unless you can average more than $285, or whatever your actual costs might be, in commissions over a reasonable period of time for each new account from your marketing programs, it would be foolish to spend very much on these efforts.

The financial industry continues to promote heavily, increasing its marketing expenditures regularly, so it can be reasonably assumed that its marketing results are at least marginally profitable. With a little practice, you can most likely achieve results that will make your own marketing programs worthwhile. Let us see how that is possible.

The factors that affect how much is made or lost on a promotional campaign include:

- Cost per sale
- Size of sale(s) made to new accounts
- Net commissions earned

Notice that cost per lead is not listed here since it does not really determine the program's profitability.

Keep in mind that for every extra dollar you pour into a program, you need to earn it back before you start making a profit. Therefore, one goal should be to keep your cost per sale as low as practical, which means less must be earned to recoup and profit from the program. In fact, costs are the only component here that you really can control. You cannot (generally) dictate how much business a new client may give you, nor how much you will earn from the transactions. The less you have invested in the lead when you close the sale, the easier it is to profit.

Cost per sale is, in turn, determined by the expenses of running the campaign, the response rates achieved (number of leads) and conversion rates (number of leads converted into sales). Here you can affect each component to a large degree. The expenses of the campaign are, of course, determined by you. You decide what the budget will be, and how much of it will go for the various parts of the campaign.

The response level and closing rates are also fairly dependent upon your actions. A superior campaign will draw more and better leads, that is, leads that are easier to convert into sales.

Later chapters of this book will describe techniques which will help you keep your costs down and your sales up. For the moment, assume that you can do at least as well as the averages indicated here. An example will demonstrate how marketing can be quite profitable.

ONE SALESMAN'S MARKETING SYSTEM

Joe, a salesperson in the Miami office of a major brokerage firm, has developed a campaign of advertising and direct mail. Joe mails weekly and takes out a small ad in the local paper about once a month. He says leads cost about $21 each, a little more than average, and he has a closing rate of 8%, also a little above average. Since leads cost him $21 each, he is paying about $263 for each new account produced from a lead ($21 per lead divided by the 8% closing rate).

Joe says he usually sells $10,000 worth of securities on the first trade and another $20,000 on the second trade. Subsequent business typically brings him another $30,000 to $50,000 in volume over the next six to 12 months. He hasn't kept track of additional business beyond that, but believes that much more comes in from these now established accounts.

Joe estimates his net payout to be about 1% on average. So he earns $100 on the first $10,000 trade and about $200 on the second $20,000 trade. Another $300 to $500 is made on subsequent trades. On average, therefore, a new account produces a total of $600 to $800 in proceeds after roughly the first six months that the account is open.

Since the average new account produced by a lead cost Joe about $263 in this example, he appears to be profiting at least modestly on all parts of his marketing programs and earning a high return on many of them. And he has acquired quite a few new accounts which should continue to generate additional income over time.

It's easy to see how programs like Joe's can be very beneficial. While he did not share the amount of income he earns from this program, we can make a reasonable estimate.

Assume his weekly mailings include about 100 pieces. He did not mention having any assistance, so it would not be likely that he could do more than about 20 letters a day continuously on his own. Therefore, in the course of a year he probably mails in the vicinity of 5000 pieces. If he gets a 2% response rate, he has 100 leads, about two per week.

His monthly ad is a little more difficult to judge, but we will guess it costs Joe about $200 for each run. At $21 per lead, his average cost, he must get about ten leads a month from the ads, or nearly 120 a year from this activity. Therefore, Joe probably receives 220 total leads per year, 100 from the mailings and 120 from the ads. Since he claims to close 8% of his leads, he probably ends up with about 18 new clients. His programs apparently cost him in the vicinity of $4600 annually (220 leads times $21 apiece).

According to Joe, he nets $600 to $800 per new account after about six months. That suggests that his 18 new customers have produced over $10,000 in income from their dealings with him thus far. And it is reasonable to expect most to continue adding to his volume. We can reasonably conclude that he has more than doubled his $4600 estimated investment in the marketing programs and the money continues rolling in! While we have had to guess at many of the figures in Joe's program, and those estimates may be off by a fair amount, we can see that in all likelihood he is doing quite well from this activity.

Building new accounts economically is what marketing is all about. The concepts and techniques presented in this book will help you maximize the effectiveness of your promotional dollar and permit you to earn more by marketing wisely.

Direct Mail

2

A Review of Direct-Mail Marketing

WE WILL BEGIN our discussion with a review of basic direct mail and then explore some important aspects that can make it particularly useful in financial marketing. Direct mail is the use of printed materials, generally mailed or physically delivered by other means, to prospects in an effort to solicit their business. Direct mail can take many forms, sizes and shapes, but the vast majority of direct-mail marketing programs have four basic components in common. These are:

1. A clearly defined target audience of prospects selected by you, typically a compiled or purchased mailing list.
2. An outgoing promotional package which conveys the offer to the prospects, primarily through literature, samples, etc.
3. A motivator or other technique to spur response, often an incentive such as a free offer, etc.
4. A response vehicle: a coupon, prepaid reply card, telephone number, or an address to which to write, enabling the prospect to inform you of his interest in your offer.

TARGET AUDIENCES

The target audience will most likely be selected through a specialized mailing list that can be rented for a fee. It is also possible to compile your own mailing list from a phone book, directory, etc. Whatever the source of names for your target audience, you will generally control who will receive the promotional piece. Of course, your direct-mail package might be passed along to another party, but for the most part it does not reach anyone you have not specifically selected.

The fact that you reach primarily only those you have chosen to reach gives you tremendous control. You can select your audience by geography—perhaps just those in your sales territory; by their profession—only lawyers for example; by investment experience—only those who have previously purchased mutual funds; or by a combination of these and other criteria. The possibilities are endless. Obviously, getting your message to a receptive audience can make the difference between a profitable campaign and an unsuccessful one. As you will see, proper audience selection is a key to superior response rates.

THE DIRECT-MAIL PACKAGE

There are many different physical forms of direct mail. The most common would be an envelope containing information about your offer. Another possibility might be a "two-way" mailing card. This is basically two postal cards attached back to back, one providing the outgoing address and message and the other providing a means of responding. It is often used to keep costs down. You might also consider sending a single post card containing just minimal information about your offer. The card might request that they call you or write to you for additional facts. There are other formats of card mailers as well. Figure 2-1 shows some typical mailer formats.

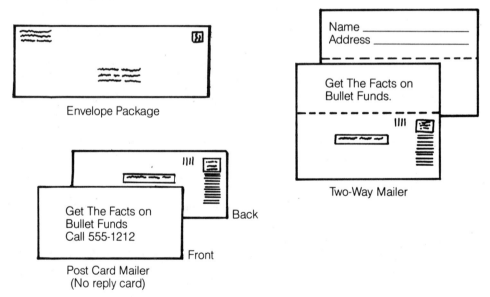

Fig. 2-1. Card mailers and envelope packages.

A direct-mail package does not necessarily have to be printed materials. You could potentially send out an audio cassette explaining your services and requesting a response. You might even use a video tape now that short blank tapes cost just a few dollars. Quite a few marketers have used thin plastic "records" which could be played on a phonograph.

While these materials are all legitimate marketing methods, they tend to be much more expensive than printed matter and have not been shown to be particularly effective. They might be employed in your fulfillment materials, however, where the required quantities are much smaller.

OPENING THE PACKAGE

The most important initial step to accomplish is enticing the prospect to open and review your mailing. If they do not open it there is no chance they will respond. Most people look at their mail quickly and take only a few seconds to decide if a piece is worth saving. If it is not tossed in the trash, they must make an evaluative judgment about what to do with it next. Three possible actions include:

1. If they think it is important they will probably open and read it immediately.
2. If it just appears interesting they might save it in their reading material file.
3. It does not appear to apply to them, but they think it might be of interest to a friend or associate, so they pass it along to them.

To help ensure that your package is opened and reviewed, it should look good and prompt interest. Obviously, sending the mailing to well-qualified prospects is a major step in the process. If you can personalize the package, at least by using the prospect's name, that will help. Letters to "occupant" or "The Investor At:" will not do much to pique interest.

Using postage stamps can often make a better impression than a postage meter or a bulk imprint. And your return address and logo will build confidence and raise the specter of potential benefits waiting inside the package. You might even select an unusual package, like a gift-wrapped box, which certainly will get the prospects' attention, but at a significant cost.

Whatever form of direct mail you select, the package should attract the prospect's interest and encourage them to open it and review your offer. The appearance of your mailing should be different from other mail so that it does not seem to be just more "junk mail." A recent trend has been to send direct mail by an "express mail service," or to give it a "telegram" look. The majority of people assume something sent this way must be important and they tend to give it top priority in their mail processing. While this idea does have its merits, the cost can be significantly higher than ordinary direct mail. Unless a very large increase in response levels can be achieved, this is rarely worth the extra cost.

A good mailing should include something to motivate the prospects to act on your offer. While you are probably promoting an excellent product or service truly needed by the prospect, that is often not enough to get many potential customers to reply. Something that really entices them to respond is usually needed. It may be a free offer or a special bonus to those who do respond. Or it may be additional information prospects might require. In one way or another, the prospects should feel that they can benefit by responding to your offer. In many cases a limited-time offer can help push the prospect toward responding when they might otherwise postpone action, or not reply at all.

Finally, the prospects must have a way to respond. A postage-paid reply envelope, postal card, or telephone number are the most common response vehicles. The easier it is for the prospects to reply, the better the chance that they will do so. The more work they must do to respond—i.e., addressing an envelope, paying postage, or visiting your office—the less likely they will be to take action. If prospects need only check a box or two and drop a card in the mail, the greater the probability that you will get them to reply. Providing more than one way to reply, in most circumstances, can be advantageous and permit the maximum number of prospects to reply in the manner they prefer.

In other cases, however, it can be beneficial to make the potential client exert some effort so you can screen out those who are simply curious. Occasionally a mailing contains no response vehicle, only information. This sets up the prospect for a sales call or it might motivate the prospect to try to contact you. Providing no response vehicle can be an effective marketing technique, but it does force you to follow up on nearly every prospect on your list rather than just those who responded.

As shown in Fig. 2-2, a typical direct-mail package would, therefore, consist of an outgoing envelope in which the package is sent, a letter describing the offer, another enclosure with additional information or a particular offer, and a reply card or envelope enabling the prospect to respond.

A direct-mail package is not generally designed to actually make a sale, but only to whet a prospect's appetite for more information. The materials sent in the initial mailing usually include only a brief description of the opportunity and the offer would typically be for additional information, often including a prospectus or other in-depth materials. If the prospect requests the new materials, they would be sent the appropriate information and then followed up with a telephone call. The pattern of contact is illustrated in Fig. 2-3.

Although there are many variations on this type of direct-mail program, essentially you are trying to elicit a response at minimal cost, and create a reason to make personal contact with the prospect. We will explore many techniques and variations to optimize responses in later chapters.

DIRECT-MAIL COSTS

Like all marketing, there are costs associated with a direct-mail program. The charges for various items needed for a mailing have all been rising rapidly in recent years. This makes it even more critical that direct mail be highly productive and that you get the most for each dollar spent. The expenses for a program fall into four primary categories:

1. List rental or compilation expenses
2. Postage or other means of delivery
3. Materials (envelopes, literature, reply cards, etc.)
4. Labor (folding, stuffing, sealing, addressing, etc.)

Whether you rent a list or compile one yourself, there is likely to be some expense in procuring the names, although probably less if you compile your own. Renting a list might cost in the vicinity of $60 per 1000 names, for a single use. If you create a list, you might have to pay for a directory from which names are obtained, or you may pay someone to type names from a phone book, etc. In addition to the basic list rental, you are

BULLET TAX FREE FUND

A TARGETED APPROACH
TO TAX FREE INVESTING.

Key Benefits:
- High tax-free return, currently 26%
- A high level of risk for those willing to take chances
- Convenient payments every 69 days
- Not a shell game
- Carefully managed by pros who are quick on the trigger

If this fund sounds like it is on the mark for you, shoot the reply card back for more information. Or call: 800-555-1212.

Information Enclosure

Please send me complete information on Bullet Tax-Free Funds.

NAME _____

ADDRESS _____

CITY _____ STATE _____ ZIP _____

Please send me other investment information on: _____

RETURN THIS POSTAGE PAID CARD FOR YOUR FREE INFORMATION KIT.

BB Best Brokers, Inc.

Reply Card

BB Best Brokers, Inc.

48 Kenilworth Terrace, Kenilworth, IA 60048

June 11, 1996

Mr. and Mrs. Roll D. Dice
1601 Financial Way
Snakeeyes, ID 41600

Dear Mr. and Mrs. Dice:

As one of your Newcomer sponsors, I want to welcome you to the Snakeeyes area.

I have had the pleasure of helping many area residents with their financial needs. Best Brokers is the number one name in financial services in the Snakeeyes area. We've been here since 1776.

Best Brokers is a full service firm with discounted commissions. We can save you up to 99% off the regular fixed commissions by having you act as your own floor broker. We also provide complete insurance services through our "Protection" arm.

If you would like to discuss your investment needs, or just talk about our beautiful area of the country, use the handy postage paid reply card, or give me a call.

Again, I would like to welcome you to Snakeeyes.

Sincerely,

Douglass Flywheel, XXIV

Douglass Flywheel, XXIV
18th Vice President

P.S.   Our special of the week is the 26% Tax Free Bullet Fund. For more information call me or return the enclosed card. The brochure included with this letter gives some basic facts on this "investment."

Encl: Brochure and reply card

Sales Letter

Fig. 2-2. **Typical promotional package.**

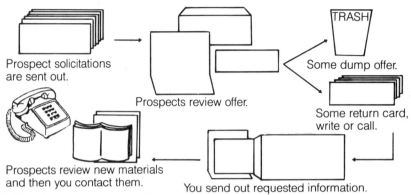

Prospect solicitations are sent out.

Prospects review offer.

Some dump offer.

TRASH

Some return card, write or call.

Prospects review new materials and then you contact them.

You send out requested information.

Fig. 2-3. Direct-mail program flowchart.

bound to run up a few additional costs related to the way the names are ordered in the list and how the list is delivered.

For example a *ZIP code* order, useful for reducing postage costs, will typically add another $5 per 1000 names. As a result, you should estimate your cost per name at somewhat over $.06 perhaps $.08 each to play it safe.

A significant direct-mail expense will be postage. If you send out a large number of relatively light-weight mailers, you will probably qualify for special mail rates which can be dramatically lower than regular postal rates. See the chapter on *Postal Services, Rates and Regulations*, or contact your local post office for current rates and requirements.

Sometimes, especially on smaller direct-mail programs, it is worth paying for regular first-class postage. This makes it less obvious to the recipient that they have received part of a mass mailing and usually gets the letter to them sooner as well. A first-class letter can reach a recipient several days or a week prior to one sent using bulk rates. In programs where time is critical, you simply may not be able to use the slower means of delivery.

For example, if a new investment fund is going to be released on May 17 and you wish to inform potential customers about its availability a week prior to that date, it may be too risky to depend on slower bulk mail to get your notice there on time.

When estimating the costs for postage, figure $.25 each unless you plan to use special postal rates, in which case the cost might be closer to $.17 each.

The cost of the actual direct-mail package materials vary greatly depending on quality, quantity, and other production factors. If you are printing 100 letters, your total cost will not be much less than if you were printing 1000 because the expense of setting up a print run can be hefty while the actual printing is fairly inexpensive. As the quantity increases significantly, each piece will be cheaper, but the total cost will, of course, rise.

If you are likely to do another mailing in the near future using the same materials, you might consider printing a larger quantity and saving it for the next program. You must, however, balance the advantage of lowering your cost per printed piece against the risk of wasting the additional printing if it is not used or if the information contained in it changes.

If you plan to print an extra quantity for future use, do not include a date or other indication of when it was first printed. A code to help you identify what these materials are would be acceptable.

Tip: If you cannot justify printing extra quantities, at least save the printer's negative and/or plates from the first run. This will eliminate the cost of that preparation on the next printing.

Printed letters might cost anywhere from a few cents each up to perhaps $.10 or $.15 depending upon the specifics of the job. For example, a two-color run with your signature printed in blue and the letter in black on high-quality paper will cost you much more, probably more than twice as much as a one-color job on cheaper paper. Your local printer or in-house print shop, can give you more precise quotes for your needs. For estimating purposes you might use $.04 each as an average which is roughly the cost to produce these items in limited quantities of 1000 or so.

The insert describing your offer (if you use one) will also vary significantly in cost. Often you will be using materials provided to you by your firm or an outside investment packaging firm, in which case this item might not cost you anything. If you have to produce your own information, you will probably be limited to a fairly simple flyer since the cost to produce a slick, multicolored brochure would be prohibitive in quantities of much less than 5000. For estimating purposes you could use an average figure of about $.10 each, if you have to make your own flyer and the quantity is about 1000.

The envelope will cost between $.01 and $.03, but you would most likely use your firm's envelopes and they probably cost you nothing. If you must supply your own, estimate $.03 in smaller quantities.

The reply card or envelope and form will add another $.05 or so to your costs in quantities of about 1000. This, of course, does not include reply postage for those who do respond, which will run roughly $.40, but that will total a small amount since it only affects actual responses.

The labor of actually assembling the packages and mailing them can be tedious, but usually it is not that expensive. To do the mailing, you might enlist the help of your spouse and children, working over a weekend stuffing envelopes. Or you could have a mailing house prepare and mail it for you at roughly $.10 per package, provided you have enough total pieces to make it worth their while to take on the job. If you have 25 pieces, it is unlikely that a provider of mailing services would be interested in your project, even at $1.00 each! But, if you wish to mail to 1000 names, they might be glad to do it all for $100.

You might also be able to have the mailing services vendor sort the packages to qualify for discounted mail rates that could save you enough to offset a large portion of their fee. If the volumes you want them to handle are significantly larger than the ones mentioned here, you can probably negotiate a much more favorable price. In general, figure about $.10 each to get the assembly done on a volume of 1000 or so.

The various costs and averages for a direct-mail program are reviewed in Table 2-1.

These figures suggest that you can expect to spend between $360 and $800 to reach 1000 prospects via direct mail, with $600 being the expected average. If you were selling products that cost just a few dollars, it would be very hard to justify that level of expense. But since your typical order probably involves tens of thousands of dollars, if not more, the cost of direct mail can easily be justified if you can generate enough business to offset those expenses.

You will have additional expenses for those prospects who do indeed respond. These costs include the reply postage from the prospect (if you use postage-paid cards

Table 2-1. Typical Direct-Mail Costs.

Expense Item		(In cents)	
	Low End*	Average	High End**
List rental	6	8	10
Postage	17	22	25
Materials			
Envelope	0	2	3
Letter	3	4	6
Insert	0	7	10
Reply Card	4	5	7
Total Materials	7	18	26
Labor	5	10	15
Total Estimated Package Costs	35	58	76
Fulfillment Costs	1	2	4
Total Estimated Costs	36	60	80 cents each

Notes: *Low end of estimates reflect items supplied at no charge, high volume discounts and better mailing rates.

**High end of estimates reflect cost of all items used, minimum fees and low volume usage.

or envelopes), and the mailing of the fulfillment materials—usually a prospectus and other literature. The postage costs here will depend on how you handle inquiries and what you send them. If you use a postal reply permit number for your incoming responses and minimize the weight of the fulfillment package, you can probably keep these costs to about $1.00 or so per lead.

However, a lead is valuable, so do not try to skimp on the quality of your fulfillment package. You will have already invested perhaps $20 in each lead, reflecting the total costs of your campaign to the number of responses (cost per lead), so another dollar is a small price to pay to keep the prospect on track.

Financial services salespeople typically get about a 2% response rate to direct-mail programs. Amortizing the added dollar in fulfillment costs over the number of prospects required to generate a lead, you can calculate an average added cost per prospect of $.02 ($1 × 2%). In other words, if you mailed 100 letters and got two replies, you would then spend $2 on fulfillment ($1 each). The extra $2 translated into an extra $.02 for each of the 100 original prospects.

DIRECT-MAIL ALTERNATIVES

Although there are many variations on the basic direct-mail program just outlined, three specific approaches are worth considering for the marketing of financial products and services.

Card Packs

Group mailings consist of a package of various solicitations from a number of sources. These packages are often called card packs because they are essentially a package of information cards. For example, your mailer might be included with 40 different offers—perhaps others are selling attaché cases, desks, or printing services, etc. The usual restrictions require no directly competitive offers in the same package. That protects you against another securities salesperson making a competitive offer in the same mailing. If you use a card pack, be sure to check if this limitation is in effect.

The primary benefits of mailings can be summarized as follows:

1. Cost savings
2. Access to attractive markets

Since many offers go in the same package, the cost for you to reach each individual should be considerably less than the $.58 we calculated previously for an average direct-mail campaign. The cost can be as low as a nickel or less per prospect. You are also able to reach exclusive target audiences that these services have compiled. Further, their audiences often have requested the mailing—so the odds of the prospects reading the enclosures are pretty good.

For many years card mailers were considered unsophisticated and inappropriate for the marketing of financial products and services. In recent years, partly driven by the cost spiral of conventional direct mail, card packs have become quite acceptable.

Despite the apparent advantages group mailings can offer, they are not always the best choice when marketing financial services. While it is acceptable to sell tools, furniture, and soap with flashy cards in "special offer" packages, not all prospects will look with favor upon a salesperson who markets securities the way kitchen appliances are sold.

Some of these group programs are devoted solely to financial products, so insurance, financial planning, accounting services, and home value appraisals might be lumped together. While there may be some competitive overlap, this grouping will most likely be more appropriate for your purposes. Other group efforts focus on upscale products, like designer items or exotic cars, and an offer for investment opportunities could fit nicely into those programs as well. Card packs are usually inexpensive enough to be worth a test if they look interesting. Figure 2-4 shows a typical group mailing.

Take-Ones

"Take-one" mailers are the second major variation on direct mail. Instead of sending a promotional package to a selected list, the materials are placed in a special stand and the public is encouraged to take one if interested. Take-one mailers are commonly found in taxi cabs, grocery stores, and convention halls. A postage-paid card is typically completed and returned by the prospect if he is interested.

This form of promotion is attractive primarily because it is inexpensive. You completely eliminate the outgoing postage in return for a nominal fee for use of the location

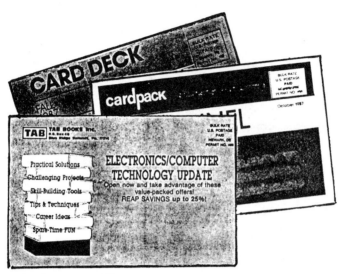

Fig. 2-4. Example of a group mailing.

for the stand. Finding a location appropriate to attract financial services clients can be a major problem often encountered with the use of take-one mailers. Many investors would be hard pressed to entrust their money to a salesperson discovered between the potatoes and the carrots at the local grocery. There are many locations where this approach can work well, such as at a financial show or seminar that tends to draw a highly qualified group of prospects as participants and where offers relating to financial products are more or less expected.

Another problem with the use of take-one stands is that it is often associated with the marketing of consumer products and other relatively utilitarian and inexpensive items. The image conveyed by this method is somewhat contrary to the traditional personal and professional marketing approaches used in the financial services industry. On the other hand, many means of offering services have become more acceptable today, and the take-one stand is certainly not an unacceptable method of marketing. Caution is probably the best advice one can give when considering this concept. This form of promotion is usually inexpensive enough to test if a situation arises where it looks like it may be worthwhile. Figure 2-5 shows a typical ''Take-One'' display.

Statement Stuffers

Statement stuffers are the third direct-mail variation worth considering. Essentially a take-one or card mailer, these promotional devices ride along with some other mailing (most often a monthly customer statement). The inserts are structured to make a brief pitch and provide a means to request further information, usually in the form of a reply card.

Statement inserts are a very inexpensive way to generate potential interest. You will typically have no outgoing postage cost, as long as the insert does not push the weight of

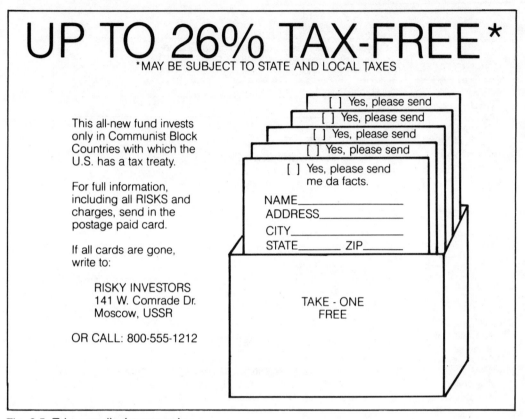

Fig. 2-5. Take-one display example.

the carrier package into the next postal bracket. The card itself might cost $.05, or far less if very large quantities are printed.

Stuffers can be used effectively in brokerage statements, monthly bank statements, insurance billings, etc. This is a low-cost, low-risk approach to marketing. Figure 2-6 shows a typical statement insert.

In addition to creating your own mailers, you will quite often be offered preprinted direct mailers. These items are usually provided by your firm or an outside investment packager in an effort to encourage you to promote a particular product.

Mailers Provided By Others

Mailers provided by someone else may cost you little or nothing—they often will even imprint your name and address on the reply card, etc. You will usually, however, have to pay the postage costs yourself. Since the mailer probably costs only a few cents, and the postage may be $.10 or more depending on the specifics, the risk is much more yours than theirs.

Front

GET THE FACTS
ON OUR BAG
HIGH YIELD
FUND — NO
TAXES! NO
FEES! NO
PROBLEMS!
NO INCOME!
Return the
card today.

[ ] Please send me complete information and
    an application for BAG HIGH YIELD FUND!

NAME _____

ADDRESS _____

CITY _____ STATE _____ ZIP _____

MY RISKY INVESTORS BROKER IS: _____
Use this postage paid card or call us at
800-555-1212. Ask for Guido.

BF-7

Back

DETACH CARD
BEFORE MAILING

Send for your
free investor
kit today.
There is no
obligation!
Hurry while
supplies last.

RETURN ADDRESS

PERMIT
#235

POSTAGE WILL BE PAID BY

RISKY INVESTORS
123 Bet Em High Rd.
Ulose, NV 91567

Fig. 2-6. A statement stuffer.

While using mailers supplied to you can be a worthwhile marketing effort, care must be taken not to assume that because they are provided free they must be a good deal!

As you can see, there are many ways to utilize marketing. Each of the primary techniques we have discussed can be applied advantageously to the selling of financial products and services. With experience you will likely find that each method is especially suitable to a particular situation and that, sometimes, several programs used simultaneously will further extend the benefits that can result from a campaign.

3

Planning Your
Direct-Mail Campaign

EVERY MARKETING CAMPAIGN should begin with a plan. Knowing what you are going to do and how you will do it is essential to a successful promotional effort. This chapter will discuss how to develop an effective direct-mail marketing plan, as well as concepts and specific ideas that can make your programs really pay off.

SETTING GOALS

You should start by setting specific goals that you hope to accomplish. While these will necessarily evolve as you develop a plan, you should try to define what you want from the program. This might entail such things as the number of new accounts you would like to open, the dollar amount of transactions, the products or services you wish to market, or perhaps the amount of commissions you hope to generate. Your goals will probably involve several of these and perhaps other things as well.

It is important that you establish what you want to attain so that you can determine what must be done to achieve it. Goals also permit you to evaluate how successful the marketing program has been. Review the list of things you want your direct-mail program to accomplish and make sure you are comfortable with what you have set out to do.

Teaming Up With Others

An early decision in the planning process is whether to work alone or to team up with other salespeople, perhaps your entire office, to plan and execute a program. The key advantage to teaming is that you share the effort and costs, making your proportionate share of the expenses less than if you worked on your own. But you also must share the leads, sales, and new accounts.

If you want to work with others, the optimal strategy is to get some of your fellow employees to join you, but target a different geographic territory or different audience than they might target. For example, if you work in Cincinnati and you intend to mail to a list of local business people, reserve that list and territory for yourself. Then join only with those who want to mail to other lists in other areas. That way you can share the cost of preparing the materials and achieve some economies of scale in printing and mailing, without competing for the same customers. In a shared effort, your costs should end up being lower and you may be able to execute a better program than if you had worked on your own.

DETERMINING A BUDGET

Whether you work in a group or alone, the next major decision you must make concerns the budget for the program.

Tip: If you are able to put together a group, it is easier, and usually fairer, if everyone puts up exactly the same amount of money and shares equally in the quantity of leads. Unequal participation often results in feelings of unfairness, especially if the plan is very successful.

Your budget will determine what types of programs you will be able to use and the quality of those marketing efforts, so coming up with a reasonable amount to spend is quite important. While there can be no assurance that the money you spend for promotion will bring you large returns, a good pay-back is often the result of a well-planned program. So allocate as much money as you comfortably can risk. The amount of your budget will also determine how close you can come to accomplishing the goals you have set for the program. Lofty goals and a tiny budget can rarely coexist.

Determining a budget is a function of available funds, your willingness to risk some or all of them on marketing, the goals you have set for the program, and the type of marketing you wish to do. You will necessarily spend more to mail a high-quality package to a rented mailing list of 10,000 names than you will sending a postal card to a few hundred prospects taken from the local phone book.

Table 3-1 will give you some idea of the budget you should plan to spend to effectively execute various types of marketing programs. These figures, established from much field experience, indicate minimum amounts to be spent to use a particular medium. Your budget will determine as much about your marketing program as other considerations such as the availability of particular media, appropriateness of the method of reaching your target audience, legal restrictions on how you may sell, etc. The viable options that you may reasonably consider based on a particular budget range are indicated by an ''X.''

One conclusion that can be drawn from the table is that one should not attempt to promote actively without planning to spend a minimum of $500 for a program, including materials, postage, etc. The exception might possibly be telemarketing, as discussed in the chapter: *Telemarketing—Using The Telephone In Marketing.*

Since advertising tends to be more expensive and generally requires frequency (the running of several ads at close intervals), those contemplating budgets of $3000 or more should consider advertising. If you wish to utilize advertising for all or part of your marketing campaign, please refer to the chapter: *Planning Your Advertising Campaign* for detailed advice on using advertising.

Table 3-1. Promotional Budget Guide.

Dollars Available For Campaign	Telemarketing	Direct Mail	Premiums	Print Advertising	Radio	Misc.*	TV
$ Under $500	x						
500 – 3000	x	x	x				
3000 – 10000	x	x	x	x	x	x	
10000+	x	x	x	x	x	x	x

*Misc. includes billboards, sponsorship of events, etc.

While you can certainly spend less on a mailing, to get real impact and effective communication, at least $500 should be budgeted for a direct-mail program. Another conclusion that can be drawn is that, at least for the individual salesperson with a limited expense account (or one using his own funds), telemarketing and direct mail may be the most practical options.

Budget Analysis

You can do some preliminary analysis to see if the budget you have set and the specific benefits you expect from the program are a reasonable fit.

For example, if you have decided that you want to open 10 new accounts and sell them an average of $30,000 worth of mutual fund products over the next few months, you know that you hope to do a total of $300,000 in sales volume. Assuming a commission payout of 1% to you, you can reasonably expect to make $3000 from the sales if you are able to achieve your sales goal ($300,000 × 1%). These figures exclude follow-up business that might subsequently come in.

This information tells you something about how much you should be willing to spend on the program—probably less than $3000 since that is what you hope to earn! It also tells you that your sales can cost you up to $300 each ($3000 budget divided by 10 sales).

As we have learned previously, financial services salespeople typically close 7% of their leads. This suggests that if you want 10 sales, you need about 150 leads. If you are able to achieve a 2% response rate from a mailing, you would need to mail to approximately 7500 prospects to produce 150 leads (7500 × 2%).

You had set your budget at $3000, so you will have a maximum of $.40 per name to spend on this program ($3000/7500 prospects). A cost of $.40 per piece is probably only feasible, including postage, if much of your package is supplied to you at little or no cost, or you use bulk mailing rates or inexpensive mailers. Since the figures make sense, your program can work. However, you would require ideal circumstances (minimum costs and maximum results) to have it perform the way you plan. So you may want to go back and set different goals or develop an entirely new program.

If the available budget cannot realistically achieve your goals, you must reevaluate the program and look for alternatives that have a greater chance of achieving the things you have set out to do.

As one alternative, you might decide to spend more on your program, say $4000, which would be roughly $.50 per prospect ($4000/7500). While you will quite likely lose money on the initial volume of sales that result, you might reasonably expect to make it up in subsequent business. If each new customer that resulted from the program simply did another $10,000 in volume with you over time, their sales would then total $400,000 (10 clients × $40,000 in business). At a payout of 1%, you would recoup all of the costs of the program and have ten new clients!

Figure 3-1 is a worksheet that will help you analyze your proposed programs.

Use this worksheet for a preliminary test of how reasonable your direct-mail plan may be in light of the funds available.

Step 1. Determine how many sales or new accounts you want.
> *# of Sales = Dollar Volume/Average Sales per Account*

Two of the three figures here will be assumptions that you must make based on subjective estimates. You probably have a pretty good idea what your average sale of a given type of product has been in the past.

Step 2. Determine the number of leads you require.
> *# of Leads = # of Sales/Closing Rate*

The closing rate will vary, but a reasonable initial assumption, until you gain further experience, would be 7%.

Step 3. Calculate the size of audience needed.
> *Audience Size = # of Leads/Response Rate*

The response rate can also vary considerably. As a start, estimate 2% for direct mail.

Step 4. Figure your budget per audience contact cost.
> *Budget Each = Total Budget/Audience Size*

The result should be in the $.30 to $1 range for direct mail. While your results may differ somewhat and these figures are only guidelines, if you calculate costs much lower it is unlikely you will achieve them. Higher costs probably mean you cannot make any money on the program.

Step 5. Determine potential profitability of the program.
> *Profit = (Dollar Volume × Net Payout Rate) – Budget*

Payout depends upon what is sold, etc., but 1% to 1.5% is a good initial estimate.

Fig. 3-1. Budget analysis worksheet.

Sensitivity Analysis

A variation on the budget analysis is the testing of incremental additions (and deductions) in the planned expenditures to see what effect they will have on a program's costs and required payback.

Adding another $.25 in materials to each package can seem unimportant. But when that figure is multiplied by 2000 or 5000 mailers, suddenly some significant money must be recouped from the program.

For example, if you spend just an extra $.01 per piece on a mailing of 1000, the total is only $10. However, at an expected response level of, say 2%, that translates into an additional $.50 per lead (2% × 1000 = 20 leads, $10 additional expense divided by 20 leads equals $.50).

Further, even if you successfully close 10% of those leads (a very generous estimate), you will have made two sales. That means you will have added $5 to the cost per sale ($10 additional divided by the 2 sales).

At a payout rate of 1.5% on some financial product you might sell (again quite generous), you would need to sell an additional $333 to each of those new customers to recoup the extra costs! Obviously, at a lower closing rate and smaller payout level, the required sales to make up the additional cost would be even greater.

It is the leverage that extra spending causes in required payback that makes sensitivity analysis important. In this case, a $.01 extra cost per piece translated into a required additional $666 in sales ($333 each multiplied by 2 sales). While you may be able to justify the cost in terms of greater expected response or other benefits, it is important to understand this cause and effect relationship.

A handy formula for calculating sensitivity is shown here. No one can tell you that a specific added cost will or will not be worthwhile. But this formula can help you analyze whether an extra expenditure, or a cutback in costs, is justified.

Step 1. Additional Sales required =
[Additional Cost per piece × Number of pieces] /
Net payout rate percentage

Step 2. Additional Sales required per new customer =
Additional Sales required (from Step 1) /
Number of sales

PREPARATION FOR A DIRECT-MAIL PROGRAM

Once you have settled on your direct-mail budget, you will need to sketch out the details of your program. Your next step in planning your campaign would be to select a specific target audience, that is, the prospects you feel have the greatest potential to do business with you.

You have two basic choices at this level. You can do your own mailing or you can utilize a group mailing using a card pack or some such package of many offers.

Doing Your Own Mailing

While your budget is important in determining what you will be able to do, the actual decisions involving how and what your program will look like will be affected greatly by the prospects you wish to reach (target audience) and what you are trying to sell. Keep in mind that a mailing can be somewhat more directed than most advertising, so you may be able to more precisely choose the individuals to whom you will convey your message by doing a mailing.

Say you are offering a tax-free investment. Because not everyone is a candidate for this type of product, you might choose a list of high-income executives because they probably have a greater need to reduce their tax burden. The next chapter, *All About*

Lists, will give you greater insight into how to select an appropriate list for your particular needs.

Next you must allocate the cost of renting the list (or lists) so that you know how many names you can mail to given your budget. You know from Chapter 2 that a direct-mail package can cost anywhere from about $.36 to about $.80, with $.60 being about average, including fulfillment. To be on the safe side, always assume your package will be expensive. It is better to find out that you did not spend your entire budget rather than to discover that you ran out of money before the program was completed! If your package will weigh less than an ounce and you will not mail using bulk postage rates, estimate about $.80 for the package and postage, at least until you have done a few mailings and know the actual costs more accurately. If your firm is supplying some or all of the materials, or a group is sharing costs, you can probably assume a much lower figure.

Now divide the dollars you have budgeted by the $.80 estimated cost per package, or whatever figure you have calculated for your average total cost per name, and you will know approximately how many names you can mail to on your budget. If you have a budget of $500, plan a mailing of about 600 pieces.

Tip: You may only be able to rent lists in minimums of 3000 or more, so be sure to check this. If you rent more names than you need, save the excess for a future mailing. See the chapter *All About Lists* for more discussion on this matter.

After determining the number of pieces you will most likely mail, you should next determine the contents of your package. You determined the size of the mailing first because the size will affect what is reasonable to consider including in your package. Larger mailings can afford options that do not make economic sense in smaller quantities. Table 3-2 suggests approximate costs for various inserts you may use. Since printer's charges will vary considerably, and the particulars of your project may involve some unusual work, these can only be rough guides.

Table 3-2. Estimated Materials Costs for Direct Mail.

Approx. Mailing Quantity	Preprinted Letter (cents)	Personalized Computer Letter (cents)	Two-Color Brochure (cents)	Reply Card (cents)	Printed Envelope (cents)
500	6	-	-	7	3
1000	4	-	-	5	2.5
5000	3	15	7	4	2
10000	2	10	5	2	1.5
20000	1.5	5	4	2	1
50000	1	3	3	1.5	.5

Some of the spaces in the table are blank because in small quantities you cannot, practically, use fancy brochures, unless they are already available. At low volumes it is also difficult to justify using personalized computer letters, unless you are able to generate them yourself, perhaps on your personal computer.

Preparation and Printing Services

There are many services available to assist you in preparing your materials. These include ad agencies, direct-mail designers, graphic artists, mailing houses, etc. Generally they will not be worth the expense for small projects. It costs an agency about the same to write your copy as it does to prepare similar materials for a large corporation which would use them in huge quantities. The agencies' overhead have been established by the larger clients they serve, so it is unlikely that you can get significant professional assistance for less than $500. While this advice would be useful, it is doubtful that it would be worthwhile to spend that kind of money on a campaign that might total only $1000 or $2000.

If you feel you absolutely need outside assistance, use a free-lance writer or designer. Their work can be excellent, sometimes superior to big agencies, and a great deal less costly. If your budget is larger, it can make sense to use an agency.

Tip: Be sure to have any mailings or other direct-mail materials cleared by your compliance department or firm's attorney.

Most printers can set up and print your work. Use a small printer in your neighborhood. Big operations cannot make much money on your small runs and they will treat you accordingly. Your local resume printer should do nicely and value you as a client. They may even become a prospect for financial services.

Remember that a very large percentage of your printing costs are in paper. Try to minimize wasted paper by discussing the details of your job with the printer. He may be able to offer you paper he stocks at a better price than a special paper you may have selected previously. Also try to use his standard inks, special mixing of inks can get expensive.

Try to see a proof of your materials before they are printed. This is an actual run of the piece before the full quantity is produced. It is a last minute check against printer error, or your own mistakes. A proof also shows you the quality of the piece. The paper should not feel cheap, the printing should be clear and clean. Take the time to examine it carefully. Not all printers will run a proof copy—it costs money to start and stop the press. But better printers usually will do this for you, although they may insist on a few dollars for the effort. It is worth it.

It has been estimated that nearly one-sixth of third-class mail is not delivered. A postal delivery test indicated that mail that appeared to be more important (to the postal carriers) was delivered more often than mail that did not appear to be important. There is probably a general truth to the fact that, no matter how a package is sent, it stands a better chance of getting there if it looks important than if it appears to be junk mail. So do try to make your mailing as attractive as possible, both for the prospect's benefit and to help ensure its delivery.

Desktop Publishing

Many financial services salespeople either own or have access to a personal computer or other word processing equipment. With recent advances in desktop publishing, it is now possible for you to do much if not all of the copy preparation for direct mail (and advertising) and deliver materials ready for production to a printer.

If you can put your copy on a diskette, printers are often able to use the information directly in their typesetting systems, cutting down substantially on the time and cost they require to produce your work. If you have access to a desktop publishing system you may be able to generate work that is basically camera-ready. It is definitely worth your while to investigate your options in this regard.

Coding and Dating Materials

However your materials are produced, do not date them. The temptation to put a date on a letter or other mailing piece can be great, but it can only cause you trouble. If your mailing is delayed (the names you ordered do not arrive on time), you must toss the dated materials or look silly. Also, if the prospect puts the piece in his drawer for a month and then finds it, he may assume it is old news that is no longer relevant. And if you have materials left over you cannot use them again if they are dated.

Although dating is undesirable, you will want to code your reply cards or other reply mechanism so you know which mailing produced the inquiry. A simple *1* for your first mailing or *2* for your second mailing will suffice. These can easily be updated to *1A* or *2A*, by hand if necessary, for future use if you have extra items left over. Figure 3-2 demonstrates typical coding methods.

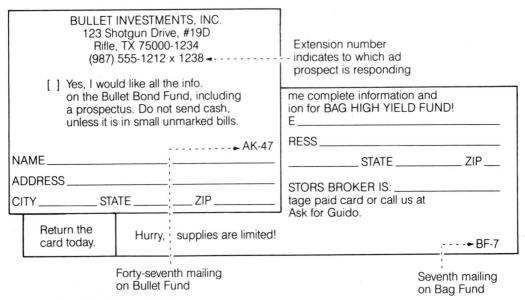

Fig. 3-2. Typical coding methods.

THE MECHANICS OF A MAILING

Your mailing plan should be carefully thought out. The arrival of labels, materials, and the actual mailing must be well timed. If some parts arrive long before others do, you will have to store them and risk misplacing some items for your campaign.

When you have all of the pieces of the package ready, you need to assemble (in some cases, fold), insert into an envelope, affix a label (or have the envelope typed), bundle, and mail. Do not underestimate the work involved in preparing a mailing of just 500 pieces. And if your mailing is significantly larger, it will be a time-consuming job. Perhaps you can have people in your mail room, your assistant, or an outside service do the assembly? Give thought to how you will get your package put together and mailed.

One way to reduce the burden of the mailing is to stagger it over a number of days or a week or two. This not only helps you cut down the crunch on the outgoing end, but may make it easier for you to deal with the incoming leads.

Assume you mail 4000 pieces and get just 1% to respond (a low estimate). That would result in 40 leads you would have to follow up. This number of leads may not seem like a lot, but to send out fulfillment materials and call them all within a few days (before the leads get cold) is not that easy. Most securities salespeople find they can reasonably follow up 10 to 15 leads a day, factoring in the leads not reached, busy signals, call-backs, etc. So it may take you three or four (or more) days to contact the leads you get from this type of program. This activity is in addition to maintaining your regular business schedule.

Of course, if you obtain a much higher response rate, say 3% (which is not all that rare), you could be buried by 120 leads. While that is a nice problem to have, it is a problem! So you may want to stagger your mailings over a few days so that your expected returns do not inundate you.

However, like most decisions, staggered mailings have trade-offs. One important trade-off is that you may not qualify for bulk mailing rates if the mailing is split into smaller segments. If you did not plan to use bulk rates this will not be a factor. Another trade-off is that the job will drag out. Instead of one marathon stuffing and sealing session, you might end up with three or four, and a similar number of trips to the post office or mail room. But a staggered mailing will help protect you against a huge response rate that you cannot efficiently deal with. After you gain experience with several mailings you will be better able to gauge what to expect in return volume and plan your mailings accordingly.

Personalization

Most mailings are generic. That is, the same exact package goes to each prospect. Every item is produced in bulk and designed to be general—appealing to common interests or needs of those on the list. It is more difficult to persuade someone that you can help them when they are referred to as "you" or "them." They would certainly feel better about your offer if you were able to call them by their name and perhaps if the sales materials reflected something about them specifically.

Personalization is the process of inserting certain key names or phrases into your direct-mail pieces to make the prospect feel like you sat down and wrote an individual letter to him. One way to accomplish this is to address your letter correctly. That is, name and address on the letter in addition to the envelope.

Another personalization technique would be to incorporate some fact about the prospect into your letter or other materials, such as his occupation, type of car he drives, his birth date, children's names, etc. Most of this information is readily available along with many lists and some of it may even be relevant to your sales pitch.

Advances in computer technology have enabled us to generate letters that seem as if they were typed just for the recipient. Sometimes your signature can even be written (by machine) on the letter for added authenticity.

Since personalization adds to marketing costs, the most economical way to accomplish this is to personalize one key insert in the direct-mail package and use generic items for the balance. The letter is the most sensible item to choose for the following reasons:

- It is usually seen first, so you create the right impression immediately.

- Most important letters people receive are personalized. In fact, a non-personalized letter is one good way to define junk mail. So a personalized note reduces your mailing's solicitation appearance.

- Personalizing the letter allows you the most flexibility. The other components of your mailing may have legal requirements on what they must, and must not, contain. Personalization of a prospectus or sales brochure would be a tough legal maze to work through. But letters, within limits, have little if any rules governing their content. A personalized reply card would be of questionable value.

A personalized letter can also contain some particular information relevant to that specific prospect. For example, you are a banker wishing to market to a list of homeowners. You also have access to real estate sales in a particular development or town. You might indicate in your letter that the average home in that individual's neighborhood has risen 14.7% in the past year and, based on the average values, means they probably can now qualify for an additional $20,000 home equity loan.

Another prospect, in another location, might be told they potentially could qualify for as much as a $40,000 home equity loan. This effect can be much stronger than just telling all prospects that they may be able to obtain a home equity loan.

To get some other ideas on how you might personalize your direct mail, talk to your list broker or vendors who specialize in generating computer letters. Ask to see samples of what they have done for others. This will not only give you ideas, but you will be able to see what kind of work they turn out.

Remember that personalization can also mean mistakes. A specific piece of information may not be available, or be incorrect, for some prospects. They will laugh (or worse) if you tell them that they can get an extra $100,000 equity loan when their house has recently been appraised at $75,000!

What happens if there is no Mr. or Ms. attached to the name and their first name is Chris or Dana? You may offend a potential customer when you address your letter to Ms. Leslie Rosen and *he* realizes you have no idea who you wrote to. It takes away the very personal touch you hoped to accomplish! Review every personalization item and try to arrange a fall-back position, something safe to use if the information is in question. In this case, eliminating the title may be the best way to go.

Also keep in mind that in smaller volumes, unless you are able to generate them on your own computer, personalized letters can add another $.10 or so to the direct-mail package cost. And personalization may add further to your cost if you have already ordered labels and will need to have the list entered into a computer to generate letters. You might be able to order lists on magnetic tape, which many mailing houses can use to produce your personalized letters. Check on this and ensure that if you use a list on magnetic tape that the format is acceptable to the mailer. His equipment may not accept certain types.

The extra $.10 personalization cost, assuming a 2% response rate, means your cost per lead would rise by $5 ($.10/2%). Further, at a 7% average closing rate, it would raise your cost per sale by a whopping $71 ($5/7%), or about 25% of the $285 average cost per sale.

So you should believe that a personalized letter can raise your average sale, or closing rate, by more than 25 percent to make this approach appealing. It is doubtful that this particular personalization program would be cost effective. However, if your added costs to generate a personalized letter were in the $.01 to $.05 range, the benefits would likely outweigh the added cost. A personalized letter can often raise response rates by 10% or more, from two to 2.2% for example!

HOW TO SEND YOUR MAILING

A mailing can be sent through the post office in a variety of ways. It can also be delivered by means other than the U.S. Postal Service. While these other services may be appropriate for certain direct-mail efforts, they are quite expensive and generally not cost-effective for most investment marketing.

For an in-depth discussion of mailing options, be sure to see the chapter on *Delivering Your Direct-Mail Package* as well as the appendix, *Postal Services, Rates and Regulations*.

When to Mail

Direct-mail experts will tell you that if mail is addressed to the prospect's home, they probably have more time to read and consider an offer on the weekend. However, when mail is delivered to the office, people are more responsive to mail early in the week, before they get busy or start thinking about the weekend. Thus, if you are mailing first class, delivering the mail to the post office on a Thursday or Friday (late in the week) will usually result in a weekend delivery to a home address and Monday delivery to an office (early in the week). If you are mailing using bulk rates, you have much less control over when delivery may occur, so the mailing day is somewhat less critical. Figure 3-3 illustrates typically optimal dates to mail.

Keep in mind that this guidance is quite general. There may be many circumstances where it would be desirable to have the prospect receive the mail at other times. And holidays and various seasonal factors can affect optimal mailing dates. For example, if a long weekend is intervening when you mail, you will have to factor that into your mailing date. Mail is not usually delivered on a holiday, so you may wish to mail a day earlier to try and maintain the schedule.

Where to Mail: Home or Office?

Most prospects really have two mailing addresses: their home and their office. There are pros and cons to mailing to either of these locations. In the majority of cases you will not have a choice, the list you compile or rent will usually give you just one option and it will

SUN	MON	TUES	WED	THURS	FRI	SAT
	1	2	3	4	5	6
7	8	9	10	11	12	13
14	15	16	17	18	19	20
21	22	23	24	25	26	27
28	29	30	31			

Optimal mailing dates are usually
Thursdays or Fridays for regular
First-Class Mail.

Fig. 3-3. Suggested dates to mail.

most often be the home address. If you do have a choice, send it to the home address anyway. Five reasons for sending financial offers to the home address are outlined below:

1. Prospects typically will not have their mail screened by a secretary so the chances of your package actually reaching the addressee are better.
2. If the letter is screened at home, it will probably be done by a spouse who may be interested and would be a good prospect in their own right.
3. Your offer is personal in nature and most people would prefer to keep their finances away from the job scene.
4. If the prospect decides to respond, he can often call or write more easily at home (although a call from home is likely to be during non-business hours).
5. If the addressee is no longer at that address you will probably get the letter back if it is sent to their home address and you paid to get undeliverables returned. If you sent it to an office address, there is a pretty good chance that the letter will be delivered to the individual's replacement, or just tossed in the trash. In that case you would never know why no reply was received. The undeliverable content can often be large enough that this can throw off your analysis of that mailing list and your program.

There are some circumstances wherein a letter to an office might be appropriate, but they are not too common. For example, a solicitation concerning a cash management program for corporate cash, or a preferred stock offering of interest to the company treasurer would best be sent to the company address. Most personal appeals should be sent to the home address. Unless you have a compelling reason to use the office address, send it to their home if that address is available.

FOLLOWING UP ON YOUR DIRECT-MAIL PROGRAM

Part of any direct-mail plan must be a follow-up and tracking system. You should know what you will do when a lead comes in. What will you send them? Will you have letters typed for each? How will you know which product or service was offered to the prospect?

The easiest way to identify the offer is to code each reply mailer with a number or letter, or combination of these. You might indicate your first commodity offer with a ''C-1'' or use ''I-5'' for your fifth insurance mailing, etc. If you are running several campaigns at once, additional coding showing the media, etc., would be desirable.

Based on the coded information, you will know exactly when and to what the prospect responded and which items should be sent to them. The response levels obtained for different campaigns may also provide significant information for optimizing your future programs.

Keep track of your responses. For direct mail the bulk of responses come within the first seven to 10 days, then the responses taper off, but can continue to trickle in for a long time. Figure 3-4 shows graphically the typical response pattern from the time of mailing to about two weeks after the mailing. This applies to first-class mail only.

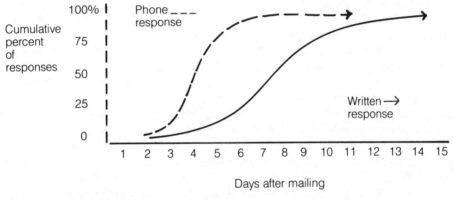

Fig. 3-4. Typical direct-mail response curve.

If you utilize bulk mail rates, slide the chart to the right by the additional number of days the mail will probably take to reach its destination. In the case of bulk mail this might be an extra five or more days. Your local post office can give you a more precise estimate based on your location and the mailing's target area.

You should count how many responses you get, how many sales, and how many returns (undeliverable). These figures will tell you if you should use the list, and, perhaps, your materials, again.

Reusing Leads

Plan to keep and reuse all leads which have not become customers after the initial campaign. Divide the results of your marketing effort into four categories. These groups should be utilized to generate further potential business as follows:

1. Respondents who became customers are now part of your *customer file*.
2. Respondents who were interested but not ready to act just yet should be kept in

a special *follow-up file* to be approached when you feel it appropriate (when they said they would have funds available, for example).

3. Respondents who were not interested should be maintained in an *old lead file*. Including them in a subsequent direct mailing or contacting them by telephone as part of an old lead revival program usually produces excellent results, far above the level of ordinary purchased lists.

4. Prospects you failed to contact (undeliverables, no answers, etc.), should be filed as *non-contacted leads* so you can check new efforts against that list and eliminate their inclusion in future mailings that you might do.

Using Group Mailings

In the event you have elected to utilize a card pack or other group mailing, a somewhat different approach will be needed.

To review, card mailers are packets of various offers grouped together in one mailing package. These would typically be cards measuring about six inches long by four inches high that often are self-mailers. One side would make the pitch or offer and the other side might be a postage-paid card.

With a group mailing, you will usually be very limited as to your options on the piece. The size, type style, perhaps even colors, will be dictated to you.

The obvious problem with a group mailing is getting the prospect to read your promotional piece. First, you must overcome the hurdle of their actually opening the package. With all the card mailers that are being used today, it is likely that the prospect has received several and may be tired of all that mail.

Second, your piece could easily be lost among the 20, 30, 50 or more other cards in the deck. You must catch the prospect's attention. Your card must stand out from the rest.

One effective approach might be to use a tin-foil wrapper for the package. This is something you probably will not control, but you might mention it to the individuals creating the group mailing.

You will have quite a bit of input about your actual card. In addition to the limited choices the mailer will offer you (color, print type, and perhaps position in the deck), you may be able to include a logo, etc. Since you will have just a moment to get the prospect to stop at your card and read it and only a few more seconds to convince them to act on your offer, before they toss it, the visual impact of your card is critical.

The headline will also determine how well your card generates leads. A strong and effective headline is a must. And to make it easy for the prospect to reply, use a postage-paid card, or possibly a toll-free number. Be sure to code your cards so you know immediately from which promotion they came and what the prospects want.

Leads generated from group mailings should be treated just like leads generated from any other source. While they may be of somewhat lesser quality (less likely to convert into a sale than leads from other sources), they definitely deserve fulfillment and follow-up.

It is not suggested that you use card packs as a substitute for other direct mail. They should be a part of your overall marketing strategy. The cost to use a card pack is close to advertising rates—just a few cents to perhaps a dime per prospect. So it is a low-risk proposition worth testing.

Another promotional approach you will want to consider is the "take-one" mailer. Take-ones located in taxis, at airports, at hotels, etc., can also provide a low-cost and productive source of leads.

The key here is where the take-one stand is located and how attractive your material appears. If positioned in quality locations—upper class hotels, for example, and if you focus on a particular product or service rather than on yourself or your firm, this type of marketing can often prove useful. As mentioned previously, a particularly appropriate use for a take-one mailer would be at a financial seminar or other financial services related activity.

Some fee for permission to place a stand in a particular location is expected, if permission is granted at all. Depending on the particulars, it might be a direct payment or an informal lunch or dinner. In any event, unless it is a very unique location, the cost should not run much more than a few hundred dollars a year. That, of course, is in addition to the cost of the materials which you will periodically have to restock.

A growing trend is to place branch banks—sometimes little more than a teller machine—in grocery stores and other retail outlets. A good potential market may be developed by placing a take-one stand near or in these branches. People doing a bank transaction at a retail store are reasonable candidates for financial services since teller machines in stores tend to be in upscale markets and people doing transactions at these "banks" are likely to be in need of some financial products.

While placing take-ones at other teller machines, at the main bank office for example, would also be worth considering, it is less likely that you could obtain their permission to do so.

4

All About Lists

PERHAPS THE MOST important part of any direct-mail campaign is the list to which the promotional package will be sent. An offer of financial services using the nicest literature, the most carefully worded letter, and the prettiest envelope would all be wasted if the letter arrives at a school dormitory, jail house, or tenement. But even a mediocre package will get attention if delivered to the right person.

As we discussed in "Planning Your Direct-Mail Campaign," one of the first steps is selecting your target audience. In direct mail, the target will become the list (or lists) to whom you mail. Selecting your list wisely is, therefore, quite critical.

Your target list can either be rented or compiled by you. If you have a source of prospects that you wish to use in a direct-mail campaign, you do not necessarily have to type or keypunch the names in yourself. Many firms (often list brokers) offer services that will put your file on computer records and generate labels and lists for you. These services typically cost from $50 to $70 per thousand names, with some minimum quantity or price required—usually at least a few hundred dollars.

LIST RENTAL SOURCES

There are two important questions to keep in mind when renting a list. First, consider who is renting you the list. Second, try to determine where the list came from.

Lists are created either because someone compiled a group of names (often from other lists) or a marketing program (mailing, advertising, telemarketing) produced respondents that indicated people were interested in a particular offer. The firm creating the lists then decides to generate revenues from rentals of their lists. They would probably retain a list manager to promote their lists. The manager, in turn, makes the list available to other firms who act as list brokers, offering the list for rental to end-users. The process is illustrated in Figure 4-1.

You can rent lists from a list broker or you can "mail order" lists from compilers of lists.

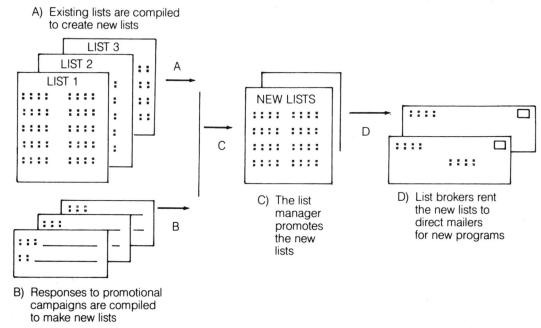

A) Existing lists are compiled to create new lists

B) Responses to promotional campaigns are compiled to make new lists

C) The list manager promotes the new lists

D) List brokers rent the new lists to direct mailers for new programs

Fig. 4-1. List creation and use process.

List Brokers

Using a list broker has many advantages. However, the broker earns his fee in much the same way ad agencies earn theirs—a percentage of the list rental. If you pay $200 for 4000 names, the list broker probably makes $40 (about 20%). So you should not expect a great deal of time and effort on those small orders. However, if you can get a list broker to deal personally with you, you will be able to take advantage of some of the expertise he has to offer.

A broker's guidance about which options are best suited for your needs can be valuable. The supplier should have experience renting to financial users so that he is prepared to help you choose the most promising list for your programs. It is also important that the list broker you deal with has many lists available, not just a few of his own for which he acts as a manager. Otherwise the source will be biased into recommending simply what he has rather than what may be best for your purpose.

The price on a given list does not vary greatly since no discount is given even if a middleman is eliminated. Sometimes it is possible to negotiate a discount on the price of a list, but it would take very large volumes of list rentals to get a broker to consider this.

A few years ago the role of a list broker was quite simple. The lists available were limited in number and it was a fairly straightforward matter for them to scan the available lists and make a recommendation based on essentially superficial clues like occupation or income level.

But the world has become more complicated with many more lists and all sorts of new indications as to the optimal list to use. One important new area of evaluation is called psychographics, which has to do with life-style. Unlike demographics which deals with specific traits like income level, etc., psychographics deals with more intangible qualities like how leisure time is spent, does the family have teenagers headed for college, etc.? These factors can be important clues in trying to maximize the effectiveness of your list selection. A list broker cannot only provide you with this information, but he can also assist you in analyzing what it means and how best to use it.

However, do not put your total faith in a list broker's advice. You should always evaluate the list yourself and test it with a small mailing before committing to a major program.

The list source is quite significant as well. Remember, even if the list broker has worked with financial clients, you know your products and markets best. Ask about the list he is recommending. Try to learn enough to make your own evaluation about its appropriateness for your purposes. Find out when the list was compiled. Is it old? Does it represent compiled names or respondents to a mailing? To what were they responding? If it is a compiled list, try to get a description of why these names were selected. Are they buyers of expensive cars and frequent travelers, mutual fund owners, etc.?

Ask when the list was last updated and how often it has been used. When was the last promotion sent to these people and what was it? If they received a tax-free mailing last week and you are interested in selling municipal bonds, you might be better off with another list, or waiting a month or so until your offer might appear fresh.

Characteristics about individuals included in lists is usually summarized in terms of buying patterns and demographics. Buying patterns refer to what they tend to buy, where, how much they spend, etc. Demographics is data about the prospect's typical age, income, occupation, marital status, home ownership and length of residence, etc. Both buying patterns and demographics can help you evaluate the appropriateness of a particular list for your purposes.

This might seem like a lot of information to gather about a list of 3000 wealthy farmers, but if it turns out that ''wealthy'' just means they have two tractors and the list was put together in 1979, you might not be pleased with the results of your mailing. Request a data card which gives the answers to many of these questions.

List Rental from Compilers

Many compilers of lists now offer them by mail. You review their catalog and select the list or lists you wish to use and send them payment. Back come the labels and lists you requested. It is very convenient. You do lose the guidance and experience a list broker could offer.

However, for small users of direct mail, obtaining lists this way may be the only viable alternative. A broker is just not going to spend much time with you if you are looking for 2500 names and might spend $150.

List Data Cards

Whatever method you use to obtain a rental list, be sure to request a list data card (Fig. 4-2) for every list you are considering. This will give you the relevant information about who is on the list, their characteristics, etc.

While the particular format of data cards will vary somewhat from supplier to supplier, the basic information presented will be fairly consistent. The *name* of the list will usually appear first, followed by the *source* of the names. Sometimes the source will be quite obvious, as in the case of our sample. However, in many cases the list might be something like "120,000 Kindergarten Teachers" and you would have to look at the list source data to find out that the list was derived from membership in the United Kindergarten Teachers Union.

The *description* of the list will generally tell you something about the source of the names on the list. It might reveal how many people are in the Teachers Union, or how its membership differs from just a list of teachers—perhaps they have higher income, are younger, that they were founded in 1988, etc.

The *quantities* section will give you an idea of how many of these prospects are available. Typically, the counts will show domestic (US), Canadian, and another category or

---

LIST: SOURCE:
Kindergarten World Subscribers   *Kindergarten World* Magazine

DESCRIPTION:
This publication is read by one million Kindergarten Teachers who receive it as part of their membership in Kindergarten Teachers United Union of America, established 1988.

QUANTITIES:
Subscribers: 897,934 (US)   102,060 (Canada)   6 (Foreign)

PROFILE:
Kindergarten World readers are intelligent, high income, active, many have advanced degrees in finger painting and pottery. Ave. income $96,000. Average annual bond investment of $23,000.

RECOMMENDED FOR THE FOLLOWING OFFERS:
Books, magazines, self-improvement, computer related products, credit cards, insurance, investments, cultural memberships, travel, furniture and supplies, saddles, mail order products.

PRICES AND SELECTIONS:		SPECIAL SELECTIONS:	
Base	$65.00/M	Story book readers	487,954
State or SCF	$ 5.00/M	Arts and Crafts	335,612
Key Coding	$ 5.00/M	Music Appreciation	94,975
Nth Name Select	NC	Music Appreciation at	
Special Select	$10.00/M	School Address	28,153
		Home Economics	211,865
MINIMUM ORDER:	.	Male	476,925
3,000 labels/$200.		Female	523,075

FORMAT:
Cheshire Labels. Pressure Sensitive Labels ($10.00/M). Magnetic Tape (9 track/1500BPI – $15.00 Flat)

LEADING LISTS, RR #7, Box A Whatchwana, IA 50232 (800)-555-1212

Fig. 4-2. Typical list data card.

TYPICAL LIST DATA CARDS

LIST LIBRARY JOURNAL SUBSCRIBERS   SOURCE LIBRARY JOURNAL MAGAZINE

DESCRIPTION For over 100 years this publication has appealed to library personnel responsible for the acquisition of book and non-book materials and equipment in libraries. It is the leading magazine in the library field.

QUANTITIES Subscribers: 20,992 (U.S.)   820 (Canada)   1,495 (Foreign)

PROFILE Library Journal subscribers are well-educated, many having advanced degrees, intellectual and cultural.

RECOMMENDED FOR THE FOLLOWING OFFERS • Self-Improvement • Cultural Memberships • Books • Magazine Subscriptions • Computer-Related Products • Continuing Education • Library and Audiovisual Equipment • Furniture and Supplies

PRICES AND SELECTIONS   BUSINESS SELECTIONS

Base
Slate or SCF
Key Coding
Nth Name Sel
Business Sele

MINIMU

FORMAT
($8.00/M). M

LIST PUBLISHERS WEEKLY SUBSCRIBERS   SOURCE PUBLISHERS WEEKLY MAGAZINE

DESCRIPTION For over 100 years this publication has kept its readers informed as to the latest developments in the American booking stories and has been the nerve center of the American book publishing industry providing innovative ideas, editorials, articles, forecasts and book lists.

QUANTITIES Subscribers: 34,027 (U.S.)   958 (Canada)   1,995 (Foreign)

PROFILE Publishers Weekly subscribers are professionals who are well-educated and culturally oriented.

RECOMMENDED FOR THE FOLLOWING OFFERS • Books • Magazine Subscriptions • Cultural Memberships • Seminars • Credit Cards • Travel • Association Memberships • Mail Order Products • Insurance • Investments • Self-Improvement • Computer-Related Products • Office Equipment and Supplies

PRICES AND SELECTIONS   BUSINESS SELECTIONS

Base
Slate or SCF
Key Coding
Nth Name Sel
Business Sele

MINIM

FORMAT
($8.00/M). M

LIST SCHOOL LIBRARY JOURNAL SUBSCRIBERS   SOURCE SCHOOL LIBRARY JOURNAL MAGAZINE

DESCRIPTION This publication has the highest paid circulation of any library publication. Most of its readers are school librarians and youth services librarians in public libraries. These individuals are responsible for the acquisition of book and non-book materials and equipment in their libraries. Their purchases amount to approximately one-half billion dollars.

QUANTITIES Subscribers: 36,333 (U.S.)   1,427 (Canada)   388 (Foreign)

PROFILE School Library Journal subscribers are well-educated, many having advanced degrees, intellectual and cultural.

RECOMMENDED FOR THE FOLLOWING OFFERS • Books • Magazine Subscriptions • Self-Improvement • Cultural Memberships • Computer-Related Products • Continuing Education • Library and Audiovisual Equipment • Furniture and Supplies

PRICES AND SELECTIONS		BUSINESS SELECTIONS	
Base	$50.00/M	Public Libraries	4,756
Slate or SCF	$ 3.00/M	Elementary School Libraries	14,842
Key Coding	$ 3.00/M	High School & Junior High School Libraries	13,890
Nth Name Selection	No Charge	Special (Business/Industry) Libraries	1,099
Business Selection	$ 5.00/M	Publishers, Government, Book Sellers, Library	
		Science Students	443
MINIMUM ORDER	3,000 Labels	Educators/Boards of Education	998
		General Company/Corporate & Business Addressed To	
FORMAT		Other than Library Outside Publishing Fields	
Cheshire Labels. Pressure-Sensitive Labels		College & University Libraries	105
($8.00/M), Magnetic Tape (9 Track/1600			
BPI—$15.00 Flat)			

Fig. 4-2. Continued.

so. Obviously if this were a list of foreign nationals investing in the United States, the listing would have some greater breakdown of quantities by other countries.

The *profile* section is supposed to give you some very basic data on the characteristics of the people on the list. For example, it might tell you that the Teachers Union has the highest paid teachers in the world with an average salary of $96,000 and that they regularly invest an average of $23,000 in junk bonds.

The *recommended usage* section was designed to give you an idea of how you might best use this list. While it can be of some guidance, the categories are usually so broad that there is little left out. It is doubtful you will want to select a list simply because the card lists "investments" in the recommended section.

Prices and selections give you the charges for the rental of the list and any extra services you may require. Each service is added to the base cost. So you may rent a list for $65.00/M ($65 per thousand) and then pay another $5.00/M to have the list sorted by ZIP code. If you also want certain selections, say for example, Music Appreciation Teachers as illustrated in the sample card, you would pay another $10.00/M in special selections as well.

Often you will be offered "Nth Name Selection." This simply means that you want the names selected from the master list to get a cross section. So you might ask for every 100th name in a list of 100,000, giving you 1000 names, but spread throughout the list. That way, if that mailing works well for you, you can be reasonably confident that you will have similar success with another selection from the list. If you chose just a block of 1000 names, you might happen to get the oldest names, or a group that all came in from some activity that is not a good predictor of investment interest.

The *minimum order* will usually be stated in terms of number of labels or names, but it sometimes might be stated in a dollar amount, say, for example, $200.

The *format* has to do with the type of labels you will be receiving and with specifications of any magnetic tapes that might be ordered containing the list. Since it is unlikely that you will use magnetic tapes, it is not necessary to concern yourself with that at this time. Cheshire labels are a specific type of plain label that requires special machinery to be affixed, so you will almost always have to pay an extra $5 or so for self-adhesive labels or another form.

DESIRABLE CHARACTERISTICS

For securities promotions, the names on a target list should have a number of basic characteristics. These fall into three broad categories:

1. Wealth or earning power—those with money or high income are much more likely to need and use financial services.
2. Previous investment experience—people who have already made investments are typically better candidates for additional transactions.
3. Expensive buying habits—individuals who spend lavishly probably have available funds for investment.

If you examine your present client profile, you will most likely see these characteristics fairly often. One key indicator of wealth would be the geographic location of the prospect—an expensive neighborhood for example.

Earning power would primarily be implied by the prospect's type of occupation—a doctor or lawyer, etc.

Indications of investment interest or experience would be primarily shown by previous transactions (tax shelter buyers or mutual fund owners) or inquiries about these types of investments.

Expensive purchasing habits are usually readily apparent in the ownership of a luxury car, yacht, or private club.

Most of these indicators of good financial services prospects are public information that have already been compiled into useful lists. For example, you can easily find lists of doctors, boat owners, or people who have purchased mutual funds, etc.

Of course, you may be selling an insurance policy geared for lower income families, or accounting services that might not benefit from all the characteristics listed here. But by and large you will be looking for prospects with above-average incomes and wealth to become customers. And these people tend to fall into one or more of the three categories discussed here.

Despite the obvious desirability of selecting only those prospects that are most likely to be interested in and qualified for your offer, you may not want to use a source that has been overworked. For example, it is doubtful that a list of known options speculators would prove productive for an options offer if that list had recently received many other options solicitations. The audience would be tired of options promotions and would quite likely have had their needs in this area already fulfilled. Your response rate would suffer as a result.

You should be striving for a list that is current (created in the past few years or later), updated recently (so as to avoid excessive undeliverable names from old addresses), and a list that has not been used heavily for financial offers (so that recipients have not been inundated with similar offers).

UNDELIVERABLES

It is not possible to avoid undeliverable letters altogether. People move fairly often, and marriages and deaths do occur. Your goal should be to keep your returns down to less than 5% which is considered quite good. The more often a list is "cleaned"—the process of updating information and removing those names that do not have deliverable addresses—the fewer returns will occur. Your mailing to the list and reporting any undeliverable names to the list broker is a form of cleaning.

List brokers typically give few guarantees on the quality of their lists or results expected. Some do try to protect you from excessive returns due to undeliverable names by offering some sort of a refund policy. This would typically be for the rental costs only for returns above some limit—often as high as 7 to 8%. In other words, if you pay $70/M (seven cents per name) and got back 10% undeliverable on 3000 names, they might refund the cost of the returns above 6% or 120 names (10% × 3000 = 300, 6% × 3000 = 180, 300 − 180 = 120). At $.07 each, that totals $8.40 (120 × 7 cents). Meanwhile, you probably spent $.60 per piece mailed or $180 on the 300 undeliverables! While a guarantee can give you some reassurance, it will probably be of limited value.

Save your returns (those that were not delivered). By calling directory assistance you can often locate the new phone number, particularly if the party has moved locally.

Call the prospect and indicate that you had attempted to mail them an informative brochure but could not get it delivered. It is amazing how many people will give out their new address and thank you for calling.

Tip: Saving your returns can also mean recycling some of the materials used in the mailing. The generic parts of your mailing package that came back undeliverable can probably be used in your next direct-mail program.

List Recycling

Remember that a list of respondents to a previous mailing is usually more desirable than the original list from which they came. This is especially important if the response would tend to qualify them for investments. For example, if the list you are considering consists of the replies to a financial publication solicitation, you have a high probability that these people will be interested in offers like yours.

The same principle is at work when you mail to one of your files of respondents from a previous campaign. Typically, you can expect significantly higher levels of responses to this type of mailing than that of an average newly rented list.

First, you have eliminated the undeliverables, which should boost the response level relative to the number mailed (you do not waste as many).

Second, a list of respondents to a previous mailing have all indicated a fairly high level of interest in your offers, (you have already screened these prospects through your previous marketing programs). A new list that you simply rent will have lots of names in it that have no interest in financial matters whatsoever. So the odds of getting responses from an old lead file are much greater than most any other type of list.

THE LIST RENTAL PROCESS

From the renter's perspective, the list rental business is not very complicated. If you want to use a particular list, you order it and pay a rental fee. The fee varies depending upon the list and other factors. A very popular, hard to compile list that has proven itself over time might rent for $75 to $100 or more per 1000 names, for a single use. A more typical list that is used only occasionally may cost $50 to $60 per 1000 names or possibly even less. List rental fees are quoted on a per thousand basis, even though you might be required to rent 2000, 5000 or more names in many cases.

The fee paid for a list rental is for the right to use the list just once. The temptation, after you have the list in your possession, to make a copy and use it again can be great. Many renters figure they can use the list again without the list broker ever knowing. But there are some precautions list managers and owners take to protect their lists. One is to "seed" the list with names of people who will alert the owners if they receive an unauthorized mailing. The owner can then check if that particular mailing was approved and rental fees paid.

Usually, each mailing you make must be submitted to the list broker for approval. Technically the broker is suppose to show it to the list owner and obtain his approval. Despite the fact that this seldom actually happens, the risks involved in using a list without paying for it, or without obtaining proper approval for your specific mailing, are far greater than any possible benefits. Don't do it!

However, do try to get a set of $3 \times 5''$ cards printed with the list names so you will have a complete record of who received your mailing. Or photocopy the list for your records only. This will be useful in tracking and following up on your inquiries. Using a copy of the list for record-keeping purposes is perfectly acceptable. It is when the list is reused for more direct mail without paying additional rental fees that you may be committing a crime.

If you are in doubt about the proper ways to utilize a list, you might obtain a copy of a booklet titled *The List Practices Handbook*. The Direct Marketing Association issued the 47-page manual to foster understanding in using lists and how to avoid problems in their rental.

Additional Costs

The rental fee for the list is not the only cost you will face to obtain a usable list for your direct-mail campaign. The basic rental fee is generally for ungummed (no glue) Cheshire labels which can only be affixed by a special machine. For convenience, you will probably want your list on adhesive peel-off labels and that will probably cost you another $5 or so per 1000 names.

If you desire a special sorting of names, perhaps in ZIP code order for a bulk mailing, that might cost another $5 additional per 1000 names. And if you require titles or other specific additional information like individual's names in alphabetical order within each firm for some sort of executive promotion, you should figure as much as an extra $10 or $15 per 1000 names, in addition to the base rental fees, etc.

This will typically raise your average cost per name by a cent or two and that should be considered when doing your budget. This is especially important if you plan to have an expensive process included in the list order, perhaps the addition of phone numbers or job titles. The list broker can quote you more precise costs for your specific needs.

Tip: Phone numbers are often available with many lists for an extra $25 or so per thousand. This can save you a lot of work later.

Minimum Quantities

The rental of a list usually requires some minimum quantity or minimum dollar order. These vary depending on the list, list broker, and even the geographic territory you require. The minimum quantity is almost always at least 3000 names. Quite often the minimum may jump to 5000 or even 10,000 names. Or the smallest order may be $200 or some minimum combination of a quantity and a dollar amount.

There is nothing to stop you from ordering 5000 names if you must, despite the fact that your mailing plan calls for mailing only 2500. If you do another mailing within a reasonable time period, before the list gets too old (less than a year generally), you can probably use the balance of the names and not waste them. In any event, since the vast majority of lists cost well under $100 per 1000 names, wasting 2000 or 3000 names is not a terrible disaster.

If you retain some labels for future use, do be careful. While using a portion of the names for a later mailing should be OK, you may upset the list broker if that subsequent mailing is very different from the one you proposed originally. Also, some of the recipients may have forgotten that your use was authorized and alert the list owner to a potential problem. It would be wise to discuss your intentions with the list supplier and get permission in writing to use the names over a period of time in several programs.

Selecting a List

Since the success of direct mail is predicated on the concept of reaching as few prospects as possible and gaining the most sales, the selection of an appropriate target list is perhaps the single most important factor in determining how well the program works.

Your actual choice of a mailing list (or lists) will be based upon a range of considerations. First, the nature of the individuals on the list must be matched with your ideal target market. If you sell annuities, the list should have characteristics which suggest that individuals on that list would want to purchase an annuity. Probably one strong indicator would be that they are older. A list of recently retired individuals may, therefore, be of interest.

Another consideration would be the number of names available and the minimum quantity you must rent. If you are unable to rent a sufficient quantity to satisfy your plan, some other choice would be logical. Despite the fact that most lists contain 50,000, 100,000 or more names, this can be more of a problem than might be apparent at first.

The cost of the list must also be evaluated. While the dollars involved may be small, and the differences in the costs of various lists seemingly insignificant, the price of a list does tell you something about its likely quality. If you plan an inexpensive campaign, perhaps using a low-priced card mailer, you probably do not want to pay for a very expensive list. In general, the pricing of the list should bear some positive relationship to the campaign cost. Spend more on the mailing package if the list is expensive.

Figure 4-3 shows some lists that have proven effective, or are likely to be useful, for financial services marketing. Most list brokers can provide lists like these, or they may suggest alternatives.

Most list brokers will send you a flyer describing what lists they have available, characteristics of the lists, charges, etc. Some publish catalogs of thousands of available lists and their sources. One such publication, *Direct Mail List Rates and Data*, is available from Standard Rate & Data. This is published every few months, so it is fairly up to date. While a subscription is quite expensive, it just might make your list selections easier.

Avoid lists of doctors and lawyers, everyone uses them and your welcome is probably well worn.

An important list source that does not yet seem to have been well "mined" is magazine lists: lists of subscribers to publications, particularly those that are business and financial news related. While some major magazine publishers may not rent their subscriber lists, many do. These lists are often available for under $100 per 1000 names, a bit higher than average lists, but still quite inexpensive relative to other direct marketing costs.

Some magazine subscriber lists that are available include: *Changing Times*, *Kiplinger Washington Letter*, and *Money Magazine*. In addition, *Newsweek* makes its subscribers at a business address available.

LIST NAME	REASONS RECOMMENDED
Arts & Civic Associations Members and Contributors	Wealthy and well educated tend to support the arts, etc.
Business and Investment Newsletter Subscribers	Interest and likely experience with investments.
Business Magazine Subscribers	Higher income and interest in business and finance
Classical Music Club	Older, more affluent individuals
Country Club Memberships	High income individuals
Credit Card Holders who have moved	Financial means and a likely need for a new financial salesperson
Diamond Buyers	Wealthy investors
Equus Magazine Subscribers	Many own horses (implies wealth)
Financial World Subscribers	Often more substantial investors
Government Lands Subscribers	Indication of investment funds
Luxury Car Owners	Expensive cars imply wealth
Marine Radio Buyers	Usually own boat or yacht
Noncommercial Aircraft Owners	Own plane (business or pleasure)
Pre-movers	Applied for home mortgage within last thirty days
Top Management At Home	No secretary to ''screen'' mail
Upscale Retail Credit Card Users	Buy upscale products with card
Women Credit Card Holders	Higher income women

Fig. 4-3. Some lists that you should consider.

Business and financial magazine subscribers can be an ideal target audience for your mailing. Here are just a few reasons why they make great lists for financial services direct mail offers.

- Many financial and business magazines are subscribed to at the home, making the home address available. As noted earlier, mailing to a home address is generally preferable.

- Business magazine subscribers tend to be upscale, have high earning power, and usually have funds available for investment.

- These subscribers probably read to improve themselves and their business position, keeping a sharp eye out for new ideas and trends. They are more likely to understand and act on an investment opportunity.

- Business and financial magazines are typically paid subscriptions, not usually complimentary (free), so readers have shown a propensity to pay for business related items and a greater interest in business subjects.

Another emerging and potentially valuable group consists of "empty nesters" and their offspring. The rapid rise in home values over the past 10 or so years has made many otherwise moderately well-off families quite wealthy. It is not uncommon for older folks in major metropolitan areas to have half-million dollar homes. As their need for a big house diminishes, they will come into substantial funds that are likely to be available for investment. Alternatively, their children may inherit the homes or the monies received when the homes are sold. These people make excellent target audiences that you might be able to reach effectively through direct mail.

Chances are that people who have passed their need for a large and expensive house tend to live in communities built and settled during the suburbanization of America 30 to 40 years ago, when many of them would have been in their thirties. So if you can identify areas that fit this characterization, you might have a worthwhile program.

At the other end of the spectrum, another productive technique is to use a list of the new arrivals in your town. Marketing to those who recently moved into your area gives you a good opportunity to make contact before they locate a new financial services salesperson. Some local papers pick up this information (Fig. 4-4). The "Welcome Wagon" type of organizations may permit you to participate in their newcomers programs on some basis as well.

```
            SIXTY-THREE MORE FAMILIES MAKE
            INVESTORVILLE THEIR NEW HOME!
                      by D. Jones

   Since January, 237 more people have moved to our rapidly
   growing town. That brings the total population to 238. Here is
   a rundown on who they are.

   Adams, Henry & Robbin                          23 E. Elm
   Beck, Shirley                                  24 E. Elm
   Crown, Bill & Mary                              319 First
   Dester, Wm. & Carol                            14 Collins
   Fine, Ivan & Sheba                             25 E. Elm
   Goodley, Sue                                 12 W. Shore
   Jones, Tom and Sue                               Box 43
   Knight, Wm & Brenda                               38 7th
   Lee, Ron & Debbie                           1243 Second
   Leeds, Sales                              14 W. Prospect
   Mooney, Pat & Dee                             236 E. Oak
   Nickerson, Al                                19 W. 22nd
   Nickersuds, Bud                                 159 Polk
   Quick, Leslie                           1760 Balsam Rd.

                   Continued Sec. H, page 33
```

Fig. 4-4. New arrivals listing in local newspaper.

If a list of new arrivals is not available, you might try home sales information. Quite often a local paper will publish a list of real estate transactions, indicating the sellers, buyers, and the house's address. You would, therefore, be able to compile a list of new arrivals. The title recording office in your area should also have this public information.

Locating the Lists

While national lists of 50,000 may seem large, it averages out to only about 1000 names per state (50 states). Of course most of the concentration will probably be in the major population centers. That may leave some of you in smaller towns with only a handful of names to choose from on a particular list.

Table 4-1 indicates population percentages by state. This might prove useful in estimating the probable number of names for your state for any given list. Just multiply the total quantity available by the applicable percentage. Use this only for estimating purposes. This is no substitute for obtaining actual counts before you order.

**Table 4-1.
Percent of Population by State.**

State	Percent of U.S. Population
Alabama	1.69
Alaska	.15
Arizona	.88
Arkansas	.96
California	9.87
Colorado	1.10
Connecticut	1.49
Delaware	.27
District of Columbia	.37
Florida	3.40
Georgia	2.27
Hawaii	.39
Idaho	.35
Illinois	5.45
Indiana	2.55
Iowa	1.38
Kansas	1.11
Kentucky	1.58
Louisiana	1.80
Maine	.48
Maryland	1.93
Massachusetts	2.77
Michigan	4.38
Minnesota	1.86
Mississippi	1.10
Missouri	2.31
Montana	.34
Nebraska	.73
Nevada	.24
New Hampshire	.35
New Jersey	3.54
New Mexico	.50
New York	8.91
North Carolina	2.50
North Dakota	.30

State	Percent of U.S. Population
Ohio	5.23
Oklahoma	1.26
Oregon	1.04
Pennsylvania	5.74
Rhode Island	.47
South Carolina	1.28
South Dakota	.32
Tennessee	1.94
Texas	5.56
Utah	.52
Vermont	.22
Virginia	2.28
Washington	1.68
West Virginia	.84
Wisconsin	2.15
Wyoming	.16

Table 4-1. Continued.

Depending upon the size of your sales territory, the lists you want may not be available in sufficient quantities you require for the mailing. If this turns out to be the case, you must search for bigger lists that contain the appropriate quantity in your area, or expand your marketing territory if possible. You might also use more than one list. The primary problems with using more than one list have to do with finding several "good" lists and with the minimum quantities required to be ordered.

Locating a list that has viable prospects for your offer is hard enough; finding several might be very difficult. You may have to accept lists with less likely prospects.

If one list cannot provide you with enough names in your area, you might have to order two or three lists so you can find 200 names here and 300 there, etc. However, you may still be required to order minimum quantities of 3000 names per list. While ordering 3000 names and using 2000 can make sense in some circumstances, ordering 3000 and using 300 does not. Try to work some sort of deal with the list broker since it is not your fault that he cannot supply enough names on one list.

You may often find that a list broker's help will be required to locate a satisfactory quantity of names for your targeted territory. List brokers are fairly easy to locate. Some will be listed in your local phone book, others advertise in financial publications if they rent lists useful to securities salespeople. Your firm's marketing department may also be able to put you in contact with a list broker.

Be sure you are comfortable with the list broker you select. See his operation if possible. And make your first order a small order so you can decide if the broker is worth using on a larger scale.

As was stressed previously, the margins that list brokers often work on are quite small. While having a list broker help you select your lists is usually desirable, you may just not have a sufficiently large order to justify his time and effort.

Verification

If you order a list, regardless of the source, make sure it is what you wanted. List brokers are only human. They can make mistakes. Before you blindly affix all those labels to your packages, take a moment to spot-check the names. Among the things you can verify are:

- Geography: If you sell in California only, are all the addresses in California?
- Title: If you asked for corporate treasurers, do the addresses show that title, and are they addressed to an office?
- Spelling and Punctuation: Are titles spelled correctly. Did they use Mr., Mrs., etc., or just names?
- Sorting: If you asked for ZIP code sequence, is that what you got?

After working so hard to select a good list and put together an effective program, it would be a terrible shame to find out that you mailed to the wrong list and received a negligible response rate. A few minutes of checking can prevent a wasted mailing.

5

Creating Your
Direct-Mail Package

YOU ARE MAKING excellent progress on your direct-mail campaign. By now you have determined to whom you wish to mail, what you plan to offer, and how much you are willing to spend on the program.

As discussed earlier, the ideal arrangement in direct marketing is to reach the fewest prospects and get the most to reply, since it is expensive to reach each prospect. The task now before you is to create the most favorable impression you possibly can in an effort to motivate the prospects you do reach into responding to your offer.

QUALITY

One ingredient in the marketing of financial products and services that is essential in any direct-mail package is quality. The nature of the financial services business is quite personal, requiring a high level of confidence in you on the part of the potential customer. If you were selling a commodity like toothpaste, which is generally bought almost entirely based on price and convenience, you could truly mass market by coupons and other volume builders without much regard to how the promotional pieces looked.

However, in your case, people will be trusting you with their money. The service industry requires an image of quality and respectability to win customers. Therefore, try to make your materials as professional looking and high-grade as possible. This applies to all materials. Using a quality envelope but a xeroxed letter may actually be harmful since you have set up the prospects to expect a first class presentation and then disappointed them.

Careful attention should be paid to the paper or card stock used for your materials. While it is wise to try and use stock that is readily available (this saves time and money), be sure the quality of the paper is sufficient to your needs. Printing a nice letter on cheap paper is counter productive.

If you will be printing on both sides of a sheet, be sure it has sufficient opacity to prevent the message from being visible on the other side. Your printer can provide you with an opacity gauge (Fig. 5-1) to test the ability of a particular paper to block "see-through."

TYPICAL PAPER OPACITY GAUGE

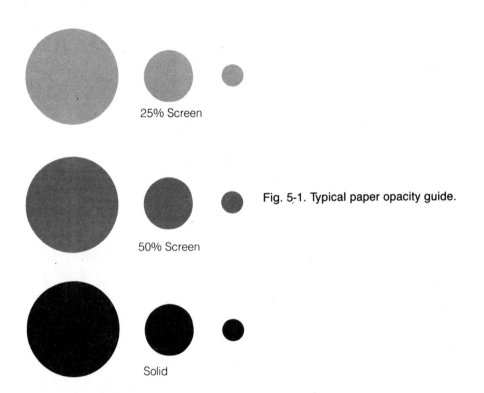

25% Screen

50% Screen

Fig. 5-1. Typical paper opacity guide.

Solid

CARD MAILERS

You will have two primary choices in developing your direct-mail package: an envelope containing various offering materials, or a card mailer which is essentially one or two attached postal cards.

There are quite a few variations on the card mailer theme that have become popular in the promotion of financial services. While all of these are based on the same premise (an easy to use and inexpensive promotional piece that can be sent to large numbers of prospects), the execution of their formats can differ significantly. We will discuss a few types here, but do keep in mind that there are many other possibilities.

The most common card mailer is a "double mailer" (Fig. 5-2). It is sent out folded and sealed (taped or stapled) with the prospect's label or typed address exposed. The prospect tears off the labeled portion, addresses the back side of the other (attached) card, where it requests name, address, etc., and mails it back. The postage is typically prepaid and the address to which it will be returned is printed on the card, minimizing the prospect's work.

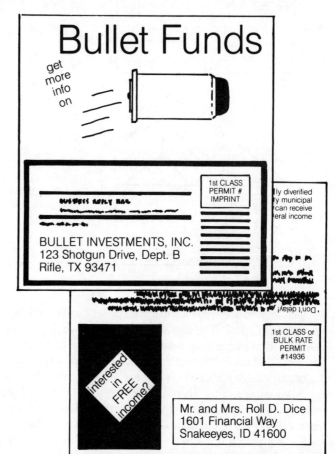

Fig. 5-2. A double mailer.

The chief advantage of the double mailer is price. In quantity, it is exceptionally inexpensive. It is also very efficient to use, requiring your affixing a label, sealing with tape, etc., and mailing. It does, however, typically cost the same amount to mail these as any mailer weighing less than one ounce, including an envelope package. As an outgoing double mailer, these do not qualify as post cards in the eyes of the postal service. The response card, when detached and mailed back, is considered a post card.

Another type of card mailer is a cross between an envelope package and a double mailer. While there is no particular term for this mailer, it sometimes is referred to as a

"Polk" mailer, probably named for the firm that first developed it, or a triple mailer because it has three sections. This format is made of sections of card folded as illustrated in Fig. 5-3. The top section is the outgoing mailing cover, with the prospect's address showing through a cutout.

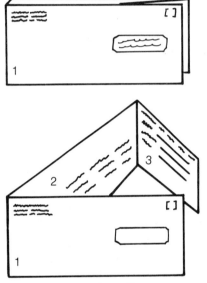

1) Face of mailer with cutout for mailing label to show through

1) Face of mailer

2) Back of mailer with sales message

3) Response Vehicle (Reply Card) already has prospect's address from original addressing label

Fig. 5-3. A "Polk" or triple mailer.

The second portion is a flap folded under the first one which becomes the response vehicle (reply card). The last section acts as a back and contains text about the offer. This type of mailer is both relatively inexpensive and has the added advantage that the prospect need not fill out anything, since his address already appears on the reply card as the original mailing label which showed through the front flap.

As discussed in the chapter *A Review Of Direct-Mail Marketing*, if you use a card mailer it is usually apparent to prospects that this was the least expensive way for you to contact them. While this approach can be useful in certain circumstances, generally it is not the impression you want to create, nor one that typically gets great results.

Response levels from card mailers will invariably be lower than from a nice envelope package including a letter, for a given quantity mailed. While it will also be less expensive to do a mailing using cards, the cost per lead might very well be more for cards.

Card mailers certainly do have a role to play in marketing, and there are many situations where they can prove beneficial. For example, if you are given a group of leads by an outside investment packaging firm, and you are doubtful of the value of these leads, you might use a card mailer to test their interest. This would be an inexpensive way to follow up without spending an inordinate amount on questionable leads.

A card mailer would also be a very acceptable method of generating leads as an add-on to some other mailing, as in the case of statement stuffers.

There is a wide variety of other card mailer options. The variations in ways the mailers can be folded and assembled are almost endless. All but the single card variety will cost you essentially the same to mail as a one-ounce envelope package, so your savings will be primarily in materials charges, not postage.

Tip: A good rule of thumb for deciding whether to use a card mailer or envelope package is as follows: If you must pay the postage to send the mailing, use a letter and a nice package. If you do not pay the postage, or pay a portion of the postage, a less expensive approach may be appropriate.

ENVELOPE PACKAGES (Envelope and Contents)

In putting together your direct-mail package, a good place to start is with your letter. You should use a letter whenever possible. This is the only enclosure that can convey the slightest illusion of personalization—even if it is preprinted in quantity.

Your letter should be an introduction, a sales tool, and an information source. The prospects should know who you and your firm are and why the offer will benefit them. They should understand how to reply to your offer and be motivated to take action. You may choose to focus mainly on your credentials, or on the benefits of your offer, or on the action needed, but cover all of the following areas to some degree:

- Tell the prospects who you and your firm are.
- Describe the offer and explain how they will benefit.
- Explain how to reply and why they should do so.

Bear in mind that you cannot sell in written form the same way you sell face to face. In person you have time to build confidence and rapport. You get to monitor the prospect's reactions and adjust your sales pitch accordingly. And you can modify your tack as the conversation progresses.

But in a letter you do not have the opportunity to react or correct your approach. Based on much feedback by monitoring direct marketing, certain methods have proven more successful than others. One general guide is to get right to the pitch. Do not waste valuable time (and the prospect's attention), by "chatting." Tell them why they should continue reading and what they will get out of it. Studies indicate that 80% of prospects read the first line, and that is all they read—then they toss the letter. So if you do not get their attention right away, it will be a lost cause.

Throughout your letter and other literature, keep reminding the prospects that they will benefit from dealing with you. Give them a good reason to continue reading and, hopefully, to respond to your offer.

Assume you offer accounting services and have decided to target new arrivals to your metropolitan area, specifically those who have purchased a new home within the last six months. You believe this makes a good prospect list since new arrivals probably do not have an accountant and the fact that they purchased a home tends to indicate financial means and potential accounting needs. Figure 5-4 illustrates one type of direct-mail letter you might use.

BIG-TIME ACCOUNTANTS
1438 Financial Way
Bearmarket, OR 91753
800-555-1212

Mr. and Mrs. Roll D. Dice
121 Easy Street
Snakeeyes, OR 91753

Dear Mr. and Mrs. Dice:

Congratulations on your new home. As one of your newcomer sponsors, I wanted to welcome you to the Bearmarket area.

I have had the pleasure of helping many area residents with their accounting needs, perhaps some of your new neighbors are my clients? Big-Time is the number one name in accounting in the Bearmarket area. We've been here since 1926.

The Tax Reform Act of 1986 changed the way interest deductions are computed on residential property and the Revenue Act of 1987 further modified such changes. We are very familiar with these laws and how they may affect new homeowners like you.

If your move has created the need for accounting services, I would be delighted to discuss this with you at a free five minute consultation. Just return the postage paid card and I will be in touch to set up an appointment.

Again, welcome to Bearmarket.

Sincerely,

Douglass J. Flywheel III

Fig. 5-4. Example of an accounting direct-mail letter.

In another case you may wish to market insurance. The product you have in mind is geared toward older people concerned about failing health and rising medical costs as well as the cost of their insurance. Your product is targeted to a select group who, by certain qualifications, are a lower risk. Presented in Fig. 5-5 is an approach you might use in a direct mail-letter.

If your letter does not sufficiently explain the offer, which is rarely possible in the limited space of a letter, some offering materials should be included such as a brochure or flyer. These items must be kept brief or securities regulations may require you to enclose a prospectus or other very detailed information. It is not desirable to send all prospects lengthy technical information at this stage. There are three compelling reasons to avoid including a great deal of data in your initial mailing:

1. It is expensive. The extra materials cost money and add to the package's weight, increasing postage costs.
2. You probably want to build customer interest and confidence in you, prior to unleashing the heavy legal disclaimers often included in a prospectus. Most disclosure forms required to be provided at some point in the selling cycle are intim-

idating and potentially can scare off prospects. While they will eventually see these items, you should develop a relationship with the prospect before providing this information.

3. You do not want to provide all of the information initially since literature rarely makes a sale. You should give the prospects a reason to respond (seeking more information) so you can personally ''sell'' them on the product or service.

ALLCITYFARM INSURANCE
1438 Financial Way
Bearmarket, OR 91753
800-555-1212

Mr. Huge Risk
121 Easy Street
Bearmarket, OR 91753

Dear Mr. Risk:

Soaring charges for procedures and medications have made medical care the number one issue among older Americans. We share the concern of people like you who must balance the risk of large medical costs against the escalating premiums for health insurance. And we have a way to help.

Our new Pacemaker Policy is specifically geared to keep down the costs of health insurance while providing the optimum in coverage. How can we do this? It is very simple. We limit who can qualify to the best risks. That means you do not have to pay for the expenses of those at greater risk!

To screen out those that are likely to have larger than normal medical expenses, we ask the following:

- Have you ever been in a room where there was smoke?
- Have you ever been to a party where alcohol was served?
- Have you ever seen a doctor?
- Are both your parents dead?

If a prospective member answers yes to any of these, they do not qualify. In addition, new enrollees in our Pacemaker Policy must pass rigorous tests including swimming the English Channel and Climbing Mt. Everest.

If you qualify, you will benefit by our low rates, often one to two percent less than average and our guarantee not to cancel as long as you continue to meet our rigorous enrollment tests.

If you would like complete information on our Pacemaker Policy, please complete the form at the bottom of this letter and return it in the postage paid envelope. Together we can beat the high cost of medical insurance!

Sincerely,

Douglass J. Flywheel III

Fig. 5-5. Example of an insurance direct-mail letter.

```
- - - - - - - - - - - - - - - - - - - - - - - - - - - - - - - - - - - - - - - - - - - - - - - - - - - - - -
```

COMPLETE THIS FORM, DETACH AND RETURN
IN THE POSTAGE PAID ENVELOPE

Dear Mr. Flywheel,

[ ] Yes, I want to learn more about your Pacemaker Policy. Send me complete information and set up my qualifications test!

NAME _____ [ ] Mr. [ ] Mrs. [ ] Ms.

ADDRESS _____ APARTMENT _____

CITY _____ STATE _____ ZIP _____

PHONE (Optional) (_____)_____

AGE BRACKET [ ] 15 – 50 [ ] 51 – 60 [ ] 61 – 65 [ ] 66 [ ] 67 – 183

ALLCITYFARM INSURANCE 1438 Financial Way, Bearmarket, OR 91753
800-555-1212

Fig. 5-5. Continued.

In the majority of cases, your best option is to offer complete details, including the prospectus or other detailed data, only to those who actually do inquire. Your offer may, therefore, be part of your letter or an insert explaining certain benefits (general or specific) of investing or dealing with you. For example, you might include a brochure about your firm describing its hundred-year history of service and success, or you might add an insert about the benefits of a particular investment which you sell, etc. Whatever you select as an offering device, it must be carefully reviewed and approved by your legal department to make sure you are not in violation of any regulations.

Response Vehicles

Your reply vehicle must be effective. Once you have convinced the prospect to respond, try not to do anything that may change his mind. Keep it simple. Pay the reply postage if you request a mail reply.

Your prospects are at a critical decision-making stage when they are considering sending back the reply. The easier it is for them to do so, the more likely they will do so. Your firm may already have an incoming postal permit number available for your use, or you can obtain one from the post office for a nominal fee. If you use a mailing permit number, you will pay postage only if the reply vehicle is actually returned. In limited quantities, you can simply pay $.40 for each reply received (plus a nominal permit fee). In larger volumes, a fixed fee can reduce the per piece charge substantially. See the appendix on *Postal Service, Rates, and Regulations* for more information on this.

Ask only the barest essential information. The prospect's name and address are often enough. Depending upon the type of direct-mail package, it is even possible to have their name and address already on the reply, so they would simply have to drop it in the mail.

Try not to request a telephone number. Asking for a phone number is like flashing a neon sign that reads, ''you are going to get a sales call from this.'' Many people will not give you their phone number anyway. The majority of numbers are listed and you can usually get this information when you require it. It is also possible that phone numbers may have been supplied with the original mailing list.

If you decide to ask for the phone number anyway, make it optional and ask for just one number. Have the prospect indicate if it is their office or home phone number. That way you will have a better idea of the optimal time to call and what to expect when you do call, i.e., that a spouse may answer if a home number or a secretary may answer if a work number. Make sure that you indicate that the phone number is optional in any case. It is a shame how many leads are lost because the prospect is interested in the offer but reluctant to give out a phone number, so they decide against responding.

It is much better to ask if the number is their home or business number than to ask ''best time to call?'' The indication of which number they have given you accomplishes the same thing (you have a better idea of when to call and what to expect), but it is not quite as blatant an indication that you will call.

If you need some other data about the prospect, keep it as short and as impersonal as possible. The prospect does not know you at all at this point. Do not ask their income level, ask for their approximate tax bracket instead. This is disarming and probably still gives you what you need.

Similarly, do not request a list of their financial holdings and values. As a better alternative ask for the types of securities they own and, perhaps, an estimate of their portfolio size if you really need it. A checklist might be useful here. Get just what you need initially. There will be many chances to learn all about the prospect's financial needs after you develop contact with them. Do not do anything unnecessary that might discourage the prospect from replying. And use good sense. If you ask any personal questions, such as their tax bracket, etc., provide a reply form and envelope. Definitely do not use a reply card in that case. People do not want the whole world to know about their financial affairs.

Another reply mechanism you might try is providing ''your'' telephone number. Make sure that you pay the ''postage'' here too—permit collect calls or use a toll-free number. Also, ensure that there will be someone available to answer the phone when calls are likely to come in. An unanswered phone is like no reply vehicle at all. Few people will try an unanswered number more than once or twice. If a person cannot answer the phone (at night for example), use an answering machine. Not everyone likes answering machines, but almost everyone would prefer them to a ''no answer.'' And be sure to provide enough lines to prevent excessive busy signals. Most people dislike busy signals even more than ''no answers.''

You may elect to use both a mail reply and a phone number, which gives the prospects the greatest opportunity to contact you in the manner they prefer.

Envelopes

The last necessary ingredient for your direct-mail envelope package is the envelope in which it will be sent. Use a plain envelope with your return address. It is best if the prospect's address is typed on the envelope, but if you are mailing a large quantity, using the labels from a rented mailing list is acceptable. One option here is to use a window envelope and place the label on a reply card (if you plan to use one). The address shows through the window making the package look nicer and saving the prospect some effort since he will not have to write his name and address on the reply card.

People are becoming more accustomed to receiving mail that appears to have been computer-generated. If you have access to a computer printer and can address the envelopes that way, your response rate should not suffer significantly and this will be better than using labels. But a nicely typed address is optimal if you can manage it.

Always use a return address. Otherwise you will not get those that were not deliverable back. As mentioned in an earlier chapter, there is roughly a 4 to 5% undeliverable count in any list. If you get more pieces that were not deliverable than this typical level, you can often receive a credit for the excess from the list broker who provided you with that list. More importantly, you will know how up to date the list was and why you may not have achieved as high a level of inquiries as you may have planned. If the list has a high content of undeliverable names, you should not necessarily fault your package for poor performance. The undeliverable count will become a valuable guide when you are considering using that list, or that list broker, again.

The most common return address to use on the package would be your firm's, perhaps with your name included as well. For effective variations, you might try your home address or your office address without your firm's name. People are usually curious as to who would send them mail and will probably open an envelope with only an address on it just to find out. They are far more likely to open an envelope with some return address on it than no address at all, particularly if the package looks like a solicitation.

The temptation to print something on the envelope like "Important Information Enclosed," or "Special Offer," etc., should be resisted. That imprint is a red flag that your letter is a solicitation and often means that it will go to the bottom of the recipient's mail pile to be opened last, or tossed out unopened. A standard number 10 envelope, the kind in which your office letters are usually sent, is quite acceptable. These probably already have your firm's return address on them. Sometimes a smaller envelope (if your package will fit) gives a personal or invitational image and this may be desirable.

The recommendation not to print messages on the envelope applies to the initial promotional mailing. Your follow-up or fulfillment package, the one sent after the prospect responds initially, can certainly indicate that this is information they requested or ordered. However, if any notification like this is used on your envelopes, it should be simple and tasteful. *Here is the Information You Requested* printed on the front of the envelope in small letters should suffice.

Tip: Do not clutter the fulfillment envelope with a large message or try to use the envelope to sell your product. That is what the materials you have enclosed are supposed to help accomplish.

In Chapter 2 the contents of a typical direct-mail envelope package were reviewed. There are many types of envelope formats that can create a variety of impressions, as illustrated in Fig. 5-6.

The envelope you use should match the letter stationery. That is, the type of paper, color, and return address layout should all be coordinated with the letterhead. A similar theme should be carried throughout all inserts. For example, if your paper is light tan with brown printing, do not use a yellow insert with green printing. Try to stick to the

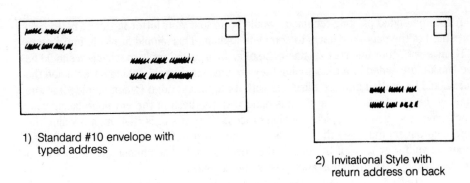

1) Standard #10 envelope with typed address

2) Invitational Style with return address on back

3) Window envelope with address on enclosed return card

Here is the information you requested

4) Fulfillment envelope with address label and reminder message

Fig. 5-6. Typical envelope package appearance options.

same basic colors and type-styles throughout the package. The exception might be the reply card or reply form since you want to make it easy for the prospect to find and use it. In that case you might use a different, but non-clashing, color. Just think of the solicitations or letters you regularly receive. Those with well-coordinated style and uniformity probably presented the most professional image.

Package Assembly

Assembling the package is also important. You probably want the prospect to read your letter first, then review the enclosures (if any) and finally use the reply card. If the reply card comes up first, they may pass judgment before having reviewed the facts presented in your letter or offering materials. The result is usually a negative decision.

Most envelopes are opened where they were sealed, with a letter opener (or fingers) used to slice across the top flap. That means the back of the envelope is usually facing the person opening it (so they can get the opener under the flap). After opening the envelope, the tendency is to pull the contents out while still holding the envelope with its back toward the person removing the contents. Thus, the insert should be positioned so that it is properly held when removed in this fashion. Try it yourself and see what happens.

A recommended packing technique would be to fold your letter in three: bottom up to one-third of the page, top down to complete folding. This should fit nicely into a number 10 envelope. Your inserts explaining the offer (if any) and reply mechanism should be placed inside the folded letter, assuming they are smaller than the folded letter. Then the letter should be stuffed into the envelope with its top most edge (when unfolded) at the bottom of the envelope. If the stuffing is done with the back of the envelope facing you, you will have reversed the typical opening process. The result is that upon opening the letter, the prospect must see the beginning of your letter before they find the inserts. As a bonus, even if they tear off the end of the envelope or utilize almost any other way to open the envelope, the result is about the same scenario.

For inserts larger than your folded letter, you should clip or staple them behind the letter, to ensure that the letter will be seen first. Fold and insert as described above.

Another option might be to use the bottom section of your letter as the response form. This could either be the bottom third of a regular letter, or the extra length an oversized page could provide. This approach would guarantee too that the prospect sees your letter before the response form. However, you would need to provide a return envelope since the form could not be mailed by itself. (A card mailer must be printed on card stock, so unless you print your entire letter on card stock, an envelope would be required.) This may add to your package's cost and it makes the prospect have to do more work, removing the form and putting it into the envelope. Alternatively, you might not give them any envelope, which would be the easiest solution. But that forces the prospect to find and address his own envelope, which would tend to reduce response rates.

You may want to try another packaging order, but the objective should be to get the prospect to read your letter first. Figure 5-7 shows the recommended assembly for a typical direct-mail package.

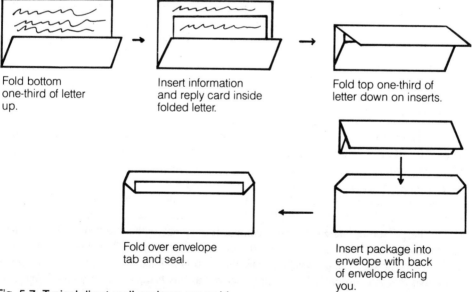

Fold bottom one-third of letter up.

Insert information and reply card inside folded letter.

Fold top one-third of letter down on inserts.

Fold over envelope tab and seal.

Insert package into envelope with back of envelope facing you.

Fig. 5-7. Typical direct-mail package assembly.

Business Cards

Including your business card with the prospecting package is usually unnecessary. At this initial stage of contact your main goal is to offer the prospect something he needs, does not presently have, and thinks he cannot get elsewhere. Thus, the main focus should be on client needs and your emphasis ought to be on a product or service.

Including a card could produce a conflict in the prospect's mind. A card may imply that the client should contact you (usually by telephone) and that your card should be kept. So if you have also provided a reply mailer for their response, the prospects may not be sure what they should do, nor will they be certain if your card should be kept since no business relationship has yet been established. Where there is confusion the probability of response goes down.

Your business card should be included in a limited number of circumstances, however. These are:

- If your response vehicle is only through telephone calls and that number is on your card.
- If you have certain important credentials such as CFA, Ph.D., etc., that would add credibility to your solicitation but would not be appropriate to mention in your letter, etc. A title such as Vice President is not enough to justify inclusion of a card since just about everyone in the financial marketing business has some such title today.

If you do include your card, be sure to clip it to the letter. Attach it at the top of the letter, where it will not interfere with the text nor drop to the floor when the letter is opened.

TESTING

You should experiment with various ideas to see what works best. Give mock-ups of your proposed package to friends and business associates and get their reactions. Watch how they open the envelope, handle the contents, etc.

Then test the actual package with a very small mailing. Send out 50 or 100 packages to part of your list. If you get a response or two, you will know the package is working moderately well. This test may uncover some potential problems you had overlooked, such as an error in the reply card, before you mail to the entire list. If you do not get any responses, review potential changes such as altering the assembly of contents and then mail another small quantity. When you achieve a few responses for each one hundred names mailed, you are ready to do your mailing.

Remember, you need to mail 1000 or more pieces to get a meaningful result which would be statistically significant in indicating if the program has been successful or not. These small tests are only a fine tuning technique. One hundred mailers could produce good or bad results which may not be representative of the larger universe.

Compiling Your Own Lists

The previous discussions focused on preparing your mailing for a rented list. You may prefer to mail to your own compiled list, to old customers, or to other sources. The basic concepts just described still apply. The thrust of your campaign may have to vary, but the packaging should follow the same format.

Here is a brief list of some potential target audiences that you can create without needing to rent a list from a list broker.

- Compiled list of your contacts.
- Telephone directory compilation.
- Old account records (your own or your firm's).
- Current, but inactive customers.
- New arrivals in the community (if you develop this yourself from newspapers, etc.). This might also be available in the form of a rental list.

In summary, your direct-mail package should convey benefits and provide information on how to learn more about the offer. The mailing should present a quality image and motivate the recipient to respond. Assemble the package carefully and keep the response mechanism as simple and easy as possible. Providing more than one way to respond can further enhance the overall response rate.

6

Delivering Your
Direct-Mail Package

ONCE YOU HAVE prepared the materials you will use in your direct-mail campaign, you are ready to assemble and send the packages.

There are four critical areas involved in the packing and delivery process of direct-mail marketing:

1. Ensuring the correct assembly of packages (the proper inclusions placed in the right order).
2. Controlling supplies (so as not to run out of, or overstock, on one or more of the inserts or mailing materials).
3. Minimizing postage costs (which are affected by both the method by which the pieces are sent and by their weight).
4. Controlling costs (other than postage) associated with the actual mailing.

PACKAGE ASSEMBLY

Previous chapters discussed inclusions and their recommended assembly order in a direct-mail package. If you are preparing a typical mailing, your promotional piece will probably consist of a letter, brochure or other insert, and a reply card or reply envelope and form. Since you will want the prospects to read the letter first, you will probably want to assemble these items as indicated in the chapter, *Creating Your Direct-Mail Package*.

Using Outside Vendors

If you use a mailing house or other outside vendor to assemble and mail your packages, you will have to give them detailed instructions along with your materials and list. Be sure to include a sample package already assembled as you wish. Check that they are doing the work as you instructed. You might take a prepared package at random and open it, verifying that everything is there and in the proper order.

Keep in mind that the package materials are just part of the mailing. The list you are using is equally critical. If you ordered a list which you will be delivering to the mailing vendor, check what form it is in. Pressure-sensitive labels that must simply be affixed to the envelopes will be a fairly straightforward and simple process. But if all you have is a typed list, you will need to tell the vendor whether to type labels or type directly on envelopes, if he should input the data on a computer for future use, etc. Perhaps the addressing will go on to a computer-generated letter? Clarify what you expect. His charges will obviously be affected by what he must do for you.

A suggested format to use when communicating your mailing instructions to the vendor is presented in Fig. 6-1 for a hypothetical mailing by Risky Investors. Each item has a check box at the beginning to help ensure that all options have been covered.

Doing the Mailing Yourself

If you will not be using an outside service for assembly and mailing, then you will not have to explain to someone else exactly how you want to assemble the package.

If you plan to do the physical mailing yourself, try to set up an efficient assembly-line process to do the project yourself. It will save you time and reduce the chances of errors if you work in a systematic and orderly manner. Rather than pile all the materials on your desk and put one package together at a time, find an available bench or conference table where you can spread out and keep the materials separated. One time-proven system organizes the various parts of a direct mail-package as follows:

- Letter—prefolded to fit the envelope
- Brochure, etc.—prefolded as needed
- Reply card or envelope and form
- Mailing envelope

This method suggests the user pick up the letter, insert the brochure and reply card in the folded letter, and then stuff the entire contents into the envelope. All inserts should be arranged so that they are facing the way you want them to go into the envelope. The process is illustrated in Fig. 6-2.

You should stuff all the envelopes first. The second operation would involve sealing all envelopes. If your office does not have an automatic envelope sealer and postage machine, sealing is best accomplished by using an envelope sealing sponge in a fixed container which sits on a table. Simply brushing the envelope over the moist sponge and folding the flap down seals it. There is no need to lift the sponge, so this simplifies the operation. Envelope sealing sponges are available at most office supply stores.

Date: July 4, 1989

From: Douglass J. Flywheel III   TO: Mailers Plus++
        Risky Investors, Inc.   1101 E. Big Apple Way
        73 Bet M High Rd.   New York, NY 10001
        Ulose, NV 94001
        800-555-1212

MAILING INSTRUCTIONS: MAILING SCHEDULED FOR July 12, 1989

[x] TIME CRITICAL   [ ] Mail Early OK   [x] Mail Late OK
                         [x] Do Not Mail Early   [ ] Do Not Mail Late

WORK TO BE PERFORMED:

[x] ASSEMBLING 7 (# of items)

[x] SUBASSEMBLY   [x] Folding letters
    REQUIRED: [x] Affixing labels to insert or reply card
                         [x] Stapling or other operations? Attach sticker

[x] INSERTING INTO ENVELOPE TYPE # 10

[x] ENVELOPE CLOSURE: [ ] Self adhesive
                      [x] Moisture activated
                      [ ] Clasp

[x] ADDRESSING BY: [x] Customer supplied labels
                   [ ] Vendor generated and supplied labels
                   [ ] Personalized letter
                   [ ] Typed address

[x] POSTAGE FORMAT: [x] Customer permit number imprinted
                    [ ] Metered postage, bill customer
                    [ ] Affix stamps, bill customer

[x] POSTAGE RATES: [ ] Regular First Class
                   [ ] First Class presort
                   [x] Bulk rate, specify which rate. 16.7 cents ea.

[x] DELIVERY TO POST OFFICE: [x] Vendor responsibility
                             [ ] Customer responsibility

[x] QUANTITIES TO BE MAILED: ___2570

[x] QUANTITIES SUPPLIED: [x] Brochure _2700
                         [x] Preprinted letter _2700
                         [x] Reply card _2600
                         [ ] Other _____ (describe)

[x] MATERIALS SHORTAGE: [ ] Do not mail   [x] Mail all finished

[x] RETURN UNUSED MATERIALS   [x] Yes   [ ] No

Fig. 6-1. Vendor mailing instructions form.

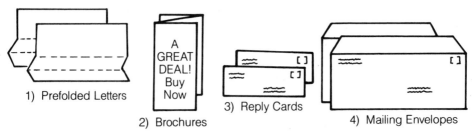

Fig. 6-2. Assembly line system for doing your own mailing.

If the envelopes were not already addressed, having been typed for example, the next step would be to affix labels (self-adhesive would be necessary in this case).

Tip: If more than one address is provided, perhaps a post office box and a street address, be sure the one closest to the city/state/ZIP line is the one you prefer for the delivery.

Affixing postage would be the final step in the assembly process. This could be done with ordinary stamps, a metering machine, or by using an outside vendor that will mail the packages for you.

MINIMIZING POSTAGE COSTS

You will have to decide which method of delivery will be most cost effective for your program. You might use regular first-class mail, or possibly bulk rate. You could also send your information by overnight letter, etc. Each of these has advantages and disadvantages.

The primary trade-off will be time versus cost. Bulk mail is cheaper, but typically adds days to delivery time. Overnight Express Mail is fast and impressive, but very expensive and usually not worth the price for promotional purposes.

Keep in mind that, for example, if you spend just one extra dollar per prospect, you will need to recoup those expenditures in sales. Even at a very optimistic estimate of a 10% response rate, that would add $10 to the cost of each lead (10 prospects × $1 additional = $10 extra. At a 10% response rate, the 10 prospects produce just one lead). Now if you were able to close 20% of those leads, again very optimistic, you will have spent an additional $50 per sale (5 leads × $10 extra = $50. A 20% closing rate on five leads produces one sale). So an extra $1 spent per prospect means 50 times as much spent per sale. It is very hard to justify the extra cost to send mail more quickly when you consider the required pay-back.

Methods of Mail Delivery

In addition to considering which method of delivery you would like to use, you must also qualify to use some of the means. This usually is based on volume (number of pieces to mail).

Smaller direct mailers commonly utilize first-class regular mail. There is no minimum number required, no sorting and no special handling. If you use a standard postage stamp for your mailing it may even create a better image and reduce the mass mailing appearance often associated with bulk postage. Figure 6-3 shows the relative appearance of various methods of paying for postage.

The cost to mail first class is currently $.25 for up to one ounce (about the weight of an envelope and three pieces of typing paper). Most direct-mail packages can be produced to weigh under one ounce, so $.25 is about the maximum you should have to spend to mail each piece (unless you are required to include a prospectus or other heavy item).

There are a number of things you can do to reduce the per piece cost of your mailing and still send it first class.

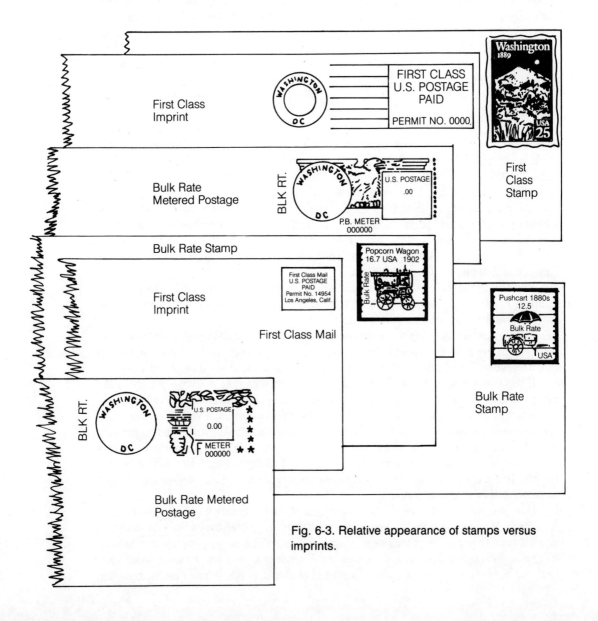

Fig. 6-3. Relative appearance of stamps versus imprints.

One potential postage saving method would be to send only a post card, which will cost you $.15 each at current rates. While this certainly reduces your cost, it is also quite likely to reduce your inquiries proportionately, or perhaps by an even greater amount.

Another option is to use first-class mail presorted in ZIP code sequence. The postal service will grant you a discount on each letter, reducing the average cost by a few cents each. This normally requires at least 500 pieces sorted by ZIP code and, for additional savings, by carrier route. An outside vendor that provides presorting services can often add your mailings to others and thereby qualify you for presorted rates.

If you are renting a mailing list, it is possible that you can order the list already sorted by ZIP code or other beneficial sequence. This will make it easier for you to take advantage of some of the discounts the post office offers. Alternatively, you can sort them yourself or hire a firm, called a presorter, to sort and mail the list for you. It has been estimated that there are well over 200 presorters in business throughout the U.S., so finding one should not be difficult. While their charges will vary, typically a presorter will charge you half of the $.04 they can save you, so you wind up saving about $.02 per piece. That still can be quite worthwhile, especially in larger volumes. They handle the mailing for you as well.

The theory is that by doing some of the work that the postal service normally would have to do, they will give you a slight break on the mailing costs. But it doesn't always work out to your advantage. For example, post cards can be mailed first class for $.15 each, but the charge is $.167 each to mail them third class, a slower method. So you should always verify that doing extra sorting will indeed save you postal charges.

If you are willing to do further sorting and do not mind your mailing taking a little longer to reach the prospects, Business Bulk Mail is an option worth considering. Bulk mail requires significant sorting and bundling prior to bringing the mailing to the post office, but it can save nearly half the postage costs of first-class regular mail. A minimum quantity of 200 pieces is required here.

Remember that bulk mailing is usually slower to be delivered than first-class mail, so if time is critical—your offer is available for a short time, for example—you may want to pay the premium required to mail first class.

Keep in mind that a high percentage of bulk mail is not delivered simply because someone in the delivery process did not think it looked important. So if you use bulk or other discounted mail rates, try to make your package look as good as possible.

If you use a mailing house to do your mailing, they can often advise you as to the most economical way to send your materials and still achieve satisfactory results.

Another important way to keep postage rates low is to keep the weight of your package down to one ounce or less. Be very careful in this matter. Weigh a complete package with all contents. Include a label if you will use an addressing label, a paper clip if you plan to use one in the package, the exact type and weight of paper your letter will be printed on, etc. If you are very close to one ounce, or slightly over, consider lighter paper stock or possibly leaving out an insert.

However, do not sacrifice the overall impact of your message to save a few pennies in postage. If you must include a brochure to tell your story effectively, then do so even if you will have to pay more to mail more than one ounce. The entire program is an investment that you hope will produce a good return. Do not risk the effort by leaving out a key item and possibly ruining your chance to get the prospect to act. In most cases, however, a slight modification of an insert can cut your overall costs considerably. Let common sense be your guide. Just be sure you know the actual postage costs and are comfortable that there is no reasonable way to cut the weight and costs of the mailing further.

The discussion here is very basic on your choice of mailing services. The appendix on postal services will provide you with much more in-depth information on methods you can use and their costs.

Supplies

Make sure you have sufficient supplies of everything you will need for the mailing. If you are planning to use company envelopes, be sure you can get 1000, or whatever quantity you plan to mail. Identify where you can obtain more of each item if you need them. If you misplace 300 reply cards, know where you can get 300 reprinted quickly.

UNDELIVERABLES

As discussed previously, in any given list some of the names will not be deliverable. The percentage typically should not exceed 4 to 5%. If it does exceed those figures, you can often get a partial refund from the supplier of the list. However, to receive a refund, and to determine how many prospects actually received your mailing, you must have the undeliverables returned to you.

If you use first-class mail and include your return address on the pieces, you will automatically receive any letters back that were not able to be delivered or forwarded. However, if you use bulk rates for mailing, the post office does not automatically return the letters that were not delivered unless you pay for that service additionally. Be careful not to agree to pay for undeliverables unless you know the list you are using is fairly up to date. The current charge to return bulk rate undeliverables (called an endorsement) is 2.7 times the single-piece rate of $.25 ($.675 each). A good list might have less than 5% that cannot be delivered. Beyond that it could get very expensive for you to find out how old the list might be.

Tip: Be sure your complete return address appears on any outgoing piece so you can get undeliverables returned. Without a return address they will not be sent to you even if you wanted that service!

To ensure that your mailing list is as up to date as possible, include the imprint "Address Correction Requested" on your first-class mail. While you will normally get undeliverables back automatically, you will not be informed of mail forwarded to a new address and delivered there. To receive notification of the forwarding address, you need the imprint. You will also have to pay a small fee for each address on which forwarding information is provided.

List Correction and Sequencing Service

The post office has a variety of services that can help you cut down on undeliverables or at least better correct your lists for future use.

They can, for a fee, remove incorrect or nonexistent street addresses, and in some cases they can insert new addresses if the customers have left forwarding instructions.

Another service called list sequencing sorts addresses on a mailing list into carrier route sequence. Undeliverable addresses are removed. If the list contains at least 90% correct addresses in a five-digit ZIP code area, missing addresses will be added and incorrect addresses will be updated where possible.

National Change of Address System

If you are a major mailer, you might take advantage of the National Change of Address System (NCOA). This is a centralized database of information from all permanent change of address cards filed at the post office. The new change of addresses are sent weekly to a central processor where they are added to the files and updated. The completely updated file is sent to about 25 computer firms that provide a service that essentially runs your list against this file and corrects or removes files before you mail. While this can save a lot of wasted postage, the fee to run a list in this system can amount to thousands of dollars. For a mailing of one million pieces it can make a lot of sense. But for 2000 it would be a waste of money.

If your firm already utilizes this service for other mailings it may make, you possibly could piggyback your mailing list on to a larger one and get the benefit of the updating and verification without the huge expense.

Other Costs

If you are expecting telephone responses, make sure that the phone number is operational and available before responses can start coming in. Do not get caught depending on your firm's WATS lines when they might be tied up because of another promotional campaign. The cost of providing a toll-free number can sometimes be minimized by joining in a shared effort. Services exist that might have just one 800 number, but it is used by 10 or 20 customers, each with an extension to identify to whom the call should be directed.

If you are doing the mailing yourself, you will incur little or no additional costs to put together the packages and mail them (except, of course, for postage). But if you use a mailing house or other service, be sure to get a firm quote on the total cost. This service will vary in cost, but $.05 to $.20 per package should be the typical range depending upon number of inserts, difficulty of assembly, etc. Most services will require a minimum of 1000 pieces or $100, so if you use them be sure to budget at least another $100 to $200 for that purpose.

MONITORING THE MAILING

Seed the list by placing your name and a few of your friend's names on the list, particularly if you use a mailing house. That way you will be able to see exactly what was sent and that it was assembled properly. You will also get an idea of when the prospects received the mailing based upon when you received it.

Be sure to examine all returns and undeliverables as well. There should be proper contents and assembly in nearly every case. If not, complain and get an adjustment to your bill.

As mentioned in an earlier chapter, try to stagger your mailing over a number of days. If you are mailing the solicitation yourself, this is especially important since you not only reduce your expected influx of leads per day to a manageable level, but your stuffing and mailing will be spread out as well. On the other hand, if you use a mailing service, you may have to have your entire mailing done at once. Those services specialize in large volume mailings and your 1000, 2000 or even 5000 pieces may represent a tiny order to them. They may not be interested in taking on the mailing in two or three sections of 500 each. Smaller mailing services may do this for you, but you should inquire beforehand rather than assuming that it can be done.

Tip: You might possibly have a mailing house stuff your mailing, return it to you, and then you could stagger the mailing yourself.

Using Your Own Lists

If you are using your own compiled list, you will need to arrange the same procedures as with a rental list in order to get your mailing sent. That often means having envelopes or labels typed from the list you have prepared. Plan time and additional expenses for this. Typing 1000 names can take quite a few hours and might cost you $100 or more. If it is your own list, be sure you have the names on file or have copies of your labels made so you can mail to these people at a later date without paying for typing costs again.

Given a choice, have envelopes typed. They look much better typed than they do with a label. While a handwritten address can add a certain personalization, it is usually interpreted as being done by someone who does not have a secretary (implying not as successful). In some cases a label will be required or it will be much easier to use, but if it does not take a great deal of effort, type the address. Your response rate should be better that way.

Tip: If your list is on computer, you may be able to use computer form envelopes and a good quality printer to give the illusion that the envelopes were individually typed.

Statement Stuffers

If you are inserting a message in statements, you will need to arrange with your firm to have inserting done in the appropriate statements. This may or may not be possible, depending upon your particular circumstances. It is best to discuss the idea with your manager or the personnel involved with statement mailings before you prepare any materials or spend any funds. Be sure your insert will fit inside the statement envelope and, most importantly, that it will fit the stuffing machine the mailer will use for your statements. Most large statement mailings are done by specialized machines which are limited in the type of inserts they are able to accommodate.

Keeping Track

Keep careful track of what you mail. Your records should show how many pieces were mailed, when, and to whom. If you obtained a 3×5" card file of your list, you already have one form of the mailing record. Otherwise, copy the list for your records only. This will be important in handling inquiries and analyzing results. A summary should also be kept in addition to the actual individual names. A couple of suggested record keeping formats are shown in Fig. 6-4. You could also put this information on a personal computer for fast analysis and use.

The importance of keeping careful records may not be apparent at this early stage of your marketing career. If you are conscientious about keeping the data suggested here, you will find your ability to execute effective programs will be greatly enhanced.

MAILING LIST GENERAL RECORD #_____

Quantity To Be
Mailed _____

List Used _____

List Source _____

Target audience or territory _____

Contents of mailing (describe) _____

Who did mailing _____ Reply Card Code _____

COSTS: Labor. . . . . $ _____

             Materials . . . .   _____

             Postage . . . .   _____

           TOTAL COSTS . . . . $ _____

Date Mailed	Quantity Mailed	Comments
_____	_____	_____
_____	_____	_____
_____	_____	_____
_____	_____	_____
_____	_____	_____
_____	_____	_____
_____	_____	_____
_____	_____	_____
_____	_____	_____

Mailing completed
on _____

Total
Mailed _____

Fig. 6-4. Suggested forms for keeping track of your responses.

MAILING LIST NAME FILE

Date Mailed _____

List Source _____

Materials Sent _____

Reply Received? [ ] Yes   [ ] No

Reply Date _____

LEAD STATUS

[ ] DEAD LEAD

[ ] UNDELIVERABLE

[ ] NEW CUSTOMER

[ ] FOLLOW-UP on

Name _____

Firm (if applicable) _____

Address _____

City _____ State _____ Zip _____

Phone (_____) _____

Comments _____

_____

Fig. 6-4. Continued.

Advertising

7

A Review of Advertising Methods and Concepts

MOST FINANCIAL SERVICES salespeople have used direct mail at least on occasion. Therefore the concept of direct mail was probably not entirely new to you. But few salespeople have ever tried advertising. This whole area may be a complete mystery to many. That is unfortunate, because advertising can be an important way to promote your services to prospective new clients.

Just as was discussed in the review of direct mail, you should have a good comprehension of what you will be doing prior to embarking on any advertising program. This understanding is the key to being able to use advertising effectively.

Advertising simply uses media such as newspapers, radio, etc., to deliver the marketing message. While the delivery system differs, the principles behind advertising are quite similar to direct mail. These general characteristics can be summarized as follows:

- A target audience you select by choosing the particular media for your advertisement
- A message to communicate your offer to prospects
- A motivator such as a free report or an offer of additional information
- A response vehicle

In addition to a different way of delivering the message, advertising accomplishes each of the elements listed here in a somewhat unique way.

TARGET AUDIENCE

Unlike direct mail, where the specific target can be selected (a particular name on a particular list), the target audience for advertising is not a specific choice. The audience must be selected based on information about the readers, viewers, or listeners of the particular media that is being considered. Advertising, therefore, does not give you as precise a choice of who will see or hear your ad. If you run an ad in a newspaper, for example, everyone reading that paper could see your ad, despite the fact that only a very small percentage might be able to benefit from what you are offering. Consequently, with advertising, you will reach many people who cannot utilize your offer.

The beneficial trade-off that makes advertising a sensible consideration, despite the lack of audience control, is the fact that it is usually far less expensive to reach a person via advertising than via direct mail. The cost often can run just a few cents to reach each person in the audience. So you can afford to "waste" the message on quite a few non-prospects in order to reach the clients with true potential, and still be cost effective.

AD COMPONENTS

The message to communicate your offer is constrained by size in print advertising or by time in broadcast advertising, not by weight as in direct mail. With size and cost working against you, you will want to limit what you say in an ad. This usually means that you will not be able to provide as much information, or communicate as complex an idea in an advertisement as you could in a mailing.

Complicating your efforts even further is the competitive environment for financial services. There is already a huge amount of financially related advertising out there. In addition, it has been estimated that most households with a reasonable credit history are already receiving as many as 10 offers in a single week at certain times through direct mail. While many of these are probably credit card and home equity loan solicitations, there are plenty of insurance plans and investment programs that also tend to clutter the landscape and make another financial services offer seem like just one more in a long procession.

Somehow, with all this marketing going on, you must try to get through to the prospects. For simple concepts you can often be more effective using an ad than a direct-mail piece or telephone call. The prospects might throw away your mailing pieces without ever opening them or they may hang up when you call. But if the prospects read the paper, they pretty much cannot avoid at least noticing your ad. The same holds true for listeners of radio commercials and viewers of TV commercials.

Advertising is also valuable if your target market is not well defined and you need to approach a broad-based audience to try and determine who makes a good prospect. This is particularly true in the case of new products or new applications of existing products. There are also many publications that focus primarily upon finance and business and these tend to minimize the scattering of your message toward unlikely prospects.

The action mechanism in advertising is similar to that found in direct mail. You want the prospect to respond and to get them to do so, you may offer a free prospectus, report or other bonus. Because advertising typically does not zero in on the best target group, an incentive is even more useful here. Since there are likely to be more marginal prospects reading your ad than your direct-mail piece, the bonus should be strong enough to push more of them toward responding.

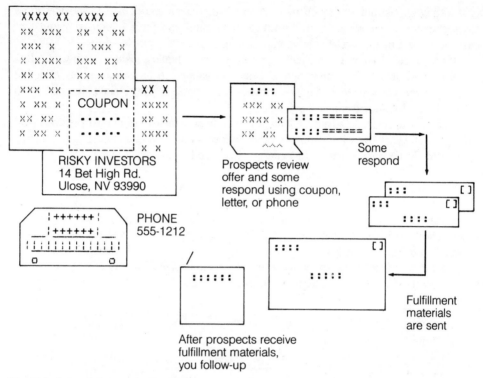

Fig. 7-1. Advertising cycle flowchart.

The response vehicle in advertising is generally a little more complicated than it is in direct mail. The prospect must write a note, clip a coupon, address an envelope and pay postage, or they must take the ad to a telephone and call to get action (Fig. 7-1). It is, therefore, somewhat harder for the prospects to respond to an advertisement than it is for them to reply to a direct-mail piece. Using a toll-free number will reduce the hurdles inherent with advertising response, but it will not eliminate them.

ADVERTISING COSTS

The expenses of producing and running an advertising campaign fall into three primary categories:

1. Creative copy and design work—what the ad will say and what it will look like.
2. Production cost—preparation and art for a print ad or the costs of producing a radio or TV commercial.
3. The actual cost for the publication's space or broadcast station's time purchased.

Creative copy and design work can be expensive, but you do not need to be an advertising genius to write a simple ad offering financial services. Ad preparation and typesetting should not run much more than $100, unless you decide to include some fancy graphics or use color. You will want to spend more in a more expensive campaign, but you can get by for a relatively nominal amount for small, simple ads.

If you select radio or TV in which to advertise, you should consider getting a professional to read or act out your script. Unless you happen to be an extremely effective public speaker, you will jeopardize your professional image fulfilling a childhood fantasy to be a radio or TV announcer.

The cost to reach an advertising audience is usually measured in cost per thousand since reaching each one often amounts to just a few cents. Cost per thousand is abbreviated CPM. In formula format, CPM can be expressed as follows:

$$CPM = (Cost\ of\ Ad/Audience\ Size) \times 1000$$

Figure 7-2 shows some approximate cost figures for a few popular financial publications. These are based upon their advertising charges for a typical full page ad and claimed circulation. CPM would be lower for a smaller ad simply because it costs less, despite the fact that small ads actually are more expensive in terms of the amount of space they use. To keep comparisons fair, full page costs are used as a benchmark.

PUBLICATION NAME	APPROXIMATE CPM (in dollars)	APPROXIMATE COST PER NAME (in cents)
Barron's	57	6
Business Week	40	4
Fortune	46	5
Financial World	40	4
Inc.	46	5
Wall Street Journal	51	5

Fig. 7-2. CPM for selected publications.

The cost of advertising space or time can be surprisingly low. There are three major factors that affect advertising costs.

1. Space size or time length (and number of times run)
2. Circulation or audience size
3. Geographic market

Space is the single largest determinant of cost for a given medium. The publication or station charges based upon the size or length of your ad. Obviously you will pay more for a full page ad than a tiny one.

If you run a small ad in a non-major market paper, your costs for space might be just a few hundred dollars, depending on its size, etc. A short radio spot in non-prime time (smaller audience) might cost even less. And late night spots on television can be purchased quite reasonably in certain markets at particular times of the year. You can easily spend $10,000 for bigger ads in more well known media. Later we will be discussing the relative merits of each medium, but generally there is little reason for individual security salespeople to advertise on TV, or for that matter on radio, since the message can usually be better communicated in print for less cost.

A number of recent trends in the cost of advertising may have an effect on your consideration of various options. The cost of advertising in media you are likely to use—newspapers, magazines and radio—have remained quite stable over the past few years. Due to the price stability in these ad mediums relative to significantly increased postage costs, you are more likely to find that advertising might be a very viable alternative to direct mail.

Meanwhile, the costs of broadcast television ads have fallen somewhat while the price of cable television advertising has risen significantly. This suggests that broadcast TV, while still relatively expensive, may be a better deal today than it was some years ago.

To determine the costs of an ad, you should request a media kit from the publisher, or station in the case of broadcast. Media kits are discussed in more detail in the chapter titled, *Selecting The Best Advertising Medium.*

Additional Costs

As in direct mail, you will face additional expenses when advertising responses come in. There will not be any incoming reply postage since you cannot typically provide a postage-paid reply mechanism, but sending inquirers requested information or accepting toll-free calls will probably cost you an average of $1 or more per lead for phone lines, postage, and materials.

RESPONSE MECHANISMS

Unlike direct mail, which can easily be acted upon, kept on file, or passed along to an interested party, advertising is harder to act upon and usually has a much shorter life. This is especially true of daily newspapers. If the reader does not work to tear out the ad, or copy the needed information, the paper is thrown out (with the ad) at the end of the day. Even a magazine which may be around for a week or more is usually read only once by each individual. So an ad should be stronger than a mailing piece because it inherently makes the evaluation and response process more difficult than direct mail usually does.

To complicate matters further, on a limited budget, advertising seldom can make the impact a direct-mail piece can make. Ads reach a lot of people, but motivating them to action is difficult. Large, major ad campaigns overcome these deficiencies with much frequency and size. But smaller advertisers with limited budgets who run tiny or short ads seldom can compete with a fair quality direct-mail program in terms of generating action.

Financial services advertising leads tend to be more expensive than direct-mail leads, occasionally as much as double the cost per lead. This is partly due to the need for frequency (more ads) and partly due to the lower relative response rates often obtained. But advertising leads are usually more qualified, having worked harder to reply, so they tend to be more serious. The cost per sale of advertising and direct-mail leads are quite comparable. It is, therefore, unfair to say advertising leads are inferior, or superior, to direct-mail leads. Depending on the campaign, products or services being offered, etc., one may work better than the other. The only way to find out which is best in a specific situation is to test both approaches. Later chapters will give you more insight into which, or perhaps a combination of both promotional methods, may be optimal.

A fundamental problem with the advertising of financial services is that it still appeals to a very small segment of the population. As a result, a large proportion of an advertisement's impressions are wasted on uninterested and unqualified "suspects," the stage before they even become a prospect.

While it is extremely inexpensive to reach each audience member through advertising, if you waste enough contacts, the effort may become unproductive. And because it is hard to select an audience accurately through advertising, the waste factor is certain to be high. Perhaps only a few percent of an audience would even remotely be interested in a financial offer in most advertising media. This is particularly true of television and, to a somewhat lesser degree, of radio.

As a result, many major financial advertisers have shifted their marketing focus away from advertising, especially broadcast commercials, and towards direct mail, where targeting a segment of the population is somewhat easier. You should bear this in mind as you consider your marketing options.

Reach and Frequency

As mentioned previously, to compensate for some of the weakness of advertising, frequency is usually required. Mailing to the same list again, or even a third time, can increase responses, but it is not generally necessary. (As we have seen, there can be some benefits in mailing to respondents again.) Advertising, on the other hand, tends to build recognition as it is seen more often. So, it is to the advantage of any advertiser to plan not just one ad in a particular media, but a series of ads over a short period of time.

Two additional measurements used in advertising should be defined at this time. *Reach* is the total number of individuals or households that are exposed to an ad one or more times over some defined period of time, typically a month. So reach is a measure of people who saw the ad.

Average frequency is the average number of times an individual or household is exposed to the ad. Frequency is a measure of how many times the typical audience member saw or heard an ad. For most ads, it is believed that a minimum of three runs are required to maximize effectiveness.

Budget constraints often limit the number of ads that can be run. It is usually better to sacrifice reach (less overall audience) and maximize frequency by running the same ad several times in media that cater to mostly the same audiences than by running ads in a number of unrelated media.

Variations

There are several variations on the basic advertising scheme and you should know about them even if you are not planning to use these techniques early in your advertising career.

Some ads do not require a response by mail. They may depend upon a telephone call, usually toll free, as the response vehicle. This is especially true of radio and TV advertising, where it is a lot easier to remember or note just a phone number rather than trying to catch an entire address in the brief moments the commercial runs. If your firm already has a toll-free telephone number available for your use, this may be a cheap and effective way for you to get prospects to reply. Or, if you expect mainly local calls, a regular phone number may suffice.

In some instances, ads provide no response mechanism at all. This is called image advertising and can be effective for major corporations in an effort to increase or improve their overall image. It is not really appropriate for the type of financial services advertising the typical individual salesperson may wish to do.

PRINT ADVERTISING

Print advertising includes newspapers, magazines, periodicals—any published material which carries ads. Catalogs are not typically considered print advertising because they are usually offered via direct mail and act as the actual offering piece in these cases.

Magazines can be consumer, business, or farming in nature. There are over 1000 magazines currently published (as best as can be determined).

The consumer group can be further catalogued as general interest (broad appeal) and segmented based on some criteria such as demography or geography.

Business publications target the business world. Some are directed at particular trades or industries. Others are aimed at particular types of job functions, usually related to management.

Farm publications deal mainly with farming business issues (pricing, planning, management).

As a result of all these specialized categories, magazines tend to be very selective. You can really zero in on a particular type of audience, almost as well as with direct mail, and for a much lower cost per contact. If you think business managers who buy office furniture would make good prospects for a particular type of retirement plan you market, you can market directly to that group through some of their trade magazines.

However, the ability to be selective with magazines is common knowledge. So everyone tries to do this and the result is magazines that are packed with ads, creating clutter and reducing effectiveness.

Newspapers are mostly general audience in nature. The primary variable in newspapers is the geographic coverage. There are some specialized papers—particularly dealing with finance and business—that can make a lot of sense for the marketing of financial products and services.

Periodicals are specialized, infrequent magazines and usually are read by a highly selective audience. While this can make them a good financial services marketing vehicle, the cost is often prohibitive.

RADIO ADVERTISING

It has been estimated that there are about half a billion radios in the U.S. (nearly six per household). So radio can certainly reach most people. With about 3500 AM stations and roughly 3000 FM stations, plus a large number of public FM stations, program formats can be found for almost any type of audience.

With so many stations and formats, listeners tend to select one or two of their favorites and listen to those to the exclusion of the rest. As a result, the market share of a given station would tend to be quite consistent, so repetitive ads tend to build frequency easily since the same people are usually listening.

Because its audience tends to be small, a given station will not get you much coverage. And since radio is generally not an "active" medium (listeners tend to have the radio on as background quite often), radio ads get less attention and recall than do TV ads.

TELEVISION ADVERTISING

There are three types of television advertising. Network ads are sent from a central location to affiliates all over the country. Spot television originates from a particular television station and is used primarily by manufacturers. Local advertising also comes from a single station, but is used mostly by retailers. Spot rates tend to be more expensive than local rates.

Newspapers, magazines, radio, and television are only some of the advertising mediums available to you. There are also billboards, yellow pages telephone directory listings, etc. How some of these can help you will be discussed in later chapters of this book.

ADVERTISING SPECIALTIES AND PREMIUMS

Sometimes, in an effort to generate interest and motivate a prospect to inquire (or even buy), a little something is offered as an inducement. This might take the form of a free report, a key chain with your name and telephone number on it, or a variety of other incentives.

An advertising "specialty item" is usually of nominal value and is offered just for showing an interest—no obligation is generally required on the part of the prospect. A specialty item might be a pen and pencil set with your name on it, etc. You hope to win favor by giving this item away and it serves as a longer term reminder of your services as a secondary benefit.

An advertising "premium item" is usually more expensive than a specialty item and premiums are related to actually doing business with you. Since there are so many restrictions on gifts and payments in the financial industry, premiums are rarely used. One concept that appears to be a premium and is winning wide approval has to do with account reports, valuations, and information. While these might be considered part of your service, they can make an excellent premium offered to prospects if they do business with you.

Tip: Advertising specialties and premiums are a tricky legal area, so do be sure to clear any proposed activity using these things with your compliance department or attorney who is versed in these matters.

PUBLIC RELATIONS

Another advertising program you might consider is public relations (PR). Essentially a direct-mail campaign, PR is an effort to get publicity in publications and broadcast media about you and your services. If your information is newsworthy or you can make it appear that way, you may be able to get coverage.

If you are marketing a unique investment product, a news release about this item to the local newspaper and radio and TV stations could generate a story about you and the investment. While this might directly produce only a few leads (if any), it certainly would not do you any harm (provided the article is favorable) and could further motivate prospects to contact you when they see your advertisements and direct-mail pieces. Figure 7-3 shows a typical format for a news release.

NEWS RELEASE

RISKY INVESTORS, INC.
13 Financial Way St.
Bullmarket, MO 19731
Phone: 800-555-1212

Contact: J.P. Flywheel III
800-555-1212

FOR IMMEDIATE RELEASE

Bullmarket, MO, September 23rd. J.P. Flywheel III announced today that his firm has just introduced a new money management fund geared for those seeking super high returns and willing to accept high risk.

Mr. Flywheel said: "We know there are a lot of people out there who are tired of keeping money in their mattress." He went on to explain how the Risky Investors' Money Management Fund achieves such high rates of return. "We give this money to our loan sharks who are able to earn 200 to 300% per month. They give us our cut of 100% and we pass along the customers' fair share, currently 26% annual return," Mr. Flywheel continued.

In further discussion, Mr. Flywheel disclosed that the returns are paid on customer's demand, but that a 927 day prior notice is required. "So far only one jerk wanted his interest paid and Guido talked him out of it," Mr. Flywheel added.

Risky Investors has two other funds that may be of interest to our readers. They are:

TAX AVOIDANCE FUND: You avoid all taxes by avoiding all income.

BAG HIGH RISK FUND: You leave your money in a bag and take a lot of risk that it will still be there.

For further information about any of the Risky Investors' products, contact Mr. Flywheel, or Guido.

– 30 –

Fig. 7-3. Sample news release.

When you prepare a news release, be sure it says "For Immediate Release" at the top. Start out with your location and the date. Be brief and cover the key items related to the story and why you feel it is noteworthy. Remember, this is not a sales piece. You should not expect anyone to call and order from you after reading it. Your goal is to get it published and thereby obtain some credibility, general awareness of your services, and perhaps some inquiries about what you are doing.

End the news release by indicating who they should contact for more information. A "-30-" is a traditional indication of the end of the news release. Using "-End-" would be perfectly acceptable as well.

The key to PR is convincing the media that your story is indeed newsworthy. Just because you would like to see your name in print does not mean the media will agree (unless you pay for an ad). Announcing that you are now taking applications for customers probably would be of little news value.

To be news, you would need to report something unique or exceptional, and timely. A significant new investment product would qualify. A new way of using an existing investment vehicle might be interesting also. Or, if you are marketing in an unusual way, it may be worth reporting to the public.

Holding a seminar on investments not only has the potential to generate new customers, it might also get mentioned in the media. It is even possible that you could receive publicity about the seminar prior to its presentation (generating more attendance) and subsequently stories reporting on the seminar itself might appear.

The primary problem in getting publicity about your seminar is convincing the media that it is newsworthy. If you can come up with some angle that makes it unique, that will help. For example, offering a seminar on retirement plans might not be news, but putting it on at a retirement home may be considered unusual. A speech on managing funds for not-for-profit organizations may bring you little direct business, but it may build good will and publicity.

Since a news release is inexpensive and there are a limited number of publications and stations in a given area, trying to get some publicity is a low risk effort. Typically, you can send out a release for $.30 or $.40 each (a decent quality photocopy is quite acceptable in this situation). There might be 20 local papers and perhaps 18 stations in your area. So for about $10 and a little effort you might get some publicity which would be worth a great deal. Be careful not to send out PR releases too often. You can wear out your welcome quite quickly. About once every six months to a year is sufficient unless you have some really important news.

While PR can be a nice image builder, by itself it is unlikely to bring you many new customers. It is suggested, therefore, that you concentrate on other marketing efforts like advertising and direct mail and use PR as additional support for those programs. A blank news release form is provided for your use in Appendix C at the back of this book.

There are public relations agencies which specialize in trying to obtain publicity for you, for a price. These firms are quite skilled in their profession and might be able to generate far more in benefits for you than they charge. However, this could be an expensive experiment. Be sure to try some PR on your own or try a very inexpensive agency before committing large resources to this type of program.

Market Reports

In some cities, local radio stations provide periodic reports on the financial markets. It may be possible to arrange your sponsorship of the program, meaning the station calls you and you provide current information, via the telephone, to the station and, in turn, to their listeners.

While this arrangement will probably not pay you directly, in fact you may have to pay the station or advertise on their broadcasts, the publicity can be invaluable. The listeners would hear from you several times a day and probably remember you when they needed financial services.

There are also numerous financial programs that bring on special guest experts. They tend to exist in larger metropolitan areas or be nationally produced. Financial News Network would be just one example of this type of programming. FNN not only has its primary cable program focusing almost entirely on financial news, but there are syndicated programs to other TV stations as well as radio business news updates. You might be able to appear as a guest expert, or possibly a guest columnist in a financial publication. While some of these possibilities are long shots, there is little risk or expense in contacting the producers and publishers and trying your luck. If you can get on one of these programs it could be quite useful.

8

Planning Your
Advertising Campaign

As DISCUSSED PREVIOUSLY, each campaign should begin by developing a detailed plan. This chapter discusses how to develop an effective advertising program.

SETTING GOALS

Start by setting specific goals you hope to accomplish, just as you would in the case of direct mail. These might include the number of new accounts you would like to open, the dollar amount of transactions, the products or services you want to market, the amount of commissions you hope to generate or possibly several of these. Establish what you would like to accomplish with your advertising so you can then determine what you must do to achieve those goals. Specific targets also will permit you to evaluate how successful the advertising program has been.

When you work on your budget, you will be determining how feasible these goals may be in light of the type of marketing program you select and the funds available for the plan.

Teaming Up with Others

An early decision in the planning process is whether to work alone or team up with other salespeople, perhaps your entire office, to plan and execute an advertising program. The key advantage to teaming is that you share the costs and the work, making your proportionate share of the expenses less than if you worked on your own.

You might take out a larger ad, which is usually much more economical and effective than smaller ones, and share the results on some equitable basis such as by the territory you serve or by a proportionate assignment. In a shared effort, your costs should end up being lower and you should be able to execute a better program.

DETERMINING A BUDGET

Whether you work in a group or alone, the next major decision to make concerns the budget for the program.

Your budget will greatly affect what types of programs you will be able to use and the quality of those efforts. While there can be no assurance that the money you spend for an ad will bring you large rewards, a good pay-back is often the result of a well-planned program. So allocate as much money as you comfortably can risk. The amount of your budget will also determine how close you can come to accomplishing the goals you have set for the program.

Table 8-1 will give you some idea of the budget level you most likely will need to effectively execute various types of advertising programs. These figures indicate minimum amounts that should be spent to effectively utilize a particular medium. The viable advertising options which you may reasonably consider are based on a particular budget range indicated by an "X."

Table 8-1. Promotional Budget Guide.

Dollars Available for Campaign	Type of Advertising			
	Print Advertising	Radio	Misc.*	TV
3000 – 10000	X	X	X	
10000 +	X	X	X	X

*Misc. includes billboards, sponsorship of events, etc.

One conclusion that can be drawn from this table is that one should not attempt to advertise without contemplating budgets of at least $3000. There may be ads available for just $100, but to get real impact and effective communication, at least $3000 should be spent on an ad campaign. This reflects not only the fact that most ads are relatively expensive, but that you should run three or more to get the most benefit through frequency.

You can do some preliminary analysis to see if the budget you have set and the specific benefits you want from the program do fit.

For example, if you have decided that you want to open 20 new accounts and sell them an average of $20,000 worth of a mutual fund product for their initial business, you know that you must do a total of $400,000 in volume. Assuming a commission payout of 1% to you, you can reasonably expect to make $4000 from the sales you hope to achieve

($400,000 × 1%), excluding follow-up business that comes in subsequently. This information tells you something about how much you can afford to spend on the program—probably less than $4000 since that is what you hope to earn, unless you consider subsequent business which could be substantial. This information also tells you that your sales can cost you up to $200 each ($4000 budget divided by 20 sales).

Financial salespeople close about 7% of their leads. This suggests that if you want 20 sales, you need about 290 leads (290 × 7% = 20). If the publication you have chosen has a circulation of 500,000, you would need a response rate of six-one hundredths of a percent (.06%), a reasonable (and acceptable) level to expect in advertising.

If the available budget cannot reasonably achieve your goals, you must reevaluate the program and look for alternatives that have a greater chance of accomplishing the things you have set out to do. If you had arrived at a required response figure of, say, 4%, you would know that is extremely high for advertising and most unlikely to achieve. Therefore, adjustment in your plans would be necessary.

The worksheet shown in Fig. 8-1 can help you analyze your proposed programs.

Use this worksheet for a preliminary test of how reasonable your advertising plan may be.

Step 1. Determine how many *sales* or new accounts you want.
# of Sales = Dollar Volume/Average Sales per Account

(Two of the three figures here will be assumptions you must make based on subjective estimates. You probably have a pretty good idea what your average sale of a given type of product has been in the past.)

Step 2. Determine the number of leads you require.
# of Leads = # of Sales/Closing rate

(The closing rate will vary, but a reasonable initial assumption, until you gain further experience, would be 7%.)

Step 3. Calculate the size of audience needed
Audience size = # of Leads/Response rate

(The response rate can vary considerably and will be much lower for most advertising than direct mail. As a start, estimate one-fiftieth (.02) of one percent for advertising.)

Step 4. Figure your budget per audience contact cost.
budget each = total budget/audience size

(The result should be in the one to ten cent range for advertising. While your results may differ somewhat and these figures are only guidelines, if you calculate cost much lower than the ones cited here, it is unlikely you will achieve them. Higher costs probably mean you cannot make any money on the program.)

Step 5. Determine potential profitability of the program.
profit = (dollar volume × payout rate) − budget

(Payout depends upon what is sold, etc., but 1% is a good initial estimate.)

Fig. 8-1. Budget analysis worksheet.

CHOOSING A PROGRAM

Once the overall budget for your advertising program is established, the next step is to choose who you want to target and how you want to reach them through a specific publication or station in the case of broadcast advertising.

While your budget is an important determinant of what you will be able to do, the actual media decisions involving how and what your program will look like are also affected greatly by the prospects you wish to reach and what you are trying to sell.

Planning a Print Advertising Campaign

The development of a print advertising program involves five stages. Each one of these is critical to creating a truly effective campaign.

1. Identifying an appropriate target audience.
2. Selection of the publication or publications through which that target audience can best be reached.
3. Determination of the ad size to be used, primarily based upon costs and available budget.
4. Purchase of space in advance of the ad run-date in order to ensure availability and optimal placement.
5. Creation and execution of the actual ad.

Target Audience Selection

Begin your selection of a target audience by reviewing the characteristics of your current customers. Since you know those characteristics will produce clients, try to match that information with the demographics of various publications in which you may advertise. The statistics about the readership showing such data as average household income, education level, employment, geographic distribution, and other information, are available for each publication you may be considering. The publishers will send you a media kit, which includes sample copies of their publications, circulation figures, ad rates, closing dates for placing ads, as well as subscriber data. These kits are free for the asking.

The major characteristics of an ideal target audience should be similar to those used in direct mail—after all you hope they will all become customers. The primary criteria should be related to wealth or earning power, investment history and expensive buying habits.

You can often gauge just how interested a publication's readers might be in your offer by looking at its characteristics. The publication's contents will indicate its type of audience quite clearly. If it has a securities price section you know readers of that section own, or at least are interested in, investments. Are there editorials on business or finance? Evidence of likely prospects would also be shown if other financial firms advertise regularly in the publication. If banks, insurance companies, and brokerage firms run ad after ad, it is a fairly safe bet that financial services sell well in that publication, otherwise they would have abandoned advertising there long ago.

You will want to use a publication read mostly by adults since young people and children do not invest very much, if at all. Circulation should be in wealthier areas. Not too many users of financial services live in ghettos or low income areas.

Do not rely totally on the publisher's claimed circulation figures. The circulation numbers can sometimes be artificially inflated by giving away copies of the publication or offering other incentives to get people to subscribe even if they would not normally do so. The readership numbers are useful, but select a publication based on other qualities first and use circulation as a backup. It is far better to appeal to a small group of real prospects than a large number of uninterested people.

A regional edition of a widely distributed publication is often preferable to a local paper. However, the distribution of a major newspaper, for example, can often be much broader than you require and the cost may not be justified. You may find that the regional edition of a national paper still has coverage well beyond your territory and you must pay for that coverage. It is an evaluative judgment which you must make based upon the costs involved and the territory you cover. You might want to analyze this decision based on the portion of circulation you are likely to utilize, apportioning the total cost to that coverage, and then calculate the required response levels and cost per lead and sale based on those figures.

Remember that it costs far less to contact each individual using most ads than it would to use direct mail or telemarketing, so even if a good portion of the audience is not suited to your product, it can still be cost efficient.

Cost will be a major factor to bear in mind. To reach your ideal audience most effectively might require television, for example. But your budget may not be able to afford television advertising. So you will have to reevaluate your target audience and objectives in that case.

Budgeting for Print Advertising

Your budget should be sufficient for at least three runs of your ad. If you run an ad only once, you have lost an important benefit of advertising—repetition. Each time your ad is run it reaches more people, but it also reaches many of the same people again (the regular readers or listeners). It is a well known fact that more people will respond if they see an ad often. So you want your ads to appear a number of times and you want them run frequently. Once a week, or even more often is desirable. Too long a period of time between ads reduces the benefits of repetition significantly.

Advertising is measured by two methods: reach—total number of people exposed to the ad each time it runs, and frequency—the number of times the ad will run. The optimal frequency is typically three to five times or more.

Once you have selected the specific media in which you will run your ad, you should budget the ad based on its size and position (location within the publication). You can control the size, but the position may be difficult to direct. We will discuss this in more detail shortly.

If you have not already done so, now would be a good time to find out the rates for advertising in the publication you have selected. A rate card is usually part of a media kit and will contain this information. You can also call the publication for rate quotes. Rates are not only affected by ad size and position, but by the timing and frequency of advertising as well. The day of the week, edition, and even the preferred section may affect your costs and your anticipated response rate. Prices are primarily a reflection of circulation and a more expensive day or time is typically worth the price. If a 10,000 person audience is worth $300, for example, then the same type of audience including 15,000 people ought to be worth $450.

Many publications offer a cash discount of about 2% for prompt payment (or prepayment), so you should factor this into your budget if it is available and you plan to take advantage of the discount.

For your purposes, it will usually be important that the ad tie in with a business or economic report, or other financial news. Even the nature of the stories can improve, or reduce, the effectiveness of your ad. Running an ad in the financial section of the Sunday paper, although it would probably be more expensive, may not be as effective as advertising on a weekday when the paper carries daily stock quotes. Further, if you invite potential respondents to call a telephone number listed in a weekend ad, you will have to man the phone on the weekend, or risk losing potential new customers.

Once you have determined the applicable rates for the publication you wish to use, calculate the size ad you will be able to afford. As mentioned previously, repetition in advertising is highly desirable. Your budget should accommodate at least three repetitions of your ad within a few weeks, or sooner. More frequency is better if you can afford it. Allocate about 20% of your budget to ad preparation, etc., and use the balance for the following calculation. Divide your remaining ad budget for media (80%) by the number of ads you plan to run (Step 1). Now divide that answer by the applicable column inch rate to determine column inches you will be able to purchase for your ad (Step 2).

Step 1: Media ad budget*/Number of ads
          = Approx. budget for each ad
Step 2: Budget for each ad (from Step 1)/Rate per column inch**
          = Est. column inches used for each ad

Radio

The process involved in the development of a radio ad will be quite similar to that used in the development of print ads. The basic steps are:

- Identifying a target audience
- Selecting a station to carry the ad or ads
- Determining the spot's length based on budget and rates
- Committing to the advertising spots
- Creation and execution of the actual ad(s)

Again, we start with a target audience. Who is most likely to be interested in what you are marketing? Certainly you should be looking for station audience demographics

---

NOTES: *After allocation for preparation, etc.
              **Use applicable rates for the number of ads you plan to run (frequency discounts).

that closely match your current customer profile. Stations that have a special financial or business news broadcast are usually preferable to music-only radio. Try to find out if other financial firms are using or have used the station with any regularity. A few other financial advertisers is a pretty good sign that the station has appropriate listeners.

Keep in mind that a radio audience is usually at its maximum in the morning when about 30% of adults tune in. The audience shrinks to about 20% by the evening.

As noted previously, there may be many radio stations in your area, but probably only a few that appear appropriate—that is, they have the type of audience likely to need financial services. Often the selection will be between just two or three stations. You must use judgment here. You may be familiar with these stations and be able to select the appropriate one without any in-depth research. If you are uncertain as to the correct choice, talk to the advertising representatives of each station and get information about their listeners, past financial advertising, etc. As is often the case in marketing, you might have to test a few stations with an ad or two to really determine if they can provide solid leads for you.

Radio ads are available on networks, in spot or in local formats. The majority of radio ads tend to be local, that is, originating from just one local station and run by retailers more than by any other group.

A buyer can possibly assist you with your selection. A buyer is an agent who purchases media time on behalf of a client. Like most things in life, there is a fee for this service.

Budgeting for Radio Ads

As with other types of advertising, the budget process for radio advertising really begins with the funding you have available. Next, you need to determine the advertising rates for the spots you wish to use. These rates should reflect the frequency of advertising you plan, length of spots, days and times desired, etc.

The broadcast day is divided into "dayparts" for radio. The charges for running an ad will be partially determined by when you wish them to run. Figure 8-2 illustrates the radio dayparts.

	DAYPART	START	END
	1) Morning Drive	6:00 AM	10:00 AM
Fig. 8-2. Radio dayparts.	2) Housewife Time	10:00 AM	3:00 PM
	3) Evening Drive	3:00 PM	7:00 PM
	4) Evening Radio	7:00 PM	12:00 AM
	5) Late Night	12:00 AM	6:00 AM

The budget computations will involve dividing your available budget (after production costs are subtracted—see Chapter 3) by the number of times you will run the ad (Step 1). You should plan to repeat the ad at least three or four times for optimal results. The calculation will give you your budget for each ad. Compare the answer to the rate for the spot length you prefer to use in order to determine which type of spot is affordable in your plan (Step 2). If your budget permits, add more spots or use better (more expensive) times rather than longer spots. There may be an occasional exception, but generally your ad should not exceed 30 seconds or you will risk boring your listeners, as well as paying for less productive air time. The calculations for the budget process are summarized below:

Step 1: Radio Ad Budget*/Number of Ads
= Approx. budget for each ad
Step 2: Budget for each ad (Step 1)/Advertising rate per spot**
= Possible ad length in seconds

If your result is less than 15 seconds you must either increase your budget or reduce frequency. If greater than 30 seconds, consider adding more spots or using part of your budget for other marketing efforts. A 30-second spot tends to be about right in terms of providing enough time to get the message out and yet not overwhelm the audience with chatter.

While a short spot of 15 seconds or less does not afford much opportunity to communicate a lot of information, there is one advantage to keeping a radio ad very short, and for that matter a TV commercial short as well. You might get your message completely told before the prospect changes channels and misses the balance of a longer spot. It is something worth keeping in mind in this age of zapping (switching) channels to miss commercials.

Once you know spot length, number of runs and ad dates, you can book the spots. Plan your spots at roughly the same time each day to maximize repetition benefits. If the ads do not pull well, run them again in different time slots or on different stations. The lead time required to reserve a specific time slot will vary from station to station. You should usually give stations a minimum of one month's notice to help ensure that you can get the times you want and that you have enough lead time to put the commercial together.

Television

If you plan to use television advertising, your approach should be somewhat different than for print or radio advertising. Your selection of a target audience will be even less precise with TV. You will get a wide cross-section of viewers with most any television ad. The only factors within your control that will affect who sees your ad will be the station selected and the timing—when the spot is broadcast.

The broadcast day is divided into six "dayparts" to distinguish when the ad will run and the applicable rates (Fig. 8-3).

A big drawback to television advertising is that it tends not to be upscale. The fact that televisions are in the homes of nearly 90% of America testifies to its broad based (common man) appeal. Further, upscale individuals tend to watch much fewer hours of TV than do others.

Thus, the average viewer is less likely to fit our ideal target audience profile than most other mediums. The need to find programs that attract a more likely viewing audience is even more critical with television.

NOTES: *Less production costs
**15- or 30-second spots

DAYPART	START	END	START	END
	(East and West)		(Central)	
1) Early Morning	Sign On	10:00 AM	Sign On	10:00 AM
2) Daytime	10:00 AM	4:30 PM	10:00 AM	4:30 PM
3) Early Fringe	4:30 PM	8:00 PM	4:30 PM	7:00 PM
4) Prime Time	8:00 PM	11:00 PM	7:00 PM	10:00 PM
5) Late Fringe	11:00 PM	1:00 AM	10:00 PM	12:00 AM
6) Late Night	1:00 AM	Sign Off	12:00 AM	Sign Off

Fig. 8-3. Television dayparts.

As with radio advertising, one of your objectives should be to purchase spots connected with a business news program, market discussions or in other ways related to the financial industry. The spots should be scheduled at the same time each day in order to maximize the benefits of repetition.

Preparing a TV ad and buying time is much more complex and expensive than in the case of other mediums. It is suggested that you use the services of an ad agency or your own in-house advertising department to prepare and schedule TV advertising.

The same basic approach to budgeting works with television as well. You must allocate your budget for television over the number of ads planned. And then you should calculate the potential length of your ads based on the funding. The shortest reasonable ad is about 15 seconds and the longest you should use is 30 seconds, primarily due to the high cost of TV advertising. A 15-second spot will probably give you sufficient time to get a brief but effective message out, so this might be a good point to begin your plan. Therefore, start by assuming you will use 15-second spots and then adjust the timing after you calculate your budget. A minimum of three TV commercials should be anticipated, but the more the better.

ALLOCATING FUNDING FOR AD PRODUCTION

Once you have selected your target audience and specific media, you need to determine your budget allocations. Table 8-2 gives some good rules of thumb for figuring the expenses of running an ad about three times.

These are only guidelines and particular instances will vary. For example, if you plan to spend $2000 on a print campaign, the allocation should be approximately $200 for

Table 8-2. Approximate Proportion of Budget for Each Type of Medium.

Item	Print	Radio	TV
Preparation of ad	10%	15%	20%
Typesetting & artwork	5	-	-
Announcer or personality	-	10	10
Space purchased	75	-	-
Time purchased	-	65	60
Production & Misc.	10	10	10
Total	100%	100%	100%

preparation, $100 for typesetting, $1600 for space, and $100 for production and miscellaneous items like proofs, reprint copies, etc.

As you can see, your ad preparation costs (non-time costs) are proportionately greater for radio and TV. This is because the overall costs for these media tend to be much larger and an investment in a quality production ever more critical. The preparation costs can be reduced somewhat by repeating a series of ads since once prepared, an ad can be run indefinitely.

According to the formula, you should spend $150 to prepare a $1000 radio ad campaign (15%), but you should spend $450 to prepare a $3000 radio ad campaign.

You may wonder why preparation costs should rise if your budget increases. You could save some costs by using an ad created for one campaign in a more expensive campaign later. However, that would be a mistake. The quality and cost of the ad should be representative of the overall campaign expenditure. If you have $1000 to spend, it would be a terrible misallocation to spend $600 preparing the ad and only $400 to place it in some obscure newspaper. But if you plan to spend $10,000 on the program, then $600 for the ad preparation may not be enough. In this case you would be spending a great deal of money on the program so you could justify putting more into each aspect of the ad campaign. If, on the other hand you are simply repeating a previous campaign from a similar medium, using a previously successful ad could be a logical and economical move.

Selecting a specific media for advertising will involve some research on costs, audience, circulation, etc. For example, if you are marketing a product geared for retirees, you should be looking for a publication that has a high percentage of retirees in its readership. The media kit the publisher will provide should give this information.

Using Creative Services

There are many services available to help you with advertising. Ads tend to be more complicated than direct mail, especially more expensive ads, so you may seriously want to consider an agency for assistance and placement advice. Unlike lists, where the list broker can advise you on which list to test, each advertising medium promotes its own advertising space. Agencies are your only real source of guidance on the appropriate media to use. Certainly if you are planning a major campaign of $5000 or more, you will want to get expert advice.

Otherwise, you can do the job using the chapter *Selecting The Best Advertising Medium* for guidance and save 10% or more of the total campaign cost. While you are not entitled to the agency placement fees even if you do not use an agency, you can save money on ad development and execution. A local printer can do the necessary typesetting and artwork for most print ads at considerably less cost than an agency (if you do the creative work yourself).

If you do not plan to use an agency, consider creating your own which will permit you to qualify for the agency discount. Done properly, this is a perfectly acceptable arrangement. Obviously, publications do not like advertisers to create their own ad agency because it reduces their charges in these cases (they know they could have collected the full advertising fee if you did not use an agency). But if you create what appears to be a legitimate agency (letterhead, business name, etc.) they will have to honor the discount.

Your firm may already have an in-house ad agency which could either do the ad preparation for you, or at least save you the agency commission. It is worth looking into this possibility.

Tip: Keep in mind that there are certain types of ads, such as classified advertising, that do not normally discount for agencies. Be sure to check on the availability of agency discounts before expending any effort trying to avoid the fee.

There has been some movement in recent years to change the traditional agency commission formula that typically ran about 15% of the ad budget plus various other fees. Advertisers did not object too strenuously since the charge was generally paid by the media, not the advertiser. That meant that a newspaper, for example, might quote $10,000 for a page ad. The advertiser was going to have to pay that price with or without an agency, so it seemed that the agency's work was free. Various pressures within the advertising industry and from external sources as well have caused this arrangement to be modified more and more often. Now agencies might simply charge you a flat fee plus the actual advertising cost, or some other formula or fixed schedule.

Despite the evolution of agency payment systems, the 15% agency commission is still quite common and you should not be surprised to have that quoted to you. However, as you can quickly figure, a $1000 ad campaign will only give an ad agency a $150 potential basic fee. Few agencies will want to bother with that small a fee. By and large, if an agency cannot see making a few thousand dollars a year on your business, they will not want to be bothered. It is much the same as in the securities business—a very small account is not worthwhile unless you can anticipate bigger things in the future. So, unless you plan a rather hefty ad budget, you should not count on using an agency or plan to pay some additional fee for their services to make it profitable for them to take on your project.

For the individual financial services salesperson's relatively small advertising programs, an agency's assistance is probably not required anyway. Agencies are quite useful for creating complicated graphics, illustrations, and catchy titles. But you certainly know your market and products better than anyone else. Thus, you should be able to prepare an effective campaign on your own.

Dating and Coding Ads

As in direct mail, it is not necessary to date your ads. The paper or magazine is dated, true, but placing the date in your ad only takes up space and gains you nothing. If it is dated and a reader clips the ad and holds it a while, you cause the ad to appear old when they find the ad again a few weeks (or months) later. And you can't reuse the ad's artwork without changes if it is dated. So skip the date in your ads.

However, do be sure to code your ad, especially if it has a coupon, so you know where and when it appeared. For example, if you advertise in *Financial News*, you might use "F8" to indicate that the ad ran in August (8th month). Any combination of coding that identifies the source is fine. Be sure the code appears in the coupon portion of the ad, so that if a prospect cuts out the coupon and sends it in you will be able to trace the source.

Coding ad coupons is important. It enables you to evaluate the success of each ad and pinpoints what information the prospect desires. Indicating the year is usually not necessary in the code since very few responses to an ad are sent in a year or more after the ad appeared. For letter or phone responses, have the prospect ask for something specific, like an extension number, department number, or a particular publication so you can identify the media source and area of interest. You might even specify a different post office box number for replies to different products, if you have these boxes available.

SIZES OF ADS

Print advertising is measured in "column inches." Publications charge a rate per column inch, which will vary depending upon position in the medium, number of times the ad is run, etc. To determine your cost for a given ad, you should measure your ad's length and multiply by how many columns wide it happens to be. This gives you total column inches. Some ads may be sold by the number of words, primarily classified ads, but the majority of publications charge for display advertising based on column inches.

Bear in mind that the actual dimensions of a column inch might vary from publication to publication. While they will all be one inch in height, the width will not be standard. So an ad designed for one particular publication might not be standard for another publication and you may have to have it typeset again.

Some major publications do have standard sized ads, which are typically measured in actual inches rather than columns, and these sized ads can probably be interchanged in a good number of print media with no modification. For example, ads measuring four inches wide by six inches high could be considered acceptable, requiring no unusual treatment or extra charges, to run in a wide variety of magazines, etc. If you can make your ad fit a commonly acceptable sizing, you will save on future rework and charges if you choose to place it in other media.

Radio and TV advertisements are measured and charged based on time. Typical ad spots are 15, 30, and sometimes 60 seconds in length. These times are standard throughout the broadcast industry.

The exposure your ad will receive will also be determined by the timing (day of week or weekend in print, time of day and day of the week for radio and TV). The placement in the publication or program will be a factor as well. Inside cover or back cover in print is usually considered optimal. The financial section would be another desirable position.

In print ads, if you will be requesting position, ask to be on the outside of the right hand page, closer to the top if possible. Studies show people are more likely to notice an ad on the right page than on the left side. If you do this, be sure the coupon in your ad is at the right or across the ad to facilitate easy removal.

For your first few ads, use smaller versions and it is recommended that you not pay extra for particular placement. While the initial results may not be gratifying, you will avoid the problem of paying a high price for poor results, or possibly being overwhelmed by a large number of responses and losing the goodwill of some qualified prospects. By testing smaller ads first, you may discover you can obtain a satisfactory response rate for a minimum cost.

HANDLING RESPONSES

Responses to advertising cannot be staggered as with direct mail. Potential respondents see the advertisement at about the same time, which could create a large number of responses at once (a nice problem, but still a potential problem if you want to be able to contact them in a timely manner).

The prospect's written replies will reach you when you are at the office (assuming the replies were directed to your office). However, if you are inviting prospects to call, they probably will try to reach you immediately after they hear or see your ad. That often means the morning for early morning radio or newspapers, evenings for late night radio or evening newspapers, and weekends for magazines. You should make arrangements for a phone answering service or someone to man the phone number you have listed. Callers are easily discouraged and will seldom try more than once or twice to reach you. A caller will also give up easily if he gets a busy signal rather than a no-answer. So make sure you have enough open lines to accommodate your anticipated responses.

An ad in a local paper might pull 10 or 20 inquiries. Larger ads in more prominent publications might attract 100 or more replies. It depends on the offer, placement in the publication, timing, etc. But the potential for a lot of leads at once does exist and you should consider this when arranging your advertising.

Following Up and Reusing Leads

Promotional campaigns should include plans to keep and reuse leads which have not become customers.

Plan to divide the results of your marketing effort into four categories. These groups should be utilized to generate further potential business as follows:

1. Respondents who became customers are now part of your customer file.
2. Respondents who were interested but not ready to act just yet should be kept in a special follow-up file to be approached at a time you feel appropriate (when they said they would have funds available, for example).
3. Respondents who were not interested should be maintained in an old lead file. Including them in a subsequent direct mailing or contacting them by telephone as part of an ''old lead'' revival program usually produces excellent results, far above the level of ordinary purchased lists.
4. Prospects you failed to contact (undeliverables, no answers, etc.) should be filed so you can check new efforts against that list and eliminate their inclusion in future mailings that you might do.

Special Ads or Promotions

If you choose to do something unusual, many of the basic principles previously discussed still apply. Of the available promotional efforts, the most viable are listing in the yellow pages and other reference sources.

Yellow page listings should be simple and direct. Look at your yellow pages for some ideas and layouts. You may only be able to afford a simple one-line listing, but some differentiation such as bold face or a block around your ad is advisable to make it stand out.

Yellow page ads are typically run for one year (one edition) with fairly long lead times. You may have to schedule an ad many months prior to publication. The listings are moderately inexpensive and can be purchased on the telephone. You, or your firm, should be listed in the yellow pages.

Some yellow pages are now accepting regular ads in addition to the traditional listings. While this may get expensive, it is a possibility you should keep in mind as you consider alternatives.

There has been a proliferation of non-phone company telephone directories recently. While usually not as popular as the yellow pages, an ad in these other directories can be useful. It is certainly worth your while to investigate these options.

Production of premiums such as key chains, imprinted pens, etc., is very straightforward. For about $.20 to $.50 each, you can obtain a nice little premium item that people will keep. Your gift not only endears you to them, but because of the imprint they are constantly reminded of you and your services.

Most premiums must be purchased in quantities of 500 or more. Sometimes an order of 100 pens is acceptable. In any event, you can do something like this and not spend much more than a few hundred dollars. Do be sure to control supplies of any premiums you produce so you do not end up being the supplier of pens to your office.

It is also possible to sponsor events or to participate in some local public activities that generate promotional value while performing a civic service. You might offer to provide T-shirts for some event—a race to raise funds for the local symphony for example. Perhaps you could have your name and firm's name imprinted on these shirts? Or you could offer to buy the trophy for the winner and get some publicity out of it. The possibilities are virtually endless.

9

Selecting the Best Advertising Media

IF YOUR MARKETING program will utilize advertising, you should first narrow your choices to a particular advertising media and then subsequently to a specific medium (the actual newspaper, radio station, etc., where your ads will appear). This chapter reviews what your medium choices might be and how you might go about making this decision.

Advertising mediums consist of the following:

- Print advertising: Magazines, newspapers, and periodicals.
- Radio: AM and FM broadcast stations.
- Television: Network, local, low power, and cable.
- Specialty items and premiums: Imprinted key chains and pens, special reports, etc.

As you will recall from an earlier chapter, your budget will be a primary determinant of which medium you will be able to use. Generally, your budget must be larger as you proceed down the list from print to radio to TV. Specialty items and premiums can be expensive or inexpensive, depending upon the form you choose. This will be discussed in greater detail in this chapter.

FREQUENCY

Frequency is important in advertising. It has been shown that repetition of an ad significantly improves the audience's recall of the ad. There are several reasons why frequency can be even more important for radio advertising than for print or TV.

First, radio does not have a visual impact. As a result, it is harder for radio ads to register with the listener. A strong print ad can really make an impression. The same is true for TV. But it is very difficult to make a big splash with radio ads. So frequency can help build the impact you require.

Second, while radio tends to have a loyal audience base—that is, people tend to listen to the same station or stations on a regular basis—there is much less chance that you will catch the same person listening at the particular time your ad runs. The same readers are much more likely to see your ad each time it appears in a given publication. Even with television, there appears to be a greater probability of reaching the same people each time an ad is run.

So it may be more difficult to achieve frequency for a given listener just by running the ad a few more times on the radio. It might take many repetitions of the commercial to catch the same people a sufficient portion of those runs to have real impact.

Clearly the particular nature of the radio station, its program format, etc., will affect how regularly its audience tunes in, but in general the listening habits of a radio audience are not as dependable as those reading the daily paper, for example.

While a single ad in print can produce satisfactory results and a few multiple print ads can be really effective, frequent repetition of ads on radio, and on TV as well, are essential to getting your message across. Since TV spots are usually more memorable than radio spots, this is not quite as critical for television as it is for radio.

The need for frequency will greatly increase your required budget, particularly for the broadcast media. Since radio and TV advertising tend to be the most expensive ways to advertise, frequency translates into significantly larger budgets in these cases.

Assuming that you have ruled out any medium which does not fit your marketing budget, your next task would be to zero in on the medium that is most suited for the particular type of offer you have in mind.

TARGET AUDIENCES

Selecting the right medium will depend upon the target audience you wish to reach, the image you are trying to create, and the frequency and length of your campaign.

If you have a very specific target market in mind, you will want to search for a particular medium that fits that group. For example, if you offer only commodities—a commodities magazine or other publication that caters specifically to commodity traders should definitely be considered. Or, if you cover a small territory, the local newspaper or radio station may be your only viable choice without incurring expenses for unusable coverage.

On the other hand, when your target is a broad range of upper-tier investors, promoting your services on a prestige radio station which broadcasts quiet music in a wealthier area would make sense. And if you are trying to make inroads into a new market area, TV may give you the credibility you need.

PRINT MEDIA

Obviously some publications will be more appropriate for financial services advertising than others.

The size of the audience will be a consideration in identifying the optimal print media for your particular purposes. The circulation data for various print media will give you some idea of how many people see the publications. Circulation figures include a variety of measurements. One figure would be the number of copies printed. Other circulation data shows the paid subscriptions and newsstand sales. If a lot of copies are given away, that figure will often be picked up as well.

The problem with circulation data is that it does not tell you very much about who is in those counts and it fails to include pass-along readers, (subsequent readers of an issue who do not buy it) which can be a significant factor for most publications, doubling the potential audience in many cases.

There are a number of ways to adjust the circulation figures to give a better measure of the true audience. These primarily consist of statistical methods that take into account a variety of factors such as subscription growth, variety of editions, pass-along estimates, etc.

Effective audience is a measure of how many people with the characteristics of your target audience will be exposed to the particular media you are considering. The fact that a publication has a circulation of one million is of far less relevance than the fact that 600,000 of them are active investors. While this does not guarantee that all those in the effective audience will read your ad, it is a fairly good indicator of potential. Arriving at this conclusion can be a fairly complicated process and would require an ad agency or other professional group to do the analytical work. However, you should bear in mind that circulation is not the only benchmark upon which media choices should be based.

In many ways the indicators of an appropriate target audience are the same as those used in direct mail:

- Wealth or earning power
- Previous investment experience
- Expensive buying habits

As we learned in the chapter "All About Lists," the indications of wealth or earning power are usually geographic location (upscale neighborhood), highly paid occupation, and ownership (boat, plane, expensive car, etc.). Investment experience shows up in previous transactions and ownership is evident by the car they drive or the club they belong to.

If you can begin to identify these qualities in the audience of the media you are considering, you can start narrowing your search.

A good indication of how appropriate a particular publication may be, for example, would be the presence of other financial services advertisers. If some advertisers are present repeatedly, that is an excellent sign that they are achieving satisfactory results, otherwise they would be long gone. Ads for expensive items in general would be another positive sign.

Sometimes a publication cross-references its readership with other characteristics. For example, you may be able to determine the average income level, education level, or typical occupation of the readers. This can be extremely useful in evaluating the value of their audience for your purposes.

Response Curves

An important consideration in selecting the appropriate type of medium in which to advertise is how quickly and for how long it is likely to continue generating inquiries. A big initial flow and quick demise implies entirely different requirements for receiving and fulfilling leads than a source that will yield a few leads daily for a long period of time. To analyze expected lead flow, a chart plotting cumulative inquiries over time is useful. You will be using these types of charts to study a variety of mediums.

A response curve tends to rise over time, finally reaching nearly 100% after some period, perhaps 10 or 20 days depending upon the type of medium and type of response mechanism. The curve rarely reaches exactly 100%, however, since a few leads often stagger in months or even years after an ad has run.

Typically, responses will come in much more quickly via the telephone than via the mails. This is primarily because the telephone is not delayed by the delivery process. It may also be due in part to the fact that prospects who call do so almost immediately, while those who write might delay their action for a short while. Figure 9-1 shows what a typical response curve would look like.

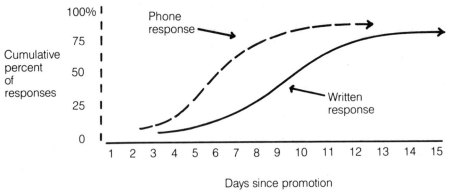

Fig. 9-1. Typical response curve.

Newspapers

In most instances, newspapers are the shortest-lived print media. Tomorrow, very few people will ever look at today's issue again. A newspaper ad provides immediate impact. People will see it today and usually act today, if they will act at all. Therefore, if you run a newspaper ad, your replies will come in quickly over a relatively short period of time. Figure 9-2 illustrates the response curve for newspapers.

There are four factors to keep in mind when deciding whether newspapers will be an effective medium for your particular advertising campaign.

1. Content of available papers (what type of information do they typically carry)
2. Target audience (who reads this particular paper; the general public versus specialized—perhaps just investors)
3. Territory covered (what geographic areas receive the paper?)
4. Costs of an ad versus the available budget (can you afford it?)

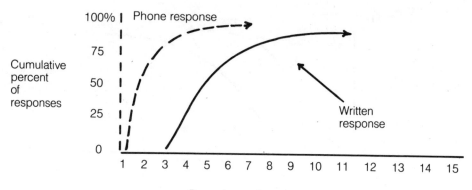

Fig. 9-2. Typical newspaper response curve.

Newspapers are usually read by a broad audience, with some notable exceptions. Most papers have at least some kind of financial report. This is important to you since publications without any financial information are probably not attracting the type of audience you should require.

Local newspapers can be very effective for financial advertisers. For a given dollar level of budget, local papers are often the best buy when covering a limited market. If you operate out of Des Moines, for example, it does you little good to run an ad nationally, or even regionally, since you must pay for coverage you do not need. The local daily may be just the right answer, giving you strong local coverage.

Magazines

Magazines present many of the same basic options as newspapers, but magazines are often more specialized and are distributed to a particular target market only. This targeting often makes them more expensive for advertisers, but the quality of the prospects can justify the cost. There might be more choices from which to select when comparing magazines to newspapers. Often, for any given area, more magazines may be available than newspapers (although most of the magazines will probably be national in scope). Remember that the cost per lead is not too important. It is the cost per sale that counts. If an audience that is more likely to buy will cost you more to reach, it could be well worth the additional price.

From an alternative standpoint, in an effort to make better media decisions, it may be advantageous for you to consider magazine advertising. Magazines have longer circulation lives, or catalog value. Think about all the magazines you find circulated in your office, your doctor's office, or how long a magazine stays around at your own home. This means that the same ad in a particular copy of a magazine may be seen by many people and even seen several times by the same person (if they reread the issue at some later time). Of course, if someone has already torn out your ad, you may not be able to reach these secondary readers.

However, in the case of magazines, as well as other long-lived publications, you do get the benefit of significant potential multiple exposures. Therefore, inquiries from magazine advertising tend to come in over a longer period of time than that of newspapers. The typical response curve for magazines is shown in Fig. 9-3.

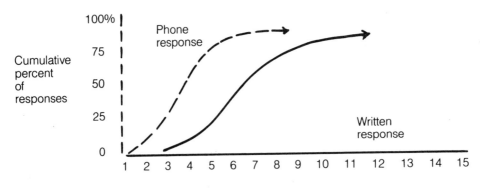

Days since ad ran (publication received)

Fig. 9-3. Typical weekly magazine response curve.

A certain amount of prestige comes with advertising in magazines. A nice magazine ad is often associated with a more substantial operation than the same ad in a newspaper.

While rates will vary, it is a good rule of thumb that an ad in a magazine can cost several times a comparable newspaper ad. While there are many exceptions to this, it will be handy for initial considerations of your budget allocations.

Periodicals

Periodicals are similar to magazines, but are published less often (monthly or semi-monthly typically) and are usually very slick and expensive. Periodicals have even longer shelf lives than magazines. Leads can come in years after an ad was run, although most will arrive during the first few weeks that the periodical was sent to its readers or released for sale.

Tip: Some readers may not want to remove a coupon from a higher-quality publication such as a periodical. You should bear this in mind and, if you do offer a coupon, also include a second means of responding such as a phone number, to permit those who do not want to tear out the coupon to reply in a convenient way.

Figure 9-4 is representative of response rates to periodicals and will be useful in guiding you should you choose to run an ad in a periodical.

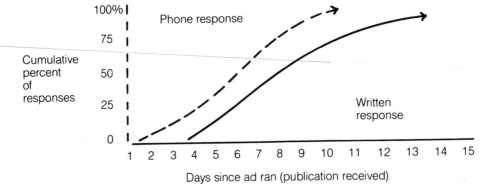

Days since ad ran (publication received)

Fig. 9-4. Response rates to periodicals.

BROADCAST MEDIA

The same considerations concerning audience selection, budgets and costs, and comparative response levels can be applied to the broadcast media (radio and TV) in evaluating the most viable methods of advertising your offers.

Radio Advertising

Radio advertising consists of spots on radio programs. A *spot* is a unit of time purchased to present your ad. Spots typically range from 15 seconds to 60 seconds. Shorter or longer times sometimes are available, but seldom are they as desirable. A spot of less than 15 seconds is usually not sufficient time to get your message across and one of more than about 30 seconds risks boring the audience (and it is more expensive as well). Fifteen-second spots are very common today and they permit a reasonable message to be communicated. Depending on what you are trying to promote, you may be able to utilize 15-second spots. More often, however, you will find 30 seconds are required.

Information on audience size is hard to verify. Some firms do offer research data on audiences and their characteristics for some selected markets, but even this is usually not terribly accurate.

A large number of radio stations are now under common ownership and this provides a potential network of advertising similar to television. While in most cases you will want local coverage, this type of network will give you the opportunity to expand your coverage if you deem it appropriate.

A single radio station has a fairly limited primary range, typically 50 to 100 miles for AM and 25 to 35 miles for FM. Thus, you automatically have a local ad when using a single radio station. You could utilize a series of stations to cover a larger geographic area.

Stations to consider would include classical music stations, all news stations and stations featuring financial information—which is becoming more common these days.

AM radio has been struggling lately to recapture market share it lost to FM and other broadcast media. AM only accounts for about 25% of radio listeners while FM is roughly 75%. The split was closer to 50–50 ten years ago.

To compete, many AM stations are focusing on business and financial matters. Consequently you may have a better opportunity finding a good target audience with selected AM stations.

One format gaining popularity on AM stations is called the Business Radio Network. You might check if its programming is carried in your area. There is also FNN Radio, prepared by the Financial News Network and picked up by many stations.

Radio has a very short response time. Listeners typically hear an ad and either act or forget about it. Figure 9-5 shows typical response levels for average conditions.

Like print advertising, radio ads will limit how much can be said due to the time constraints. Since normal speech is considerably slower than reading, it is typically not possible to communicate as much information in a radio ad as you would be able to in a print ad, for a given level of spending. You could buy an hour's worth of air time and explain in great detail every aspect of zero coupon bonds, but the expense is unlikely to be justified.

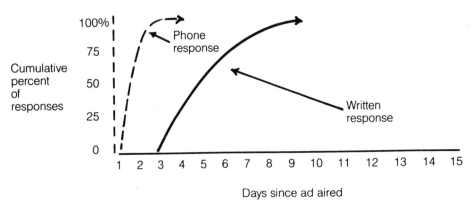

Fig. 9-5. Typical radio response levels.

In addition, for radio advertising, the listener must remember what you say (he does not have a copy to reread subsequently), and probably does not have paper and pencil available to write down the information. So you do not want to inundate the prospect by giving him too much information in a radio spot. However, in the case of radio ads, you do gain an important strength. You are talking directly to the prospect, so it can be personal, particularly if you are making your own announcement. It is almost like a telephone conversation, and this can be used to your advantage. In some cases you might have the prospect's undivided attention, such as during the morning drive to work. It is difficult to get that kind of attention and direct communication in print.

Television

Because of the broad appeal of television, the difficulty in choosing the best place to run your ad will have less to do with your selection of stations than with finding the right environment (programs) in which to run ads. In addition to the correct fit, advertisers must contend with a relatively expensive medium. This will make it particularly difficult for a smaller advertiser to find the optimal placement for his ads.

Many advertisers with very limited budgets might have to settle for late evening spots that happen to be open rather than buying in prime time. While this may be acceptable, if that turns out to be the case with your budget, you may just want to use a different medium.

In any event, the choices of particular stations and programs will be limited when you are working with TV. So most of your media selection might be by default.

One interesting development that could increase your options with television is the popularity of low-power stations. They have significantly less range than traditional stations, perhaps just 20 miles as compared to three or four times that distance for regular, full-power stations.

These low-power stations are a reasonable alternative to other local advertising on the radio or in print and are generally much more economical than ads on regular stations.

The typical response times for television ads are shown in Fig. 9-6. You can use this information to plan when you should expect most of your replies from a TV ad.

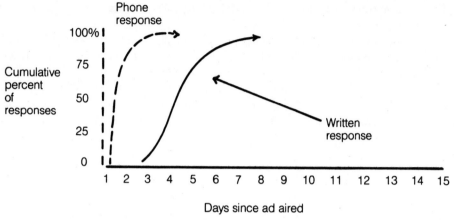

Fig. 9-6. Typical television response curve.

Television is a prestige medium. This image is partly due to the fact that it is expensive and partly because it is associated with glamour and stars. Because people will often put their confidence in a product advertised on television, you can use the fact that you ran a television ad to bolster your other promotional activities. You might include the message "as advertised on TV" and capitalize on the TV campaign even further. Care must be exercised here that such an effort fits the image you are trying to create and that your legal department does not have a problem with this approach.

Other Advertising Mediums

There are a variety of other advertising methods available to you. These include special ads and promotions as well as skywriting, loud speaker announcements, billboards, signs on your car, etc. While the list is practically endless, only a few limited practices are appropriate for the marketing of financial services.

It is doubtful that you would get very many leads from placing signs on all of your neighbors doors, but you might create a lot of angry neighbors.

Some techniques that have proven beneficial for financial services include:

- Yellow page listings
- Premium giveaways
- Sponsorships of contests and events

A yellow-pages listing can be useful. There are people who do not currently have their own securities salesperson and suddenly find the need for one. If you are listed, they may turn to you. These listings can be inexpensive if you do not get involved with big headlines or lengthy copy. However, a yellow-pages listing is not one of the more promising methods of promotion and should not be done as a primary marketing effort. In addition, your firm is probably already listed and a certain percentage of calls from that listing would go to you anyway.

Premium giveaways (pens with your name and phone number on them, for example) can be very beneficial. T-shirts are another popular giveaway, but they may not fit the business image you wish to create. You and your firm will need to decide how appropriate any of these may be.

One problem with premium items is that other employees tend to want to take one or two home for their own use. A pen here and there and soon you will not have any left for customers. So keep control of any premiums you stock.

You should also consider sponsoring a contest or show. Neighborhood kids might be planning a bike race or other sporting event. Provide them with box lunches or certain outfits, etc. You can be sure that all the parents will learn who helped the kids.

SPECIFIC MEDIA SELECTION

In previous chapters you learned that certain types of magazines can be targeted to a rather specific prospect. This ability to accurately select your audience tends to diminish as you progress through newspapers, radio, and finally TV. So one criteria for media selection might be how precisely you want to aim your message.

If you are promoting an investment with very narrow appeal to a very well-defined potential client, you will most likely find that a print ad in a publication whose audience has many of these characteristics will be a good bet (besides a direct-mail campaign).

On the other hand, if your promotion is for something new and the optimal audience is less well defined, an ad on TV, with a much broader typical audience, might be a better choice.

Your media selection process should include reviewing as many potential advertising vehicles as possible. A convenient way to do this is by requesting media kits on each candidate.

A *media kit* is a package of information about the publication or, in the case of broadcast, about the station. A media kit would typically include the following four items:

1. Sample publication (if applicable)
2. Reader, listener, or viewer data. Information about their audience's characteristics
3. Circulation or audience size and geographic areas covered
4. A rate card specifying costs and options, deadlines, etc.

The media kits will not only be useful in your decision about the best medium, they will also help you choose which specific media (radio station, newspaper, magazine, etc.) you will utilize.

There are two factors that should dominate your evaluations of potential advertising media: First, how much does it cost? Second, are their prospects worth the price?

The cost is both an absolute and a subjective matter. If the minimum cost of an ad is $20,000, you probably will not consider it even if there was a good likelihood of strong audience interest. You would probably have eliminated this option as not affordable early in your budgeting process. Advertising is always a risk. So an individual salesperson is unlikely to be willing to take a chance on that big of an expense. Fortunately, most programs will not be this easy to rule out. They will need to be considered more subjectively.

Whatever the cost to advertise, you must be convinced that the audience consists of reasonably likely prospects, i.e., potential clients. As you examine the information in a media kit, or other data, you will be looking for strong signs that the audience makes sense for your purposes.

Better statistics often translate into higher cost and the decision process can be a little cloudy here. Do you pay $45 CPM (cost per thousand) in publication number one for its $87,000 average-income reader, or do you pay $55 CPM for publication number two and its $98,000 average-income reader? The answer is, it depends. There are probably other facts that would help you make that decision, but the proper conclusion certainly is not clear from these data.

A framework for analyzing advertising options which would permit us to rate the various qualities of each media would be most useful in evaluating our choices. While it would not guarantee correct decisions, it would permit us to focus our judgments in a more formalized way. Such a system has been developed and it is presented here.

Selection Analysis for Advertising Media

Use this handy procedure for ranking advertising options and you should be able to make better media decisions.

Step 1: Is it affordable? Can you afford to advertise in this media? Considering rates, a need for some frequency of three to four runs at a minimum, and a quality ad commensurate with the ad space costs, is your budget sufficient to consider it?

Step 2: Is it appropriate? Of those media you might consider, which fit your objectives? Rule out any that are doubtful.

Step 3: Rate your options. Use the three general criteria that define your target market: wealth or earning power, investment experience, and buying habits. It may be useful to use a scale with one being the least fit and 10 being the best or most appropriate fit. Table 9-1 shows a chart that can be drawn for each media as follows.

You could then assign your feelings about each media's qualities in these categories (and any other categories you may develop). By rating each indicator from one to 10, you could get a total score.

Step 4: Ranking. Use the ratings in Step 3, you could then rank the media. This would not reflect the cost differentials, however, and therefore the question, which was the best buy, would still not be clear.

An adjustment to the ratings might be made. Suppose you divide the ratings by the cost per thousand (CPM) for each. The more expensive media would have their ratings cut by more than the less expensive media, so a fairer comparison would result. While this system is still quite subjective, it can help you focus your analysis. Table 9-2 shows the results of adjusting the ratings in this fashion.

The new ranking should give a fair measure of the optimal choices based on, admittedly subjective, variables. An example to see how this might be useful follows.

Example of Media Analysis Evaluation

Suppose you are considering four media for a $3000 advertising campaign, three newspapers, and a local radio station. Table 9-3 shows some of the vital statistics you have found for each of your choices.

Table 9-1. Media Rating Worksheet.

Criteria:	Rating									
	Worst 1	2	3	4	5	6	7	8	9	Best 10
Wealth or Earning Power										
Business Title or job (Retired)										
Education										
Geographic Location										
Home Value										
Income Level										
Net Worth										
Previous Investments										
Level of Investments										
Type of Investments										
Years Investing										
Buying Habits										
Car										
Boat										
Plane										
Private Club										

Table 9-2. Results of Rating Analysis.

Media	Unadjusted Ranking	CPM For That Media	Adjusted Ranking
Media 1	A	v	A/v
Media 2	B	w	B/w
Media 3	C	x	C/x
Media 4	D	y	D/y
Media 5	E	z	E/z
.	.	.	.
.	.	.	.
.	.	.	.

Our analysis would go something like this:

Step 1: Is it affordable?—You can afford any of them. None are beyond your $3000 budget, considering at least three runs, etc.

Step 2: Is it appropriate?—All appear to be useful at first glance. Newspaper number one might be a little questionable since income, home values, and investments are lower, but it is not clear that their audience is not worthwhile. So we may continue considering that media.

Table 9-3. Sample Medial Information.

	Newspaper #1	Newspaper #2	Newspaper #3	Radio Station
Income Level (000's)	$ 47	$ 53	$ 76	$ 57
Location	Major Metro	Suburban	Upscale Suburban	Major Metro
Some College	27%	46%	64%	39%
Home Value (000's)	$143	$197	$236	$152
Investments (000's)	$ 14	$ 19	$ 58	$ 23
Car	75%	85%	93%	72%
Luxury Car	12%	18%	39%	14%
Boat	5%	7%	12%	6%
Private Club	1%	3%	9%	2%
Ad Cost*	$930	$590	$450	$675
CPM	$ 8	$ 15	$ 29	$ 12

Note: *Cost for ten column inch ad or thirty second spot.

Step 3: Rating—You should use your chart to analyze and rate the choices. Again, this is somewhat subjective, but it will permit you to pass judgment on these options in a more formalized manner.

For simplicity, assign this simple code to each media: Newspaper One = N1, Newspaper Two = N2, Newspaper Three = N3, and the Radio Station = R.

Table 9-4 presents the information on each media rated as compared to the average of the group on each category.

Table 9-4. Rating the Media Options.

Evaluation Basis	Average	Rating									
		1	2	3	4	5	6	7	8	9	10
Income	$ 58,000		N1		N2	R					N3
Location	-					N1 R			N2		N3
Education	44%		N1		R	N2					N3
House Value	$182,000		N1	R			N2		N3		
Investments	$ 28,000	N1	N2	R							N3
Car	81%			R	N1	N2			N3		
Luxury Car	21%	N1	R			N2					N3
Boat	7%		N1	R	N2						N3
Club	4%	N1		R		N2					N3

In the case of income levels, you can see that the average for the four media is $58,000. Since the radio station's $57,000 was quite close to the average, it was rated at "5" on the scale, neither good nor particularly bad.

Newspaper number one was a fair amount below average at $47,000, so it was rated a "2." Newspaper number two was close to average, but a bit low, so it was assigned a "4." And newspaper number three was well above average, so it was awarded a "10."

The other categories were rated in a similar manner. If a specific piece of information is missing, it may be convenient to arbitrarily assign a "5" or "6" which are roughly midway on the scale and thereby neither favor nor punish the media on that item. You could also weigh certain categories that are felt to be more critical to your evaluations so that, say for example, education counts twice as much as owning a boat. That will make the calculations quite a bit more complicated, but it may be useful in some circumstances.

The result of the new ratings can be found by adding up the values assigned to each media. In the case of newspaper number one, a rating of "2" for income level, "5" for location, "2" for education, "2" for house value, "1" for investments, "4" for car, "1" for luxury car, "3" for boat, and "1" for club membership is found. These total 21. Using the same technique results in the ratings shown in Table 9-5.

Table 9-5.
Summary Ratings for Sample Media.

Media	Symbol	Rating
Newspaper Number One	N1	21
Newspaper Number Two	N2	46
Newspaper Number Three	N3	87
Radio Station	R	33

It would seem up to this point, that newspaper number three is by far the best to use. While it does appear to have the best audience for your purposes, it also costs the most in terms of CPM (cost per thousand).

Step 4: Adjust these ratings to reflect the cost to use each media, arriving at the figures in Table 9-6.

Table 9-6. Adjusted Summary Ratings for Sample Media.

Media	Symbol	Original Rating	CPM	Adjusted Rating*
Newspaper Number One	N1	21	$ 8	2.6
Newspaper Number Two	N2	46	15	3.1
Newspaper Number Three	N3	87	29	3.0
Radio Station	R	33	12	2.8

Note: * Original Rating/CPM

As you can see, the new ratings are a lot closer together and the order is somewhat different. None of these seem to be particularly bad deals now. You might still choose newspaper number three because of its audience, but you should understand that it does not necessarily make a better marketing investment than some of the other options, particularly newspaper number two.

Clearly, the subjective nature of the ranking could affect the outcome in important ways. But this process did force a fairly consistent evaluation of the options and result in some reasonable conclusions. This technique can be used with all forms of advertising media and even with direct mail.

10

Preparing Your Advertising Program

IF YOU WILL be using advertising in your marketing program and you have already selected a particular type of media (primarily print or broadcast), you will now have to develop the specific details of your campaign.

Your program should be appropriate both for the media selected and your target audience. The same ad will not usually work on television, radio, and in print, although if you use more than one, a common theme would be beneficial.

The following mediums are discussed separately because each must be developed independently, and preparation for one type will not be particularly appropriate for another type. The mediums to be considered are:

- Print advertising
- Radio
- Television
- Special ads or promotions

PRINT ADVERTISING

Once the particular media has been chosen, the next step would be the reservation and purchase of space for the ad, usually measured in column inches. As discussed previously, a column inch is an ad one column wide and one inch deep (high). A four-column inch ad could be one column wide and four inches deep or two columns wide by two inches deep, etc. It is really a measure of area and you pay based upon the area you cover with your ad. Your cost is also affected by the positioning of your ad, timing, and number of times your advertisement is run (volume discounts are often available).

Publications usually require camera-ready artwork. This means that your ad must be typeset and all necessary artwork submitted when you deliver the ad to the publication. Although some publications will prepare your ad (usually for a fee), you will probably have to have the ad prepared by someone other than the publication. This may also be more economical than having the publisher do it for you.

The typesetting might be obtained at a local printer or perhaps you could have an ad agency create and execute the entire advertising program for you. Depending on the size and nature of the account, ad agencies will charge approximately 15% of your media costs, or possibly they will bill you based upon time and materials. Sometimes both types of charges may occur. The agency usually receives its basic fee through discounts from publications for ad placement. For example, if your ad space costs $1000, the agency would probably pay $850 for the space and charge you $1000 (not considering any of their other fees which might apply).

Ad Proportions

The dimensions of your ad will be constrained by a number of factors. The amount of space you can afford to purchase will be the primary limitation. A full-page ad will obviously cost many times the fee for a one-eighth page ad. However, the rate will not necessarily be proportional. In fact, the charge for a large ad will usually be less per column inch than a smaller ad.

In addition, most publications will require specific proportions or geometric style, a rectangle for instance. Or they may insist that the ad be longer than wide. There are many ways to meet a size specification. For example, a 10-column inch ad could be 10 inches long by one column wide, or five inches long by two columns wide, or approximately three and a half inches long by three columns wide, etc. Figure 10-1 demonstrates various ways an ad could total 10 column inches.

Ads should generally be longer than wide. People are accustomed to reading things that are taller than they are wide. Most letters and books fit these dimensions. So it is a common reaction that ads that are wider than they are long look odd and can be harder to read. This is especially true for ads consisting primarily of text. Ads with extensive graphics or photos may have more latitude to deviate from this rule of thumb. Therefore, if possible, your ad should be at least as long as it is wide (square) and preferably about half again as long as wide. Figure 10-2 shows the optimal well proportioned text ad.

Of course if your ad is very brief, it may be shorter than one column wide and that is certainly permissible. But do try to stick to the formula (length should be about 150% of width) unless publication restrictions or minimum sizes prevent this. In those cases try to stay as close to that ideal as you reasonably can. Optimal layouts of ads and ways to compensate for very wide ads are discussed shortly.

Booking Space

After determining ad size and proportions, you are ready to book space in the publication and begin preparing the ad. Give the publication at least two weeks notice. Some require four or more weeks of advance commitment to get space. The earlier you notify them, the better chance you have of getting preferred positioning, or, for that matter, getting in the desired edition at all.

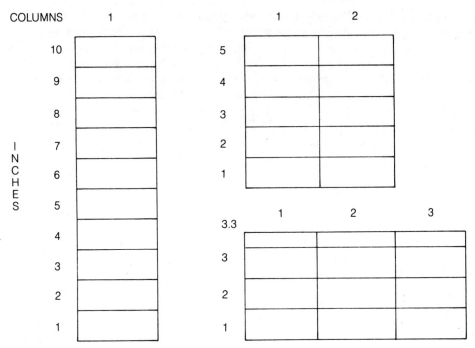

Fig. 10-1. Various proportions of 10-column-inch ad.

WIDTH IN INCHES

Fig. 10-2. Optimal print ad proportions.

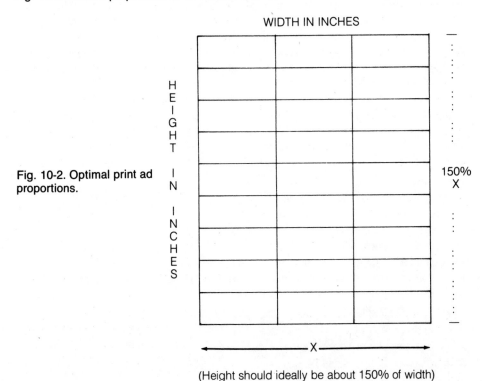

(Height should ideally be about 150% of width)

One option, if you like risk, is to book late. You might be able to pick up some remnant space that has not been sold at a substantial discount. As publications get very close to their closing deadlines (just before they print an issue) they are often willing to cut the price of space just to get some revenue rather than allowing it to go unused.

However, it is difficult to predict the availability of such space or the willingness of a particular publication to make a deal with you. The publication is obviously not going to tell you ahead of time that you should wait and get your space for a much lower rate. You may also find that no remnant space is available, or that it is in a very undesirable location. So this strategy is not without its downside.

Some publications may require total or partial prepayment, usually non-refundable if you do not run the ad. Be sure to inquire about the individual publication's policies beforehand. Get all commitments in writing, showing your ad size, dates to be run, position (if applicable), number of times the ad will be run, and all costs. Note all deadlines and specify if you are providing camera-ready artwork, or if they will do the production work for you.

Be sure you know what the publisher will do for you in the event they fail to run your ad, or run the ad but do not print it properly, etc. Will they owe you a rerun, a refund, an apology? This type of problem comes up often enough that you should inquire about it and know where you will stand.

The Ad Copy

To create an advertisement, you should consider what information you will be presenting and how it will be presented.

Identify exactly what it is you wish to communicate. Do you want to convey information about a product or service? How much information do you want to include? Is your objective to inform, to challenge a conventional belief, to help solve a particular problem, to reassure them about a concern, or something else?

Remember that the key message must ultimately translate into a benefit or benefits for the prospect. If he does not feel that what you have to offer will be of value to him in some way, you will not hear from him.

After specifying what to communicate, next decide how you would like to communicate your message. Will you be authorative? Will you be humorous? Are you going to use specific examples or generalities?

Whatever you decide to achieve with your ad, keep in mind that you are asking to become involved in some way in people's finances. You are, therefore, asking for trust. Prospects must believe what they are reading. If not, they will stop.

One way to achieve believability is to be credible. Working for a well-known firm helps. Having some special expertise that is relevant is also useful.

There are three main components to print ad copy (Fig. 10-3). These are:

1. The headline
2. The body
3. The response vehicle

BULLET TAX-FREE FUND

A TARGETED APPROACH TO TAX-FREE INVESTING

The BULLET TAX EXEMPT BOND FUND is a diversified portfolio of maturing bonds selected because they are not a shot in the dark.

Investment advantages include:

> Unreported income—What Uncle Sam does not know cannot hurt you
> Marketability—you know someone will give you something for them
> Convenience—you know the income check will arrive like clockwork every sixty years
> Minimum fees—annual fees will not exceed annual income plus 10%

The Bullet Tax Exempt Bond Fund takes a targeted approach to investing, we aim to please. We are not quick on the draw nor do we scatter your investment funds.

Get the facts on Bullet Funds today. Use the handy coupon below, or call toll free.

This is not an offer to sell or buy. It is not anything. See your lawyer.

BULLET INVESTMENTS, INC.
123 Shotgun Drive, #19D
Rifle, TX 75000-1234
(987) 555-1212 x 1238

[ ] Yes, I would like complete information on the Bullet Tax Exempt Bond Fund, including a prospectus. Do not send money, unless it is in small unmarked bills.

AK-47

NAME_____

ADDRESS_____

CITY_____ STATE_____ ZIP_____

PHONE (Optional) (_____)_____

[ ] Home   [ ] Office

Labels (right margin):
- Headline
- Body copy
- Tell the prospects how to respond
- Legally required disclaimer
- Coupon
- Second response Method (Phone)
- Ad code
- If you request a phone number, make it optional.

Fig. 10-3. Print ad.

Begin by developing your ad's headline. The following list includes just a few potential headlines you might consider using. Try variations on these as well as totally different topics you create.

- High Yields and Security
- Investment Opportunities for the 1990s and Beyond
- How to Speculate Profitably In the Commodities Markets
- Lower Fees Will Increase Your Profits!
- Research Recommendations In Primary Industries
- Unique IRA Investments Can Improve Retirement
- How To Select A Financial Advisor
- Build Your Nest Egg With Zeros
- A Government Securities Dealer You Can Trust!
- Securities Valuations For Estates

An effective headline should get attention, relate to a readily identifiable need and convey a benefit. The first example given in the above list poses an attention-getting possibility—everyone likes to earn a high return, but most do not like high risk. It also relates to a need to know how they can earn more with security, and it implies a benefit—that with your help the prospect can invest profitably and minimize risk as well. Similarly, each headline listed has these qualities, to a greater or lesser degree.

It is better to ask a pointed question or hold up a tantalizing offer than to use an undirected statement such as: "Brokerage Services Available," "Need A Financial Advisor?" etc. If you or your firm have some particular expertise or qualification, this may be an opportunity to promote it. For example, if your research department has just prepared a report on the airline industry, you might offer it this way: "Airlines—Stalled On The Runway or Finally Taking Off?" Your copy would then explain your firm's expertise and give a few points to consider. The prospect would have to return the coupon, call or write for the full report and complete information.

The copy should be brief and to the point. Be sure you cover these important areas:

- How your offer can benefit the prospect. Start with your biggest benefit and list other benefits successively.
- Why the prospect should contact you. This may be a limited-time offer or the situation is expected to last for a short time. Or perhaps this offer is not available anywhere else: your special report can only be obtained from you.
- Your firm's name: people do not know you at this point, your firm is the only credibility you can offer them. Hopefully, you do not work for a firm where that statement might not be true.
- How to contact you: coupon, phone, etc.

The response vehicle should be prominent. If it is a phone number, print it bold and clear. Use a coupon whenever possible. A coupon is convenient for the prospect; if returned it gives you a reason to contact the prospect and provides a monitoring mechanism for your advertising (i.e., which ads are generating inquiries). Further, a coupon gives prospects an impersonal way to respond if they prefer not to talk to you immediately. Replying by coupon is less intimidating to people who do not want to make an immediate commitment to buy a product or service.

An interesting theory says that if you can get the prospect involved in the marketing process, you will have a better chance of getting them to act. According to this concept, if the prospect is asked to do some small task, it actually boosts response rates.

For example, you might ask them to color in a box on your coupon or attach part of the ad to the coupon. It seems the less the task has to do with actually accomplishing something the better. In other words, it would probably be more effective to ask the prospect to color in a box (or stick on a blue dot) with little or no significance than to ask him to check off a box. But even checking a box indicating that he wants information (which is already obvious from the fact that he returned the coupon) may be better than having him just complete a form.

As crazy as it sounds, this gimmick can work. However, you do risk being considered too cute and turning off some prospects.

In your coupon, request name, address, and the specific product in which they are interested. Try not to ask anything else. Each additional question will reduce your response rate. Do not ask for a telephone number if you can avoid it. That bothers some people—you might call them. The numbers are usually available from directory assistance anyway. If you must ask for a phone number, write "optional" after it and be sure to inquire if it is an office or home number.

Tip: If you do ask for a phone number, do not ask for both home and office phone numbers. That is a sure sign that you plan to call and you will lose a lot of inquiries as a result.

Be sure your address is on the coupon. People often cut out a coupon but do not mail it right away. By the time they do get around to filling it out, your address may be lost if it was only in the ad copy and not on the coupon itself. Putting your address in the coupon and in the ad copy is optimal. In that case a subsequent reader seeing the ad after the coupon has been removed would still be able to contact you. This will take up more space, of course. It may therefore increase your budget beyond the level you wish. But putting your address in both places is desirable if the cost is not a problem. In any event, always place it in the coupon, even if that is the only place you give your address.

If you are also providing a phone number, include it wherever you show the address, i.e., on the coupon and also in the copy if possible. Of course, if you are not using a coupon the number should be in the copy, prominently displayed.

Surround your coupon with dashed lines. They have become a universal sign to cut out or detach. Figure 10-4 shows a typical coupon layout.

If you know your ad's position in the publication, locate your coupon within the ad for easy removal. For example, if your ad will be at the bottom of the page, make sure your coupon is at the bottom of your ad. If it will appear on the right, keep the coupon on the right. In the event you are on the far left, keep the coupon on the left side of the ad. A coupon across the full width of the bottom of your ad will cover you in all of these instances.

The major exception to this advice applies when you get space at the top of a page, which is quite favorable. In that instance do not put your coupon at the top of your ad despite the inconvenience this will cause (necessitating the cutting down to the coupon).

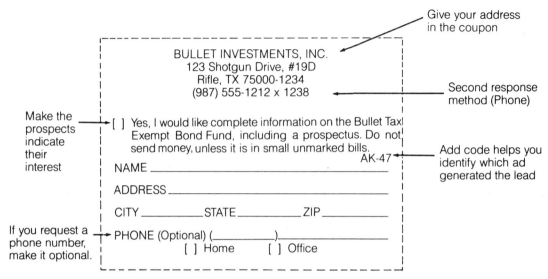

Give your address
in the coupon

BULLET INVESTMENTS, INC.
123 Shotgun Drive, #19D
Rifle, TX 75000-1234
(987) 555-1212 x 1238

Second response
method (Phone)

Make the
prospects
indicate
their
interest

[ ] Yes, I would like complete information on the Bullet Tax
Exempt Bond Fund, including a prospectus. Do not
send money, unless it is in small unmarked bills.
AK-47

Add code helps you
identify which ad
generated the lead

NAME _____

ADDRESS _____

CITY _____ STATE _____ ZIP _____

If you request a
phone number,
make it optional.

PHONE (Optional) (_____)_____
[ ] Home   [ ] Office

Fig. 10-4. Typical print ad coupon layout.

The headline and copy should come first. Figure 10-5 shows some common coupon positions.

As indicated previously, your response vehicle should be a coupon or possibly a telephone number. You might, in certain circumstances, use both. If the ad is large enough to provide for a reasonably sized coupon, use it. If not, a phone number and an address to which to write should be used. Do not expect very many replies if you offer only an address. Oddly enough, more people will write if you also have a phone number listed. You will generally get more responses overall using more than one response mechanism. This may be the result of allowing the most people to reply in the manner in which they prefer.

The coupon should have some empty space around it, especially if your ad will appear in the middle of a page. If there is plenty of space around your coupon, it can be torn out with less damage to the rest of the page. People do not like to ruin an entire page to get to a coupon. This is particularly true of magazines and publications with a longer expected useful life. Empty space around the coupon also helps to make it stand out on a crowded page.

If you believe prospects' reluctance to tear something from a particular publication will prevent them from sending in your coupon, consider using a pop-up card (a reply card bound into the magazine near your ad). While binding in a special card can be very expensive, it will make responding to your ad quite easy. The potential increased response rate could possibly justify the expense. A sensitivity analysis can help put the cost and the required benefits in perspective.

The coupon should provide adequate room for the prospect to fill in the necessary information. There is nothing more frustrating than space on a coupon so small that the respondent needs a magnifying glass to squeeze their name and address into the areas provided. This not only reduces the likely number that will respond, but it makes your job harder since the information will be more difficult for you to decipher, and the

```
XXXX XXXXX XXXXXX

XX XXXXX   XX XX X

XXX XX     XXX XX

XXX XXX    XX X XX

XX XXXX    XXX XXX
                X XX X
COUPON          XX XX X

. . . . . . .   XXX XX

. . . . . . .   XX XXX
```

Left—Bottom

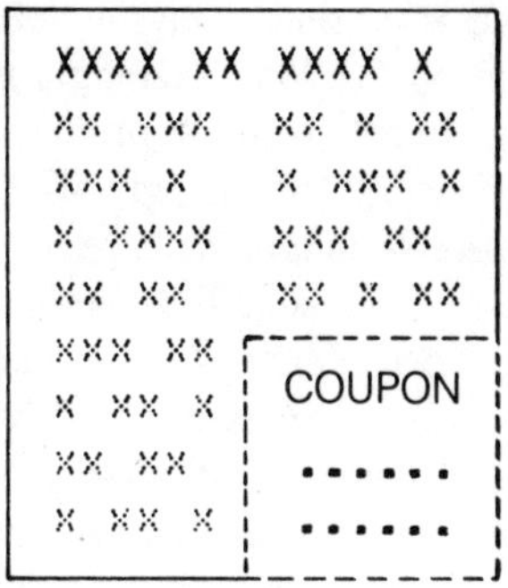

```
XXXX XX XXXX X

XX XXX    XX X XX

XXX X     X XXX X

X XXXX    XXX XX

XX XX     XX X XX

XXX XX
         COUPON
X XX X
         . . . . . .
XX XX
         . . . . . .
X XX X
```

Right—Bottom

```
XX XXX XXX XXXXX

XXX XXX   XX XX XX

XX X X    X XXX X

XXX XX    XXX X XX

XX XX X   X XX XX

XXX X X   XXXX XXX

X XXXX    X X XX X


         COUPON
```

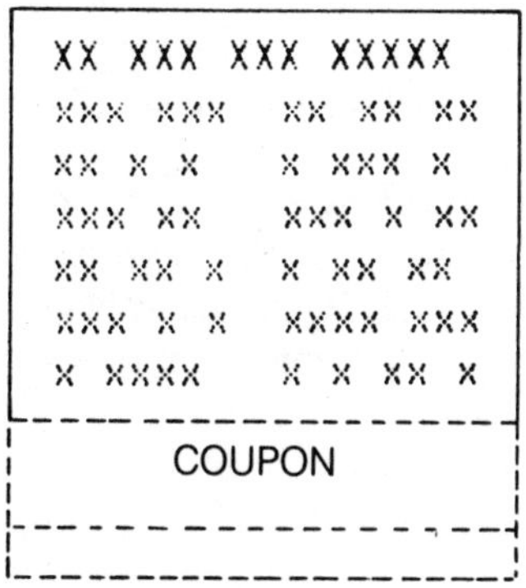

Center (Across Bottom)

Fig. 10-5. Examples of common coupon positions.

chances of error much greater. Sacrifice copy, pay for a larger ad, or do not use a coupon at all if you cannot provide enough space for the coupon to be filled in easily and clearly. Try it yourself to ensure you have left adequate space.

Your ad should use a border or other means of delineating it, particularly if it is a small ad that could get lost in the crowd.

If you choose to employ an ad agency, they can guide you through all these steps and decisions. In any event, be sure your compliance department reviews any copy before you use it.

PRINT AD LAYOUT, PRINT SIZES AND STYLES

After creating your copy, you will need to determine its layout in the space allocated for your ad. The sizes of the ad's components must also be decided.

Your headline should stretch across most of the width of your ad and should be large enough to really catch attention. The type face used for the headline should be at least three times as large as the body copy. Use clean, bold type. Avoid script, old English or other ''fancy'' type faces that are often hard to read. Headlines tend to be more readable if they are set flush-left—that is, the left edges all line up and the right fall wherever they happen to end.

The body of the ad should rarely be set in columns wider than twice the standard column width of the publication. Reading a wide column is very difficult. If your ad is three columns wide, do not stretch your copy out across the entire width, but rather use three columns or possibly two slightly wider columns with plenty of space between them. You must exercise judgment here. A very large ad may justify wider columns, especially if larger type is used. By using columns somewhat wider or narrower than those used in the editorial portions of the publication, you help set off your ad from the other things on that page. However, it will be rare that you will want to use more than two columns. Using larger type rather than more columns is typically more desirable.

Do not congest your copy. Some advertisers try to fill up every bit of their space. If your copy does not fit, do not shrink the type size! This makes it difficult to read. In all cases avoid tiny print! The size of type is the key factor in your ad's readability. Sacrifice copy if you must, but keep your print size at least as large as the regular editorial copy of the publication in which the ad will appear. Somewhat larger is better. People will not read an ad if it is difficult for them to do so. It is recommended that you size your ad's type so that letters are typically not smaller than eight or nine points. That should make it fairly easy to read.

Type is measured in *points*. The point size of a certain typeface is not a definitive measurement of the type, but rather a specification of what used to be the metal block that held type in place. While most printing is no longer done with individual letter blocks set as type, but rather by phototypesetting, this definition is still very much in use today. Figure 10-6 indicates how the measurement was created.

Fig. 10-6. A piece of movable type.

As you can see, the height of the block containing the letter determined its point size. Since the letter must necessarily be smaller than the block (to fit on it), the actual measurement of a letter will rarely be as big as its point size suggests. For example, a 72-point letter will most likely be seven-eighths of an inch high, not the full one inch suggested by the points.

A given size of type will have roughly the dimensions as others measuring the same point size, but they will not necessarily be identical. In fact it is possible to have a size of type that is defined as, say, six point, which may be slightly larger, in terms of actual letter measurements, than one defined as seven point.

Despite the fact that so much of a type's size will be dependent upon its particular style, there are some general guidelines that can help you gauge the appropriately sized type to use.

There are 72 points to an inch. A group of 12 points is commonly referred to as a pica and there are six picas to an inch. As just noted, this does not necessarily mean that you can fit 12 letters measuring six points in a one inch space.

Your local print shop will probably give you a type sizing scale. An example of a typical scale is shown here. This is basically a ruler calibrated in type sizes. The illustration in Fig. 10-7 shows one type of sizing scale. The "Ex" left-most group shows examples of various type sizes ranging from five-point at the top to 72-point type at the bottom. The right scale, called picas, will tell you how many picas will fit on a line of text. We can see that a six-inch line will accommodate 36 picas. Each type style you may consider will have a certain character count per pica. Using that figure, you can then determine how many letters will fit on a given line of space. This procedure will enable you to calculate how much copy you can reasonably accommodate for a given sized ad (or mailer for that matter).

As an example, assume you plan to run an ad that measures three inches wide by five inches high. Your headline will read: "Whole Life Beats Term" and you would like the headline to fill most of the width.

You have 18 letters plus three spaces. From your pica scale you can tell that three inches of width can accommodate 18 picas.

In addition to letters, you need some more space including some at the ends of the headline, which all together will take up five spaces, but because spaces are generally somewhat narrower than the corresponding letters, these spaces might be the equivalent of another three letters. So if we add the 18 letters to the estimated three more spaces, we need at least 21 letter-equivalent spaces. That leaves about .86 picas per letter (18 picas available divided by 21 spaces). Since there are 12 points to a pica, this suggests that we can use up to about 10 point type (.86 picas per letter times 12 points per pica). While the particular type style you may choose will affect exactly how many letters will fit, this gives you a fairly good idea of how workable your plan may be.

Since 10-point type is quite small, it would not make a good headline size. One alternative would be to use two lines for the heading, which would about double the available space and consequently increase the size of type you could use significantly.

Try it again with two lines, but use the headline: "High Rates Won't Last" instead of the other one. Here you have 17 letters plus the apostrophe and the three equivalent spaces. Thus, in this case you need to accommodate the equivalent of 20 letters on two lines, or about 10 on the first line and 10 on the second line, plus you need space on each end of each line, adding roughly four more spaces for a total of 24.

Since you are working with two lines, you have 36 picas available instead of the 18 in the previous example. So that gives us about one and a half picas per character (36 picas divided by 24 characters).

Using your rule-of-thumb that there are 12 points to a pica, we can figure a type size of about 18-point type (12 points per pica × 1.5 picas per character).

Using 18-point type would be quite acceptable for a headline, so this is a plan you can pursue.

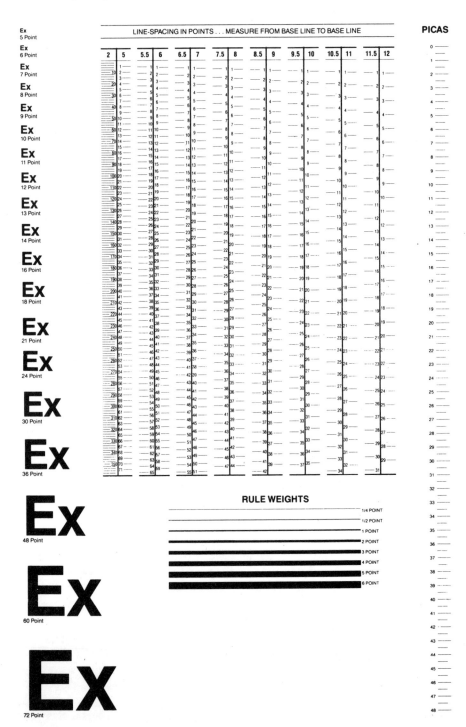

Fig. 10-7. Type sizing scale.

The same approach can be done with the copy of ads or mailers to see what can be fitted in the space allowed.

Please keep in mind that these are very rough calculations, not intended to give a precise answer. This process will simply help you estimate how much copy you can fit in the ad space available and the type sizes that might work for headlines and copy.

Besides calculating the size of type that can fit, there are some considerations as to what sizes should be used to make your ad readable. The optimal length for a line of text has been established by scientific research. In order to minimize eye fatigue and permit maximum comprehension of what is being read, the line length should be one and one half times the length of the lowercase alphabet of the particular type style you are considering. In other words, if you line up all 26 lowercase letters of the type you plan to use, and they total four inches, then the best length of text to use with that type would be six inches. There is some flexibility to this rule, so if the length was somewhat shorter, or longer, the line would still be reasonably readable.

To apply this concept, assume your ad will be three inches wide. If you plan to use type of about eight point, we can estimate that there are roughly nine or 10 letters to an inch (divide 72 points per inch by 8 points). While this is imprecise, it suggests we can fit 30 letters across our ad. That is a bit less than the ideal 39 letters (26 letters in the alphabet times 1.5), so we may want to use slightly larger letters, or perhaps go to two columns with somewhat smaller letters.

Do not use this method to calculate the exact dimensions of your ad or the precise typestyle to use. It is very rough. It does not consider the fact that an ''i'' is considerably narrower than an ''m'' nor the fact that an eight-point type might vary somewhat in actual size. But it can give you an idea of what you will be able to accommodate and how your ad might look.

Provide borders of space and some open spaces within your ad. Cut copy if necessary. Type should generally not cover more than about 75 to 80% of your ad's space. That means about 20 to 25% should be clear so as to give the ad an uncluttered look.

If you plan to use a coupon, allocate space for it. If not, you can use all the space for copy and headings. Remember, the space allocated for the coupon must permit enough room for people to write legibly.

PRINT AD POSITIONING

A very important consideration in the case of all print media is your ad's location within the publication. An ad's location is called position. There are a number of theories about what constitutes preferred position. While there are no cut-and-dry formulas for optimal position, several general rules will be helpful.

The first ad position concept says: Position earlier in the publication is more desirable than later. Being on page three is almost always better than page 33. That is because the early part of a publication is almost always read while the back parts may not be reached as often. Most newspapers have adopted sections that are numbered from one on. While an earlier position for each section is generally better, it still remains optimal to be earlier in the entire newspaper. The exception, of course, is if you are in the Financial Section, which would be more desirable than most other sections, even if it comes up late in the paper.

In the case of magazines, the back cover is a very good position despite its location at the back of the publication. This is because a magazine has a 50% chance of being put away with its cover facing down, in which case the back cover ad would be very visible.

The second ad position concept says: The higher on the page the better. The top-right of the right-hand page is generally considered most desirable. Because we read top to bottom, we tend to see things at the top of the page first.

This can be particularly true of newspapers, where being "below the fold" (the place where the paper is folded in half) makes it even less likely that the reader will notice the ad.

The third ad position theory says: The right-hand page is better than the left. As a page of the publication is turned we tend to see the right-hand pages first. We see the rest of the page successively as it is opened.

The fourth position theory says: In the case of coupon response, the closer to the edge, the better since this makes the removal of the coupon easier.

And the fifth ad position concept says: An ad placed near reading material (text of the paper) is better than an ad placed with other ads which can cause it to be lost in the clutter. The most preferred position near reading material would be those stories relating to business and finance.

Most readers scan a page, noticing ads that might interest them prior to actually reading the text of the page. Once they read the article(s) on that page, they are apt to just flip to the next page. So if you do not catch their attention as they turn to the page containing your ad, it is far less likely that they will see your ad later.

Therefore, the sooner the readers can spot your offer before they start reading the publication's text, the better chance you have of their reviewing and acting on your ad.

Optimal ad position is greatly affected by an ad's size. For small ads, the placement on the page can be absolutely critical. The larger the ad, the less important the placement, although good placement is always beneficial. In the extreme case, a spread (two facing pages) automatically has good placement on the pages, although its position in the publication may or may not be optimal.

Figure 10-8 illustrates various positions and their perceived relative desirability. Remember, this chart is only a guide and will not guarantee good (or bad) results based solely on position. It is just one important factor affecting the potential results of advertising.

Since magazines are usually read by folding the rest of the publication behind the page being read, the right side of this diagram applies to both sides of most magazines.

Most of the edges of a page are also considered quite a good location. An edge can be desirable for two reasons. First, it often has less clutter than, say for example, the center of a page where your ad might be surrounded by other ads.

Second, it makes tearing out a coupon considerably easier. A coupon in the middle of the page requires either tools (scissors, knife, or razor blade) to cut it out, or the reader will make a mess tearing out the coupon. An edge location will permit vastly easier removal of the coupon, with or without tools. You can control your position to some degree by paying an extra fee for preferred placement, or in some cases, for specific placement. This can often cost an extra 10% of the basic space cost. Considering the potential gain from convenient position and perhaps the advantage of being next to a

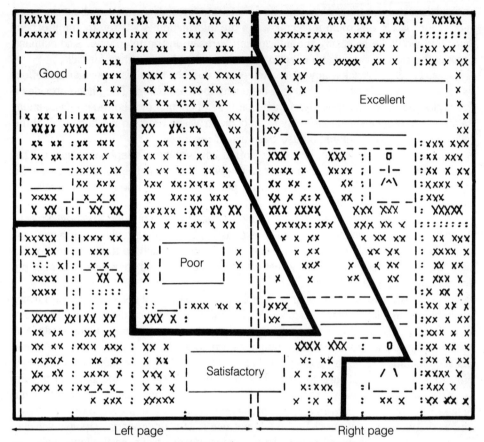

Fig. 10-8. Guide to relative position preferences in print advertising.

related article, the benefits of requesting a specific position might be worth the extra charges.

Tip: Sometimes an ad can be made to look more or less like the editorial section of a publication. If the publisher will permit this, it may increase the chance of your ad being read. However, most publications will not permit an ad that is misleading, including trying to appear like an article. So this is a difficult task to accomplish.

Print Media Reply Mechanisms

The reply mechanisms available for print advertising consist of coupons, telephone numbers to call, individual reply cards bound into the publication, reader reply cards—often called ''bingo cards,'' and addresses to which to write. By far the most popular response vehicles used are coupons, and secondly, telephone numbers (toll free where applicable).

Coupons are preferred because they are an easy, indirect way for the prospect to contact the advertiser. Prospects seem to like this indirect contact—they think they will not have to face up to a decision that they might have to make if they were talking to you on the telephone. Coupons also give you an accurate form of information about the prospect. There is far less room for error when the information is written by the prospect that there would be by taking the information verbally on the telephone. And coupons come in the mail so there is no need to stand by at the phone waiting for calls.

Despite its drawbacks, however, a telephone number to call is a popular and effective response vehicle as well. And it is becoming more common. The phone provides a direct pipeline to you for those who want that type of contact or who require fast action. As discussed previously, phone replies can come in at any time, so methods to field the calls must be in place before you use this form of response.

An excellent combination is to offer both a coupon and a telephone number. This seems to enhance the overall response rate by giving prospects the option to choose the most convenient way to reply. Be sure your phone is toll-free if long distance calls are expected, or offer to accept collect calls.

A reply card (usually postage-paid) is another good way to provide a response mechanism for an advertisement. But it can be expensive. To include a reply card in a newspaper or to bind in a reply card in a magazine can add substantially to the basic cost of the ad. For this reason, it is not usually cost effective to do this and coupons or phone reply systems should prove sufficient.

An alternative to including your own reply card is to utilize a general reply card many magazines offer. The technical term for this is reader response cards, but they are more often called "bingo cards" because of their resemblance to the bingo game cards: the reader simply must circle or mark a number corresponding to your ad, write his name and address, and mail in the postage paid card to the magazine, or their service bureau (Fig. 10-9). The requests are computerized and labels are then printed and sent to you.

This service is usually provided to advertisers in the publication at no additional charge. While it can be convenient, and probably will not do you any harm to use a bingo card as one of your reply mechanisms, do not use it as your primary response vehicle. There are some problems with using bingo card responses to financial offers.

First, most prospects who are truly interested in your offer will probably use your coupon or call you. It is generally assumed that bingo response will take a long time, if they will get their information at all. So bingo responses tend to be less serious, more curiosity seekers than average leads.

Second, bingo response is indeed slow. The magazine or its service bureau will collect leads for quite some time before they enter them into a computer and generate labels or print out lists for you. By waiting for a while they reduce the number of packets of leads they must send you as the response curve runs its course. One big envelope of all (or most) of your leads costs less and takes less effort than several shipments. In addition, the lists or labels are sometimes mailed to you by slower means than first-class mail.

The end result is that bingo card leads can take several weeks, maybe a month, to reach you. As learned previously, a month-old lead is of very limited value. While you should certainly send these leads some information, this is not recommended as your primary response system.

Bingo cards also limit how long someone can respond. Typically, when the next issue of the publication is available, they will not process requests from earlier editions.

Example of reader response ad

Example of Bingo Card

Fig. 10-9. Bingo card and ad.

So this too can limit your responses. Offering respondents only an address to which they may write is not very desirable. The prospect must produce a letter, address it and pay the postage. You have made his job very difficult and your response rate will suffer as a consequence.

On the other hand, the leads you receive this way would certainly be well qualified since the respondents clearly indicated an interest and a willingness to put out quite a bit of effort to reach you. However, the number of prospects lost because of the barrier you create by making response more difficult would probably exceed the benefits of this tough screening.

RADIO ADVERTISING PREPARATION

Preparation for radio advertising includes the following three steps.

1. Writing the ad copy
2. Testing the copy on potential listeners
3. Recording the commercial.

Preparing The Ad Copy

Writing copy for a radio ad is fairly straightforward, much the same as for print. First, develop a catchy headline that will get attention. The same discussion concerning headlines for print advertising also applies here. In radio, however, the headline is simply your opening line, so its delivery is critical. If you do not catch the listeners attention during the first few seconds of your ad, you have probably lost them completely.

The main body of the ad will necessarily contain less information than even a print ad, let alone direct mail. This is mainly due to the fact that we speak much more slowly than we read. For a given budget, you just will not be able to convey as much information via radio. Do not try to cram in all the details about the investment opportunity. Cover just the basics, giving prospects only enough facts to hopefully motivate them into calling or writing.

Here are some key items to cover:

- Why the listeners should contact you: what services you offer and what particular benefits can be obtained from dealing with you.
- Your firm's name: this makes the audience more comfortable that this is a legitimate offer, especially if your firm is well known. It also provides another way to contact you even if they do not catch the phone number.
- Your name: so they know whom to contact at the firm.
- How to contact you: read the phone number or address at least twice.

Pretesting the Ad

Read the ad copy to a sampling of several people that are typical of the radio station's audience and note their reactions. Ask them specific questions about their understanding of various points made in the ad. Are any parts of the ad misleading or confusing?

If your small sample of people are confused, chances are most of the station's listening audience would be too. This might dramatically reduce the effectiveness of your advertisement. Rewrite the copy until all problems are eliminated.

Tip: Do not forget to show any changes, as well as your final copy, to your legal department for approval.

Radio Advertising Response Vehicles

Response vehicles in radio advertising are more limited than in print ads. Coupons are clearly not an option. You are under time pressure. Many in the audience will not have paper and pencil available to write down your address or telephone number. The less information the prospect must remember, the more likely it will be remembered. And the less air time it takes to communicate that information, the less costly the ad will be.

A telephone number is more easily remembered and involves only two simple steps: remembering the number and calling. Using an address to which they should write will require three more difficult steps on the prospect's part: remembering the address (city, state and ZIP code), writing a note to you, and mailing the letter. More people are likely to remember enough information to call you than those who will be able to write down an address. If not given an address to which to write, people will make the call if they are interested, particularly if it is toll-free or local.

So a telephone number that is easy to remember is the most efficient response vehicle to use for radio ads. Be sure to repeat the number a few times in your spots to maximize the recall and to give the listeners more opportunity to write it down.

Emphasize your name and your firm's name in the ad so that an interested prospect who does not catch the telephone number will be able to look up the number later. It is suggested that you mention your firm's name a minimum of two times during the ad, three times if it is 60 seconds or more in total length.

While it is strongly recommended that you use a phone number as suggested for radio responses, in the unlikely event that you have some compelling reason to give the listeners an address to which they should write, give only the address. Do not use both an address and phone number. Using both will take more time and most likely confuse the listeners. There will be too many facts to keep straight and the need to decide whether to call or write will jeopardize your response rate.

This situation is quite different from the discussion about print ads where people may like a choice in response methods. While they may still prefer a choice, they will not want to be confused. The nature of a radio spot inevitably makes the choice confusing. Stick with a phone number response if you can.

Using a telephone number to receive inquiries will require two additional steps on your part. You should provide toll-free or collect call acceptance if long-distance calls can be expected. And you must arrange for someone to answer the calls, especially during the times when the ad is running (people near a phone will often call immediately or shortly after they hear your ad).

Plan what will be said to the callers. Ask them only the minimum number of questions required to send them whatever it is you offered, or what they requested. Do not make a sales pitch at this early stage, unless it is clear from the call that this is what the caller wants.

If you are accepting telephone responses be sure you have an orderly way of handling them. Telephone operators should use a prepared form which outlines the information you need so they can ask the proper questions of prospects. Keep the information simple. A suggested format appears in Fig. 10-10.

Recording the Ad

You might discuss with your radio station representative and your ad agency (if you are using one) the pros and cons of having your ad read by the radio station's announcer or another professional versus reading it yourself. Since you will be targeting a fairly sophisticated audience, unless you are quite proficient at public speaking, it is probably not advisable to try to record the ad yourself at the risk of sounding too amateurish.

Placing the Radio Ad

Most financial services advertisements should be run along with business news, market reports, or various economic reports. During these reports people who are most interested in financial matters are likely to be tuned in. A particularly good time might be the early market reports aired during morning drive-time, while people are driving to work. You would have a captive audience not distracted by household or office events. Audiences tend to be receptive to offers at that time.

The trip home in the afternoon usually puts people in a very different mood—anxious to get home and relax. While afternoon drive-time can be useful, the morning ads seem to work better. Do not underestimate the value of daytime radio programs which are often very inexpensive advertising vehicles. Housewives, and househusbands, are becoming more and more influential in investment decisions.

TELEVISION ADVERTISING PREPARATION

Just as in the case of radio, television ad preparation includes the following four steps.

1. Writing the ad copy
2. Testing the copy on potential viewers
3. Recording the commercial
4. Testing. However, testing a TV ad is a little more complicated than testing one for other mediums.

Preparing the Ad Copy

The same basic problem is faced with TV as with most advertising: If you do not catch the viewers' attention during the first few seconds of the ad, you have probably lost them completely.

The headline is extremely important in TV commercials. A strong headline in print media can only be seen. A good headline on the radio can only be heard. But with television you do have the added benefit that your message will be communicated both visually and audibly. This makes it a powerful medium.

Because of its dual communication methods, a television ad will be able to cover quite a bit more information, for a given amount of time, than radio could handle. While it is true that the sound portion is constrained by the fact that we speak a lot slower than we read, the visual portion more than makes up for that limitation. While you should not attempt to read a whole prospectus in a 15-second spot, you will be able to communicate a large amount of information.

For example, while the screen shows an address to which the prospects can write, the voice-over might be describing some of the benefits of the investment, or the toll-free number to call, etc.

The concept should be to elicit a response from the prospect, not make a sale. It is very unlikely, even with the strength of TV as a marketing tool, that you will have enough time to convince anyone to buy on the spot. So do not waste your budget trying to convince them to do so. Get them to want to know more.

You should cover the same key items as were recommended for radio ads.

- Why the viewers should contact you: what services you offer and what particular benefits can be obtained from dealing with you.

- Your firm's name: this makes the offer appear more legitimate, especially if your firm is well known. It also provides another means to contact you. This is easy to accomplish with TV, you need only show the information on the screen.

- Your name: so they know whom to contact at the firm.

- How to contact you: read and show the response mechanism (address or phone number, or both).

Pretesting Your TV Ad

Start by reading the copy of the ad to a sampling of several people that are typical of the TV station's audience and note their reactions. Ask them about their understanding of various points made in the ad. Are any parts of the ad confusing? Rewrite the copy until the problems are eliminated.

Then decide how the visual side of TV will be used. Will you use illustrations? Or will a spokesperson come on screen and "talk" to the audience?

When you have the visual presentation thought through, retest the ad with your sample group, actually acting out the narrative or using story boards for illustrations. You will be investing a great deal of money in a television campaign, so making it as successful as possible should be a top priority.

Tip: Do not forget to get approval from your legal department for any ads you plan to air.

Television Advertising Response Vehicles

You have two primary options for reply mechanisms in a television commercial. You can either invite phone calls, or they can write to you. It is possible to invite them to come into your office, but this is rarely an effective approach.

While some of limitations discussed for radio will be true of TV, you are not nearly as constrained. Coupons are clearly not an option here either and you are still under time pressure.

However, because most viewers will be at home when they see your ad, the audience will usually have paper and pencil available to write down your address or telephone number. So you probably do not have to dwell on that information quite as much as with a radio ad.

But do make sure you give them at least two opportunities to catch the reply procedure. If you show your address, be sure you give them the address a second time. Or provide your phone number twice. You could even use each once. Repeating the reply mechanism more times is desirable, but do it at least twice in a 15-second ad, three times or more in a 30-second spot.

The situation with TV is similar to the discussion about print ads—people like a choice in response methods. You should provide toll-free or collect call acceptance if long-distance calls can be expected.

Emphasize your name and your firm's name in the ad so that an interested prospect who does not catch the address or telephone number will be able to look up the number later. It is suggested that you mention your firm's name a minimum of two times during the ad.

Keep in mind that if you use a mailing address, inquiries will begin to arrive a few days later. But in the case of telephone calls, you might start receiving them immediately. So you should arrange for someone to answer the calls, especially during the times when the ad is running.

Plan what will be said to the callers responding to your ads. Ask them the minimum number of questions required to determine what to send them and where to send it. Do not make a sales pitch at this early stage.

If you are accepting telephone calls, use the same form presented in the discussion of radio response earlier in this chapter, Fig. 10-10.

Telephone Response Record

RESPONSES FROM _____   Call taken by _____

Date _____ Time _____ Station or Ad code _____

NAME _____

ADDRESS _____

CITY _____ STATE _____ ZIP _____

PHONE NUMBER (If given) (_____)_____

MATERIALS TO SEND THEM _____

NOTES _____

_____

_____

_____

Fig. 10-10. Form for keeping track of phone inquiries.

Production of the Ad

The station on which you plan to air your ad might be able to assist you with the production of the commercial. Alternatively, your ad agency, which you will need for TV ads, can help you create the entire ad.

Placing the Television Ad

Most financial services advertisements should be run along with business news, market reports, or various economic reports. During these reports people who are most interested in financial matters are likely to be tuned in. This is particularly true of television because of its broad-based audience. Your message would be pretty much lost if you aired it during the majority of programs. But if people are tuned in because they are interested in a business or financial topic, you have a far greater chance of finding parties receptive to your offer.

The airing of a TV commercial is much more dependent upon the accompanying programs than upon the daypart in which it is aired.

Telemarketing

11

Telemarketing

THE TELEPHONE IS a very powerful selling tool. Used properly, either in a separate program or in conjunction with other forms of promotion, telemarketing can greatly increase your sales.

Telemarketing intimidates many salespeople. Most marketers of financial services have used, or would not hesitate to use direct mail. Many would be willing to test advertising. But when it comes to telemarketing, they think it is beyond the realm of individuals or small operations to utilize that form of promotion. These people often do not realize that they have already been using telemarketing extensively, since it is just a term for the use of the telephone in marketing efforts, and we have all certainly used the phone to sell.

Telemarketing is labor intensive. It would be difficult to mass-produce telephone calls like mailers or ads. While some marketers have tried to automate telephone sales by using autodialers, or banks of operators to make initial contacts, telemarketing is still essentially a one-on-one sales process.

Because the sales of financial products and services tend to be high-ticket items (fairly large amounts of money are involved), the labor intensity of telemarketing can usually be justified. If you were selling pocket calculators for $30 each, it would be much harder to rationalize a marketing effort using the phone to contact potential customers. But when $10,000 or $20,000 might be involved in the transactions, calling can make a lot of sense. There are two basic types of telemarketing programs: those that initiate calls and those that answer calls.

PLANNING YOUR INITIATED
(OUTGOING) TELEMARKETING ACTIVITY

As in the cases of direct mail and advertising, each telemarketing campaign should start with a plan. A good place to begin is by determining the goals you hope to accomplish through your phone program. This might be the number of new accounts you would like to open, the dollar amount of transactions, the products or services you want to market, or perhaps the amount of commissions you hope to generate. Your goals will probably involve several of these.

It is important that you establish what you want to attain so that you can determine what you must do to achieve it. Goals also permit you to evaluate how successful the program has been.

Unlike other forms of promotion, teaming up with others will be of limited benefit when telemarketing is involved. You might share a WATS line, or jointly purchase a list of potential numbers to call, but for the most part you will be working on your own.

Preparation for Cold-Calling and Telemarketing

Most securities salespeople have used cold-calling for at least part of their marketing effort. The typical procedure would be to go through the phone book, selecting names that seem to have investment potential—perhaps based on where the prospects live. While this certainly can produce some new business, it is often a tedious and unrewarding experience. The major problems with cold-calling are:

- It is a very time-intensive process—each call requires 10, 15, maybe 20 minutes, and much time is wasted on those you do not reach, call backs, etc.
- There is usually little selection criteria to improve the batting average—it is difficult to know who will make a more likely prospect.
- People are less receptive to a sales call since they get so many solicitations by telephone these days.

There are ways to improve the effectiveness of cold-calling, and programs designed to boost the results of telephone sales are called telemarketing. Telemarketing, in one form or another should be part of your financial marketing efforts.

Telemarketing has three important components:

1. A carefully selected and screened list (or respondents to another form of promotion such as direct mail).
2. A script to keep the sales pitch on track.
3. A tracking and follow-up system.

BUDGETING FOR TELEMARKETING

Unlike direct mail and advertising, the costs for a telemarketing program are difficult to measure. Phone usage is hard to gauge and may not even be a factor (as far as you are concerned) if your firm pays phone costs. Other than the costs to use the phone and possibly acquire a prospect list, telemarketing usually means an investment of time more than money.

If you plan to hire someone to help you with your telemarketing effort, perhaps compiling a list or making the initial call, their salary could be considered a telemarketing cost. Listing a special phone number might also be part of your costs. The cost to rent a list would be another expense. But all of these charges are relatively minor compared with other types of marketing programs.

Financial services sellers report that they can complete about 15 calls per hour, considering those that consume time but are not contacted (the line is busy, there is no answer, or the individual to be reached is not in). Of the 15 calls, roughly five are not reached and seven who are reached are not interested. That leaves roughly three prospects per hour that spend more than just a few minutes discussing the offer, and thereby showing interest. That qualifies them as leads. Assuming average hourly earnings of $38 ($75,000 per year divided by 2000 working hours), this suggests a cost per lead of about $13 ($38 per hour divided by 15 calls per hour results in a cost of $2.50 per prospect, divided by the 20 percent that become leads).

To make a fair comparison, you should add in expenses you will incur beyond your time. These might include phone usage costs, list rentals, etc. These costs might add another $2 or $3 to the cost per lead, making an estimated total of about $16.

The success rate of telephone sales is about the same as for other marketing means, roughly 7%. So this suggests a cost per sale of $230 ($16 per lead divided by 7%), somewhat less than for most sales resulting from direct mail and advertising leads. Thus, telemarketing can be a very cost-effective marketing method.

Renting a telemarketing list is quite similar to renting one for direct mail. In this case, the phone number is the primary information rather than an address. Expect to pay about $80 per 1000 names for list rental. The cost tends to be higher because you are essentially renting a direct-mail list where phone numbers have been added at an additional cost. As with mailing lists, some error rate is expected—not every phone number will be correct, or even present. As long as the rate is fairly low (about 5%), that is about as good as you can expect. If the problem rate is higher, you might be able to get a partial refund from the list supplier on the rental costs.

The cost to use a phone for an outgoing telemarketing program would depend on the type of phone service and whether you must pay those charges or if they are picked up by your employer. If you must pay the costs, you will have to analyze where you will be calling and how long your typical conversation is likely to last.

One way to keep your phone costs down is to use a WATS line, which stands for Wide Area Telephone Service. This is essentially a volume discount from the phone company. For a given monthly fixed charge, you can use the phone for a certain amount of time, which works out to a big savings from ordinary rates. But you must pay the fixed charge regardless of usage and any additional usage costs beyond the package of time you bought.

Target Audiences

If you have decided to use telemarketing for any portion, or all, of your marketing effort, you will need to select a target audience. As opposed to randomly calling names from a phone book, a telemarketing approach might involve renting a list of prospects with certain characteristics that improve their chances of doing business with you, and then contacting them by phone. The list probably would come from a list broker who selected it because of certain prospect qualities such as previous purchases of financial instruments, etc. Or the target audience might be respondents from a direct-mail campaign who you now wish to contact in a follow-up program.

Tip: If you are renting a list for telemarketing, make sure it comes with phone numbers. Many lists do not and you could be stuck calling information or looking up numbers in the phone book!

To use telemarketing effectively, it is important that you understand your potential customers. You will typically have just 10 or 15 seconds to convince the prospect that he should talk to you. Being able to size up the best approach in each call will improve your success rate dramatically.

The singlemost important thing you can do in the first few moments of that initial call is make the prospect feel comfortable. If they feel good about your call they will be less likely to hang up and more likely to openly discuss the matters you have called about. Your telemarketing script should provide the basis for keeping the conversation on track and provide you with alternatives should you meet resistance.

Legal Considerations

Because of widespread abuses of some dishonest and inconsiderate telemarketers, a variety of legislation has been passed, or is pending, that greatly regulates what telemarketers can and must do.

While not every state has adopted each and every rule, about 35 states have some sort of regulations. It is, therefore, best that you try to abide by these guidelines. Most of them are good common sense anyway. You might want to investigate exactly what regulations your jurisdiction may have in effect or is considering enacting.

Some of these rules are incorporated in pending Federal legislation that may affect all telemarketers in the country. The Telemarketing Fraud Act of 1989 would give the Federal Trade Commission a great deal more clout in fighting telephone crime and it would also empower states to prosecute across state lines. Most of these rules, if they are in effect, are punishable by fairly severe penalties. You may even have to pay the attorney's fees of a disgruntled prospect if you get sued and lose. So be careful and try to incorporate these points into your telemarketing:

- Callers must identify themselves and the company on whose behalf they are calling early in the call (usually within the first 30 seconds). In some cases a registration number might have to be obtained for telemarketing and given to those called.

- You should give the prospect an opportunity to terminate the conversation early in the call (no intimidation to keep them on the line).

- You may not call any person once they have designated their desire not to receive calls. This would apply to their telling you not to call them as well as a possible master list of those not wanting calls.

- There may be limitations to the hours you can call a person's home, typically not after 9 P.M. and not before 8 A.M., sometimes not at all on Sundays.

- There will be severe limitations on Automatic Dialing Recorded Message Programs (ADRMP). These are automatic dialing machines that verbally walk prospects through some basic screening process and identify those that might be worth a personal call. While it is unlikely that you would use one of these machines to call and solicit prospects, just in case you consider it, keep in mind many restrictions will apply.

- While transmitting promotional messages via a Fax machine may be more of a direct mail than a telemarketing activity, legislation is pending in a number of states to ban it under telemarketing regulations.

TELEMARKETING SCRIPTS

Creating a script for your telemarketing campaign is the key to making it a successful program. The script provides a structure to your program. If you have carefully thought out what you want to say to prospects, and how you will respond to specific questions and objections they might raise, it will make your telephone work go much more smoothly.

Another advantage of having a script is that you might be able to have someone else to do some of the telemarketing for you. For instance, your sales assistant might be able to make the initial call and screen the prospect, having you speak only to those that are interested and sound qualified. This would cut down on one of the big problems with phone work—time consumption. While this approach has its downside, it is an option some salespeople have used successfully.

The script should be short, direct and simple. Know what you want to say and what information you will need from the prospect to qualify them and to be able to place an order. If their age will be a factor in the discussion, figure out ahead of time a pleasant way to inquire about their age—perhaps something about what they do for a living if you are trying to determine if they are retired.

Try to build in a hook early in your script to get the prospect to agree with you and be in a positive frame of mind. Think of several benefits that can be used early in your conversation. You might not use them all, but they will be available should you meet resistance.

Make sure prospects will understand what you are offering. For example, do not assume they know what is meant by a zero coupon bond.

Some of the issues you should consider when preparing a script are as follows:

- Making the prospect comfortable—be sure that you have identified your target market carefully and that the particular prospect fits that market. If you are offering something applicable to the prospect, they will feel better about the call, and you will have a better chance of making a sale.

- Explaining early on in the conversation why you are calling—this helps the prospect focus on what you want to talk about, and if there is no opportunity to convince him to buy, you will not waste a lot of time chatting.

- Tell the prospect why he will benefit from talking to you and that you will not require much of his time (if that is true).

- Be sure to give the prospect plenty of chances to ask questions and make comments. Prepare alternative rebuttals to negative responses—have answers to likely potential questions or objections already worked out.

- Make sure that you are comfortable—use the type of script that will work for you—should you write it out word-for-word or perhaps use an outline form? Will you put the script on paper, $3 \times 5''$ cards, a computer screen, etc.?

- How long will your typical conversation last. Make sure that you will not drag out the conversation and risk boring the prospect. An initial call should not usually last more than 10 minutes, preferably less.

- Try to cover only one product or service at a time. Otherwise you may confuse the prospect.

Prepare the actual script so it does not sound like it was carefully written and practiced. Try to make it sound natural and conversational—not like a speech. Worry more about it being understood than about grammatical perfection. It is OK to use incomplete sentences and colloquialisms. Keep your sentences brief and keep the other party talking. Remember, you are supposed to be having a conversation, you are not giving a political speech.

Test the script, both on yourself and on others to get reactions. Make sure others understand what you are saying and feel it is effective.

There is a lot of talk these days about psychographics-based telemarketing—that is, scripts and programs that react to the specific type of prospect and his personality. Proponents claim that by quickly sizing up the kind of person you are dealing with, you can tailor your pitch to optimize the chance of success. This is basically what most salespeople do anyway, even if they do not spend a lot of time thinking about it.

You may, however, want to develop a variety of scripts for different situations and types of prospects.

As an example, suppose that you have rented a list of new members who recently joined a retirement organization fostering better health care benefits. You wish to inform them of a new single-premium annuity your firm markets that gives triple death benefits to the spouse and they can have the balance in their account paid out at any time should the need arise or if their plans change. Figure 11-1 is a sample script designed for this situation.

SCRIPT TEXT	COMMENTS
Hello Mr. Prospect, this is Dough Neighbors with Best Brokers, Inc.	Identify yourself and firm early in the call
We have developed a new retirement program that features TRIPLE DEATH BENEFITS and you can withdraw at any time and receive a FULL REFUND of your balance. Would you like the peace of mind in knowing your spouse will receive a minimun of $300,000 when you die and you can withdraw your current balance at any time?	Give them the key benefits right away.

Fig. 11-1. A telemarketing script.

SCRIPT TEXT   COMMENTS

ANSWER: YES   ANSWER:NO   Have alternatives
                                            thought out for
                                            various problems
                                            or questions
The ANNUITY HEAD   Why don't you   they may have.
START program is   think this program
sponsored by one   is right for you?
of the oldest and
largest insurance
companies, BULLET
ASSURANCE. The   Give the benefits
triple death benefit   again.
pays out three
times your current
balance at the time
of your death. And,
best of all, you can
terminate the plan
at any time and
receive your current
balance (less the
7% origination fee).

May I send you an   Keep it short
informative brochure   and direct.
that explains the
ANNUITY HEAD START
PROGRAM in more detail?

ANSWER: YES   ANSWER: NO

Where shall I send it? Why do you want to Get the information
                        miss out on this   you need to keep
Name   important retirement the transaction
Address   opportunity?   moving forward,
City   State   Zip   but no more than
                                            is necessary.
When is the best
time to contact
you to answer any
questions you may
have?

                        May I just send you
                        the information;
                        there is no
                        obligation?

Fig. 11-1. Continued.

Where to Call

Just as most prospects really have two addresses, they probably also have two phone numbers: one at their home and one at their office. There are pros and cons to calling a prospect at their office or home. In most cases you will not have a choice, the list you compile or rent will usually give you only one, if any, option and it will most often be the home phone. The home number is generally the preferred number to call.

Even if you do have a choice, call the home first. The reasons for calling about financial offers at the home are essentially the same ones supporting sending offers to the home:

- The prospects probably will not have their calls screened by a secretary or other person, so your chances of actually reaching the prospect are better.
- In the event the call is screened at home, it will probably be done by a spouse who might be interested in the offer and would make a decent prospect in their own right.
- Your offer is personal in nature and most people would prefer to keep their finances away from the job scene.

There are some circumstances where a call to an office might be appropriate, but they are not too common. For example, a solicitation concerning a cash management program for corporate funds, or a preferred stock offering of interest to the company treasurer would best be discussed on company time. However, most personal appeals should be made at home. Therefore, unless you have a compelling reason to use their office number, call their home first if the phone number is available.

An interesting new development that affects where you might call has to do with electronic mail and fax machines, variations on telemarketing. Since many people now have fax machines or computers and modems either at home or at work, or both, you can potentially ''call'' them on these machines. While this changes the nature of the communication, it can be an efficient way to make initial contact. You could generate an effective message and send it to a large number of fax machines and then wait for responses, just like direct mail. These technologies are too new to have developed any track record on how they can perform in the marketing of financial services. It is doubtful that these new marketing methods will work much better than the more traditional techniques of financial marketing, but they may be worth a try. Do check into any legal limitations on this type of activity.

Follow-Up for Telemarketing Leads

Part of any promotional plan must be a follow-up and tracking system. Obtaining leads is the foremost purpose of an outgoing telemarketing program. But utilizing those leads to generate sales will be critical if your program is to be successful.

The first step in trying to turn a lead into a sale is the fulfillment of any requested information. What will you send them if they indicate an interest? Will you have letters typed for each? How will you keep track of which product or service you offered to the prospect? When should you follow up if they are not currently ready to act?

The second step you should take in herding your leads toward sales is to keep careful track of the status of each lead. Certainly every party you contact should be kept on a list showing what happened with the call. Perhaps you did not reach them—making them a potential future telemarketing prospect. Or maybe they were interested but not ready to act now. A tickler file of those people and when to recontact them would be useful. Even people who were not interested could make good prospects for other types of investments.

You should develop a complete list of all prospects contacted showing the date contacted, what was offered, the results of the call, and what will be your next step (send information, call back, etc.).

Other information you should capture in your records would include the following:

- Total number of calls
- Count of calls that reached a prospect
- Number and size of sales
- Number of prospects requiring follow-up and when
- Number of prospects not reached and why
- Number of those not interested (dead lead)
- Number of those that cannot be reached (moved, deceased, etc.)
- How long it took you to make the calls and, perhaps, the average length of a call as well.

This information will prove useful both for your sales efforts as well as for analyzing the effectiveness of your telemarketing campaign.

Combination Programs

Outgoing telemarketing is not only an effective marketing tool by itself, it can be quite useful in conjunction with other promotional programs. In many cases, calling prospects to whom you have already sent information, either as part of a direct-mail effort or from another source, can effectively get them to become customers without waiting for some of them to contact you. It is usually better to precede the call with direct mail or advertising than the other way around. (If you were not able to convince them to buy with a personal call, they are unlikely to respond to your mailing or ad.)

One reason direct mail followed by telephoning may work so well shows up in a recent survey. Nearly 60% of those surveyed wanted to receive information on financial services and sales materials through the mails rather than any by other means. Only 2% wanted to get these things via the telephone. By mailing the information and then calling the prospect, you might improve your sales rate by phoning only those who may want you to do so.

PLANNING YOUR INCOMING TELEMARKETING PROGRAM

In addition to initiating sales calls, the telephone can be used to accept inquiries from a variety of marketing efforts. In this regard it acts as a response vehicle.

Incoming telephone calls can be produced as the result of advertising, direct mail, premiums, or even from outgoing telemarketing (you might have left a message, for example). The use of a telephone number in an ad (as a response means) will produce inquiries via the phone. You should carefully plan what you will do when a phone inquiry comes in.

If you are inviting prospects to call, they probably will try to reach you soon after they hear or see your ad. That often means the morning for early morning radio or newspapers, evening for late night radio or evening newspapers, and weekends for magazines. If you will not be available to answer the telephone at those times, you should make arrangements for a phone answering service or someone to take calls for the phone number you have listed. Callers are easily discouraged and will seldom try more than once or twice to reach you if they do not get an answer.

A caller will also give up easily if he gets a busy signal. So make sure you have enough open lines to accommodate your anticipated responses.

Toll-Free Numbers

If you want to maximize response levels, you should pay the ''postage'' in a telemarketing campaign as you would in direct mail. In the case of the telephone, that means accepting collect calls or providing a toll-free number.

The decision to employ a toll-free number involves an assessment of the expected relative volume of local and long distance calls. If the vast majority of your calls are likely to be local, it is probably not worth the expense of offering a toll-free long-distance number. In that case you can just accept collect calls, which will most likely be more expensive per call than toll-free, but should not amount to very much if they are limited in number.

If, on the other hand, you anticipate a lot of toll-call respondents, you really should try to make a no-charge number available. The increase in the response level when prospects do not have to pay for the call can be dramatic. Your firm might already have a toll-free number which you can use. Alternatively, many services offer shared toll-free lines that are charged to you on a per call basis with some minimum monthly fee applicable as well. While the costs will vary, expect to pay $2 to $3 per call, and perhaps a minimum of $200 to perhaps $500 a month for the service.

Beyond the direct increase in response rates that offering toll-free can produce, there is also a prestige factor that goes along with the use of an 800 number. It seems to suggest that you are important, substantial, and trustworthy. This is probably due to the fact that major companies use toll-free numbers while smaller ones tend not to use it. While this benefit is quite subjective, it can add to your program's overall effectiveness.

Following Up and Reusing Leads

A good telemarketing plan should include a system to keep and reuse all responding leads which have not become customers after the initial campaign.

The form shown in Fig. 11-2 is a suggested method of keeping track of your telephone leads.

As with other marketing programs, divide the results of your telemarketing program into four categories:

- Respondents who became *customers*.
- Respondents who were interested but not ready to act just yet and will require *follow-up*.

Telephone Response Record

RESPONSES FROM _____   Call taken by_____

Date _____   Time _____   Station or Ad code _____

NAME _____

ADDRESS _____

CITY _____   STATE _____   ZIP _____

PHONE NUMBER (If given) (_____)_____

MATERIALS TO SEND THEM _____

NOTES _____

_____

_____

_____

Fig. 11-2. Form for recording telephone inquiries.

- Respondents who were *not interested*.
- Prospects you *failed to contact* (no answers, not available, etc.).

These groups can be utilized to generate further potential business. Clearly, respondents who became customers are now part of your customer file.

Respondents who were interested, but have not yet purchased, should be kept in a special follow-up file to be approached when you feel it appropriate (when they said they would have funds available, for example).

Those who were not interested in that particular offer should be maintained in an old lead file. Including them in a subsequent direct mailing or contacting them by telephone as part of an "old lead" revival program usually produces excellent results, far above the level of ordinary purchased lists.

And those you failed to contact, after some reasonable period of time, should be filed so you can check new efforts against that list and eliminate their appearing on future calling programs that you might do.

Combination Programs

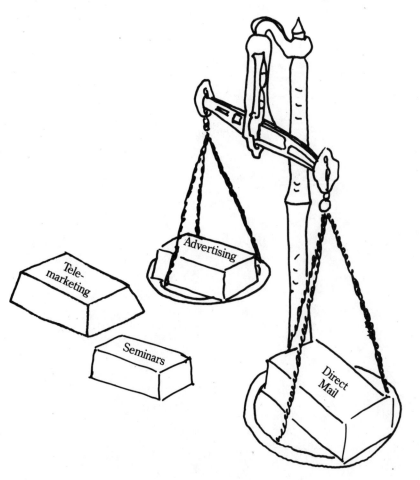

12

Coordinating Direct Mail, Advertising, and Telemarketing

THERE ARE SEVERAL theories of marketing that suggest that using a number of promotional activities together or in sequence can create a much more effective campaign than just running the occasional ad or doing a mailing once in a while.

You have already learned that frequency is essential to most advertising programs. Running an ad three, four, or more times helps it make an impression on the audience that it would not have been able to do without frequency.

Continuity of marketing implies that a marketer should be delivering his message regularly to potential audiences. The idea is predicated upon frequent reinforcement of the offer just as a prospect might be forgetting about it. This is not the same as frequency, which has more to do with making an initial impression on a prospect.

The running of several ads to make sure that your message registers and motivates the prospect is called frequency. Each successive promotional activity raises the overall awareness level somewhat. The more times a specific audience is exposed to a message the more likely they are to respond. Keeping the impression you have already made upon the prospect as strong and fresh as possible is continuity. In diagrammatic format, continuity works as shown in Fig. 12-1.

In addition to strengthening the impression by using multiple ads, a multi-part program of ads and mailings together, as a package, can produce a multiplier effect. The impact created by one part of the program is reinforced and strengthened by the other parts, usually well beyond what just more ads, or in the case of direct mail, just more mailers, would have accomplished on their own.

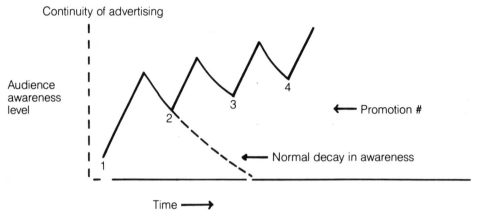

Fig. 12-1. Continuity of advertising.

STRENGTH IN NUMBERS

As an example, suppose you run an ad in a local newspaper and do a mailing to local residents. If coordinated properly, the audience would see your ad and get the mailing at about the same time. The effect is to cover the market so that some see the ad, some get the mailing, and many see both. For those who do see both the mailing and the ad, the probability of responding is much greater, usually even greater than seeing two ads or getting two mailing pieces at somewhat different times.

After seeing all of your promotional activity, the audience will think you are everywhere. In the right combinations of mixed mediums, one plus one can truly equal three as illustrated in Fig. 12-2.

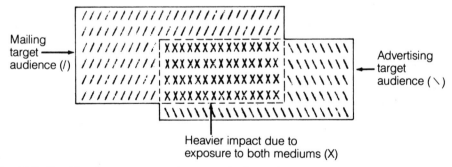

Fig. 12-2. Combined programs can have greater impact.

These effects build even further if you do several ads and several mailings. This is probably due to the fact that you are achieving both frequency and continuity, so the beneficial effects are maximized. The most common combination is direct mail and print ads. Radio and direct mail is another effective match. And telemarketing and direct mail work

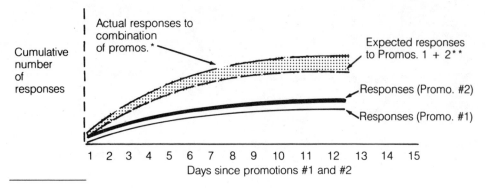

Fig. 12-3. Typical response levels to combination programs.

NOTES: * Shaded area shows "bonus" response level resulting from a combination of programs.
** Response level if Promos. #1 and #2 had been done independently.

particularly well. Figure 12-3 illustrates typical response rates and how the use of two or more mediums can increase overall response.

Another benefit from a program utilizing multiple media is some economies of scale. You need only create one theme, have one phone number for incoming calls, one fulfillment package, etc. This can reduce your costs per lead, as well as make your entire program more efficient. In some cases a lower combination rate may apply if the media have common ownership. This can cut your costs even more.

In an effort to accomplish some continuity of marketing without the enormous outlays that would be required by running continuous marketing programs, two advertising approaches were developed: *flighting* and *pulsing*.

Flighting uses heavy marketing for some period of time, a break with no promotional activity, and then a lot of activity again. During the break, the awareness levels on the part of the audience begin to decline because they are not being reinforced. The next blitz of advertising brings up the awareness level, usually beyond the previous rate, and then the cycle repeats.

Pulsing uses heavy marketing followed by a much lighter schedule (as opposed to none) and then heavy marketing again. It has been found that the concentration of ads builds impact and the subsequent group of ads reactivates that impact. The low level of ads between campaigns in pulsing keeps the awareness level higher during the break period. The effect is much the same as continuous advertising, but the cost is generally less. Figure 12-4 demonstrates the similarity.

While flighting and pulsing could be used in campaigns involving just one media and one particular ad run repeatedly, they are particularly relevant to multi-media efforts that not only strengthen each other, but keep your message in front of potential customers for a much longer period of time.

If you are planning to run ads in more than one media at the same time (combination advertising) or as part of an overall marketing program along with other efforts such as direct mail (duplication), special planning will be necessary to maximize your results and minimize problems.

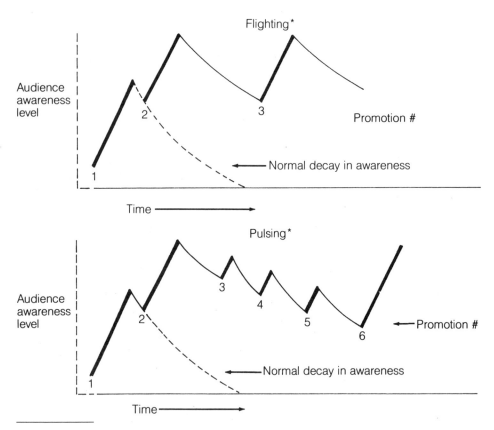

*NOTE: Promotion numbers 1, 2, and 6 are major programs; promotion number 3, 4, and 5 are minor activities designed to maintain some awareness.

Fig. 12-4. Flighting and pulsing programs.

PLANNING COMBINATION PROGRAMS

To coordinate such programs requires a great deal of planning and organization. Your materials must be ready at the same time. To maximize the benefits, the promotions must be run close in time to one another. And they should be similar enough to create instant recognition that they are part of the same program. A logo and common theme can help keep the continuity.

Since the primary advantage of multiple programs is their audience overlap and thus additional exposure to your message, any marketing effort that enhances the overlap is bound to produce better results. While using the exact same list for a second mailing, or running the same ad in a given publication several times is the surest way to make multiple impressions on the same audience, the benefits of this approach can be enhanced with additional activities.

Any combination of advertising, direct mail, premiums, and telemarketing can be used. However, the most effective mixture seems to be telemarketing and direct mail.

The practicality of this may preclude you from utilizing it. Telemarketing is time and labor intensive, so you cannot expect to contact nearly as many prospects as you could using other marketing means. Therefore, if you want to mail to 2000 prospects and then call them all, unless you have a team of operators working for you, it might take you months to make all those calls.

Advertising and telemarketing can work quite well, but typically this is not quite as rewarding, perhaps because the odds of the same individuals seeing an ad and getting your call are much less than if you had mailed to a specific list and then called that same list. Again, calling anywhere near the number you can reach through advertising would be a monumental task.

Since telemarketing will often not be a practical component in your combination programs, there is nothing wrong with running combinations that do not necessarily maximize multiple exposure. Just be aware that you may be sacrificing some potential benefits if you go that route. Advertising and direct mail would be an example of two mediums that do not necessarily maximize overlap, but that can work well together.

Another option is to run your multiple campaigns in the same medium, all advertising or all direct mail, for example. In the case of multiple ads, running the most prominent ad first should produce the best results. The impact of this first ad will provide the recognition you need for your subsequent advertisements. As a measure of prominence, you can use cost. The more costly ads are usually the ones seen by more people.

In the case of multiple direct-mail programs, the order sent is less significant. However, it is generally better to send the more expensive package first and follow up with a cheaper reminder. Also, use the larger of the lists first and smaller ones subsequently. That way the better package is being sent to more potential clients and should produce higher response levels.

If you plan to use a combination of advertising and direct mail, you should typically run the ad first and follow up with the direct mailing. This is because direct mail is one of the easiest promotions to act upon. A prospect already primed by your ad or ads will be more likely to review your mailing and respond. Since it is so easy to send back a postage-paid card, they are more likely to do that. Time your mailing so that your package arrives within one to five days after your ad has run. The timing of the two parts of the program should be fairly close together, a few days is usually optimal. Certainly no more than a couple of weeks should pass between elements.

If your marketing campaign will consist of multiple ad runs and direct mailings, alternate them. A print ad should be followed by a direct mailing, then another print ad and direct mailing, etc. This seems to work even if the direct mailings are going to entirely different lists each time. Some of the people on the list are bound to have seen your ads and this will help you. The optimal scheduling for multiple campaigns is shown in Fig. 12-5.

You should not spend a tremendously different amount on the components of your multiple campaigns. In other words, do not allocate 90% of your budget to advertising and just 10% to direct mail or outgoing telemarketing. Since you are trying for multiple impressions on the same individuals by covering the same basic target audiences (probably identified by geographic area), you should spend enough to cover those areas adequately in each part of your campaign.

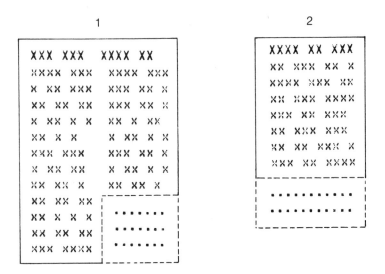

Run your more prominent (larger) ad or bigger direct mail program first, followed up by smaller ones.

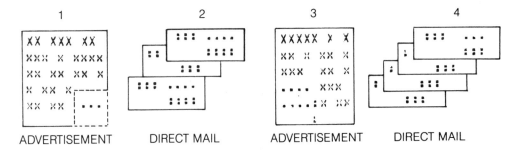

If your campaign consists of multiple ads and mailings, intersperse them.

Fig. 12-5. Scheduling multiple campaigns.

One good rule of thumb is not to spend less than you would if you were doing just one component of the program independently. If you plan to spend $5000 on a total program, do not spend $1000 on direct mail and $4000 on advertising—you would probably not bother with a $1000 direct-mail campaign if you have $5000 to spend. But you might spend $2000 on direct mail anyway, so a $2000 and a $3000 split might be reasonable.

An effective way to allocate your multiple program budget is to attempt to obtain a similar number of leads from each portion of the program. As noted in a previous chapter, leads tend to cost $20 each in the financial services industry. Advertising leads usually cost a little above this average; direct mail and telemarketing leads often cost a little less than this average. While your results will probably improve in time, assume for planning purposes that your phone leads and your direct-mail leads will most likely cost a little less than advertising leads. (As noted earlier, the quality of advertising leads tend to be higher, however.)

If you assume a direct-mail lead will generally run $18, a telephone lead will cost you $17, and an advertising lead will cost $21 (reflecting print and broadcast rates), you could spend about 47% of your budget on either a direct mail or telemarketing effort and 53% on advertising, and this should tend to even out the lead quantities, on average.

Do keep in mind the minimum budget guidelines discussed in earlier chapters. It was recommended that not less than $500 be allocated to a direct-mail program and not less than $3000 be available for print advertising including several runs for frequency. While some minor downward adjustment in these amounts might be acceptable considering the multi-part nature of the combination program, it is not recommended that you allocate a great deal less to each part of your program despite their use in a broader marketing strategy.

Leads from broadcast advertising (radio and television) typically are even more expensive than print-generated responses, so your allocation should be somewhat greater for those media, allowing a smaller percentage for direct mail, telephone, or print ads and a larger percentage for broadcast advertising.

A simple formula to help make this allocation easier is as follows:

Percentage of budget to Medium 1/Cost of average lead from medium 1 =
Percent of budget to Medium 2/Cost of average lead from medium 2

With this formula, you can estimate the appropriate allocations to obtain similar lead counts provided you have a reasonable estimate of lead costs. Of course the two percentages must total 100%. If more than two mediums are involved, each portion could be leveled using this formula and the three (or more) percentages would still have to total 100%.

Until you gain personal experience, you can use the very rough estimates based on industry averages that are summarized in Table 12-1.

	Marketing Medium	Typical Lead Costs
Table 12-1. Typical Lead Costs from Various Mediums.	Direct Mail	$18
	Telemarketing	17
	Print Ads	20
	Radio Ads	25
	Television Ads	30

The figures shown in the chart should only be used for estimating purposes. Each category has a very wide range with much overlap among the categories, so it is possible for direct-mail leads to be even more expensive than leads resulting from TV advertising. But typically, these numbers do suggest what you might find from experience.

Tip: Of course, if you have experience that indicates that your lead costs are different than these averages, use your own figures for the calculations.

Once you have determined the dollars available for each form of promotion, your next task would be to determine the advertising space or the quantity of names you can purchase. You then will have to book space or rent the required lists with plenty of lead time to finish the production of the copy and materials. You can review previous discussions in other chapters on these points.

A Common Theme

A common theme is a must in a multi-part program. If your radio ad promotes tax-free income, your print ads should do so also. A common theme helps the two ads reinforce one another. Use the same style and wording as much as possible. If in print, for example, you say "Discount Commissions Add Up To Real Savings!", then use the same headline wording for your radio ad or other promotions. And if you use more than one print ad or mailing piece, design them similarly. Try to use the same type styles, layout, and even the same colors if applicable. However, do not carry this concept to an extreme by, for example, paying for an extra color in your ad just because your direct-mail piece was on tan paper. A general similarity is important but your program's parts do not have to be identical.

Be sure to code each component of your overall program so you can determine which activity produced each lead. This will be very important when you want to determine how well the marketing effort worked.

The illustration in Fig. 12-6 shows one possible combination ad and direct-mail campaign to promote a new blind pool offering.

MULTIPLE REPLIES

With two promotions working at once, be careful to avoid the confusion that can occur by receiving two (or more) inquiries from the same person. It will be quite common for

SPECIFICATIONS

	DIRECT MAIL PORTION	ADVERTISING PORTION
Target Audience	3,000 Blind Pool Investors	Financier Magazine
Promotion	Invitation to Seminar	Quarter-page ad: Invitation
Cost	$1,500 (3 mailings to one third of list each time—1000/mailing @ 50 cents each	$2,100 (3 insertions @ $700 each)
Scheduling	Each mailing to immediately be preceded by an ad	Ads scheduled for July, August, and September
Coding	BM-1 (blind pool mailing 1) BM-2 (blind pool mailing 2) BM-3 (blind pool mailing 3)	BA-1 (blind pool ad 1) BA-2 (blind pool ad 2) BA-3 (blind pool ad 3)

Fig. 12-6. Combination advertising and direct-mail program.

Hot Money?

COLD CASH!

Experts at Risky Investors are at it again. Contrary to popular belief, they think there are huge profits to be made in Panama especially in non-prescription drugs.

The Panama Investment Group Off-shore Unit Trust (PIGOUT) will attempt to take advantage of the investment climate down there.

This opportunity may not last. We have already been asked to halt the distribution. So act now!

Our informative investor kit will give you all the facts. Use the handy coupon below to order your PIGOUT Kit or call toll-free.

This is not an offer to sell or buy anything. See your lawyer.

BA-1

RISKY INVESTORS, INC.
12397-A Manual Drive
Panama City, Panama
(800) 555-1212 x 1238

[ ] Yes, I would like a PIGOUT Kit. Do not send cash, except small unmarked bills.

NAME _____

ADDRESS _____

CITY_____ STATE _____ ZIP_____

PHONE (Optional) (____)_____

[ ] Home   [ ] Office

Fig. 12-6. Continued

RISKY INVESTORS, INC.
12397-A Manual Drive
Panama City, Panama
(800) 555-1212 x 1238

E YOU HEARD ABOUT HOT MONEY?

ay have seen our recent ad in Fin-
er Magazine describing our new
mian investment fund looking for
rtunities in Panama, particularly
e non-prescription drug field.

anama Investment Group Offshore
Trust (PIGOUT) will attempt to take
ntage of the investment climate
there.

elieve that a relatively small in-
ent in this undiscovered haven can
you big rewards in the future.
there are certainly risks involved
s sort of situation, we know you
e taken lots of chances on before
his is just one more.

s opportunity may not last. We
e already been asked to halt the
ribution. So act now!

informative investor kit will give
all the facts. Use the enclosed
age paid card to order your PIGOUT
or call toll-free 800-555-1212, ex-
ion 1238.

Sincerely,

: Copy of ad
enclosed   E. Mentwell

me a PIGOUT Kit containing
and other information.

BM-1

_____ STATE _____ ZIP_____

al) (____)_____

[ ] Home   [ ] Office

RISKY INVESTORS, 12397-A Manual Drive
Panama City, Panama

some prospects to see your ad and respond and then see another promotion of yours and respond again. This can happen for a variety of reasons:

- They forgot they had already responded. (A similarity of ads will reduce this problem, but not eliminate it.)
- They have not received the information requested from the first ad and want to be sure you hear from them.
- They want additional information for a friend, etc.
- They did not realize it was the exact same offer and figured they could get information on something else.

Of course the same thing could happen from repeating one ad several times, but that is less likely to produce multiple responses from the same prospect than if two different mediums, or significantly different promotional pieces, are used at the same time.

You should develop a master file of respondents to check against each new lead so as to ensure that you will recognize any duplication. This can save you some expenses and make you look very efficient in the eyes of the prospect when he realizes that you know he has responded again.

REFERRING TO OTHER PROMOTIONS

It is sometimes effective to mention other promotions you have done in the ads you run. You could possibly even refer to the other parts of your multiple-part campaign in each portion. For example, by indicating in your ad that the prospect may be receiving a mailing piece shortly, you set up those who do indeed receive the mailer to be more interested. This helps emphasize the importance and wide scope of your campaign in addition to reminding prospects of another way to reply if they do not act on the present ad. And for those who do not receive the mailing, some may even contact you to find out why.

If you are advertising in a well-known and respected medium, you can get additional benefits from those ads by mentioning them in your other promotional activities. An ad in a local paper might be strengthened by reminding readers of your other recent ad in a prominent paper. Do not be arrogant. Something to the effect that the response to your ad in *The New York Times* was excellent and so you are making the same offer available in this other publication. Limited space may preclude mentioning other ads, or it may not be appropriate in all situations, but it can be a worthwhile technique.

Another proven method is to actually picture one ad in another. The example illustrated in Fig. 12-7 is a typical approach that capitalizes on the recognition of the previous ad, the prestige of where it ran, or the impression that you must be relatively successful to be able to run all these ads. While this technique can work for a one-shot campaign using an older ad as the illustration, it is best when the pictured advertisement was run fairly recently, so it still has current interest.

You could also include a reprint of an ad in your direct-mail campaign.

It is possible to run more than two campaigns simultaneously. The same concepts and procedures apply to this type of promotional effort as well. However, unless your budget is very large, it is more effective to limit the overall campaign to one or two pro-

WE TOLD YOU SO!

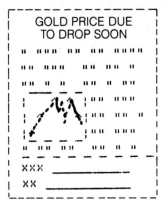

DO YOU REMEMBER THIS AD WE RAN LAST MONTH?

You had your chance to make a bundle and blew it by not contacting us about our new Gold Fund. You were stupid enough not to listen then, we hope you won't make the same silly mistake again this month!

Find out about our all new Gold Fund and how it can make a dumb investor into a not-so-dumb speculator.

Our experts take your money and gamble in the gold futures market! Sometimes we gamble in Las Vegas if we have any money left over.

All you need to do to trade gold like the pros is to buy this fund. We make money for you or you don't get your money back. That is our promise!

For all the scoop on this ''deal,'' send in the coupon.

NAME _____

ADDRESS _____

CITY _____ STATE _____ ZIP _____

Send coupon to: G-1

　　RISKY INVESTORS, INC.
　　21 Bet-It-All Street
　　Ulose, MP 54903

Fig. 12-7. An example of an ad within an ad.

motional activities at a time and to increase the ad frequency (run more ads in the same publication instead of using more mediums, for example). Remember, repetition is the most important ingredient in any advertising campaign, followed by wider exposure. So do not sacrifice repetition for an impressive sounding campaign by spreading your budget too thinly over many mediums!

Following Up Leads and
Learning from Experience

13

Following Up Leads

THE MAJORITY OF this book has been devoted to procedures and techniques best suited to generating leads. You have seen how cost-effective methods to locate interested parties and optimal strategies for communicating our marketing messages are developed. However, as everyone knows, the distance between a lead and a sale can be considerable. This chapter is devoted to keeping the gap between leads and sales as narrow as possible so more of the leads you have worked so hard to generate might become sales.

There are four components to the follow-up process. These can be summarized as follows:

1. Fulfillment—sending the prospect the information or materials requested. Regulations may require you to include a prospectus when fulfilling a specific request for information.
2. Sales calls—the phone calls, letters or visits in which you answer questions and attempt to close the sale.
3. Record keeping—the careful maintenance of lead files and a record of contacts and results.
4. Analysis—use of the experience and data from previous campaigns to maximize effectiveness of future efforts.

FULFILLMENT

The most important single action you can take to help persuade the prospect to do business with you is to act quickly. No one likes to wait for the information they requested or the opportunity to discuss it with you. So the fulfillment materials should be sent as soon as possible after you have received the inquiry. It is quite probable that your ad was not the only one the prospect answered. If someone else can get to the prospect first, that salesperson will have a better chance of making the sale than you. Therefore, fulfill as soon as possible—ideally within a day of your receipt of the lead.

The prospect may have waited a few days before getting around to sending in a coupon. His letter probably took another two to three days to reach you. If it takes just a day for you to fulfill the lead and two to three more days for your materials to reach the prospect, it is easy to see how a total of a week or more could elapse between the prospect's inquiry and his receipt of the requested materials. If you had waited another few days before fulfilling the inquiry, the process could stretch out the response time to nearly two weeks. By that time the prospect may not even remember responding to your ad.

In the case of telephone inquiries, the response time can be even more critical. While two or more days may have been cut off of the inquiry time (no incoming mail delay), prospects who call are usually looking for faster response times and might expect an immediate reply to their phone inquiry.

Prompt fulfillment is important, but what you send them is equally critical. Sending out a disclaimer filled prospectus, and nothing else, is probably worse than not fulfilling the lead.

Your fulfillment package may be required to include a prospectus or other detailed information, but you have plenty of room to "dress up" the package. Here are some tips on fulfillment procedures that will enhance your odds of closing the sale.

First, make sure the prospect knows that he requested the information. A notice on the fulfillment envelope to the effect, "Here Is The Information You Requested" will help separate your letter from other mere solicitations and remind the prospect that he wanted this material.

Second, remind the prospect what it was he inquired about. He may not recall. Do this in your enclosures, not on the envelope.

Third, encourage the prospect to ask questions. This is your best chance of getting him into a dialog when you call.

Keep in mind that your fulfillment materials do not necessarily have to be all printed matter. You could use inexpensive records, audio cassettes, video tapes, and possibly floppy computer discs, if appropriate. Depending on the potential benefits and type of customer, the cost might be justified. You will only be sending these things to actual respondents to your ad, typically a tiny fraction of the original prospect universe, so the added cost may not be a huge amount in total dollars. You should do a sensitivity analysis on the added expenses to see if it can make sense.

Fulfillment can be accomplished in-house or by an outside vendor. In-house fulfillment usually means that you or your secretary are busy stuffing envelopes, etc. It may be possible to have your firm's print shop or mail room stuff envelopes and mail information for your inquiries. If you are working with relatively small mailings, 1000 to 2000 for example, the number of inquiries may only be in the 30 to 50 range, so fulfillment of the materials might not be a terribly onerous task, although it should be done promptly.

If you expect hundreds of inquiries over a short period of time, an outside vendor may be appropriate. You can hire a firm to just send out your materials to inquiries at very reasonable prices. Charges may run just $.25 to $.50 each. Some minimum dollar amount will probably apply, perhaps $75 or $100 or more, however.

Outside fulfillment can be part of a larger service in which labels are generated, records kept, and reports generated. The cost is likely to be a few dollars per lead.

Bear in mind that your prospects will not realize the fulfillment may have been done by an outside vendor. If the packages are not assembled logically, items are missing, contents are dirty, etc., this will reflect on you, not the vendor. So choose a firm carefully and monitor what they are doing for you.

SALES CALLS AND FOLLOW-UP

After sending out a fulfillment package, you should not let too much time pass before contacting the lead. Once the inquirers have received the information requested, many will review it. Your call to them should be made about four days after you have mailed out the literature. That reflects a mail delay of two to three days and one to two days for the prospect to read the materials.

You should allow prospects a chance to review the literature you have sent them prior to discussing it with them. Few will want to talk to you about the matter until they have at least looked at the information. If, for some reason, you want to reach them before they have had a chance to read the materials you have sent them, which might be appropriate in certain situations involving very complicated deals, call about two days after mailing. By then they will have probably received the information but are unlikely to have read it.

Calling prospects before their receipt of the fulfillment package is usually not worthwhile since few investors will discuss the opportunity without having seen something about it. If you believe they do not need to receive the information to accept your offer, then try to close the sale immediately after you get the inquiry and do not bother sending them a fulfillment package. This rarely works, however.

When you do contact a prospect, be sure to indicate that they responded to your promotion and requested information. This identifies your call as not being a "cold-call" and will make the prospect more receptive to discussing the subject with you.

Many leads will come in without a phone number indicated. This might be because none was requested (OK) or because it was requested and not given (not a good indication). While this might suggest that they do not want you to call, you risk little by trying. If you cannot talk to them you probably will not be able to make a sale anyway. In any event, the number is often available. A simple call to directory assistance or the use of a phone book will usually reveal the phone number.

Sometimes you will have the phone number, but still not be able to reach them—perhaps there is no answer repeatedly. If you cannot reach the prospect by phone, do not give up. Send them a note stating that you want to make sure they received the information they requested and that you wish to answer their questions, but have been unable to reach them. The problem could be as simple as they were away on vacation. Or they may have an unlisted phone number. In these cases, prospects may appreciate your follow-up and contact you if interested.

It is also possible that the prospect may not have received your first fulfillment package and this new contact might make up for that oversight. In any event, what have you got to lose? A letter might cost you a few cents plus postage. You will have already invested about $20 in the lead so protect that investment with a small additional outlay.

Leads over three weeks old can generally be considered dead. If you have not had contact by then, these should go into a dead lead file, unless you believe there is a good chance you will succeed in reaching the prospect. Never throw away an old lead. They can produce new leads from revival mailings sometime in the future. An old list of leads who did not buy will often produce very high response rates if mailed another promotional piece a month or two later.

The sources of leads for a revival mailing are not too critical—they could be from advertising, direct mail, promotion, etc. If a typical list might yield a few percent response rate, a revival mailing to older leads from past programs will usually yield much more, often double or triple the average rates. This revival process can be repeated two or three times before you wear out your welcome and the list must be allowed to rest for a year or so.

It stands to reason that the response rate should be higher from old lead files—they showed an interest in your services once before. You have already screened them so your target market is very accurate.

RECORD KEEPING

The other important follow-up procedure that should be a part of your routine is record keeping. Monitor your responses very accurately. Measure the number of leads and sales, as well as the reasons for lack of sales. Figure 13-1 illustrates a good way to keep track of this information. The Appendix C at the back of this book includes this form so you can photocopy it for easy use.

Your records should be maintained a minimum of six weeks, longer if you run your ads in a monthly magazine, or other medium where lead flow might continue for an extended period of time. You can stop the detailed record keeping for a given ad when the lead flow and follow-up information tapers off to an odd lead now and then. The figures in the records are relatively easy to compute and will be important to your future promotional campaigns.

Completing the chart is quite easy. The ad code is simply whatever you used to identify the replies. If you used C-1 for your first commodities ad, C-1 is your ad code.

The media where the ad ran might be *The Boondocks Times*, or in the case of a mailing list you may have used *Mail Order Buyers of Tractors*, etc.

Cost is your space expense, or air time cost. Do not include production costs here (artwork, typesetting, etc.) because they are onetime expenses and will be amortized over the entire campaign, if you use the ad more than once. While this may skew your results slightly, the inclusion of these figures will make your initial ad placement appear expensive relative to subsequent placements, since the production costs would be included in the first ad and not affect the costs of later ads.

Do not include artwork and production costs when calculating the costs of your direct-mail campaign either. Include only what you would spend if you repeated the mailing, including the recurring charges of postage, collating, printing (if you reprint) etc. This approach will provide a fairer comparison between direct-mail pieces and/or advertising. The number mailed, or *circulation*, are simply the quantity mailed in a direct-mail campaign, the circulation figure for a publication, or the audience size for broadcast media.

AD CODE: _____

MEDIA AD RUN IN OR LIST USED: _____

COST OF PROGRAM: $_____ NUMBER MAILED OR CIRCULATION: _____

| Week # | LEADS | | | | COST PER LEAD | SALES | | AVE. SALE | COST PER SALE | % LEADS CLOSED | FOLLOW-UP | | INCOME FROM SALES YTD | PROFIT/ (LOSS) | RETURN ON INV. % YTD-RC |
	C O U P O N	P H O N E	O T H E R	T O T A L		#	$ (000's)				#	%			
1															
2															
3															
4															
5															
6															
7															
8															
9															
10															
11															
12															
13															
14															
15															
TOTAL															

Fig. 13-1. Advertising and mailing record.

Leads received to date is simply a cumulative total of incoming leads. If you offer more than one way to respond, you will want to separate the results by response type so you will be able to determine which methods are working best for you. The form provides for coupon, phone, and other types of response.

The *cost per lead* is simply the cost of the ad, as indicated earlier, divided by the number of leads you received. It will decrease over time as you receive more leads from the same campaign.

The *number of sales* is the figure representing how many leads became customers and made purchases. Since opening an account may take much longer than six weeks, it is suggested that you review the file periodically, but certainly at six-month intervals, to get a really clear picture of the conversion rates from leads to sales.

If you receive more than one sale from a given lead, count them all. They are a benefit of your prospecting efforts and contribute to your payoff. In fact, research shows that the largest benefits from marketing occur in the repeat business generated by newly opened accounts. Indeed, follow-up business can be many times the first order volume.

The *amount of sales* is a cumulative total of the dollar volume of all sales resulting from the campaign. This includes business from all new accounts, including multiple orders.

The *average sale* is calculated by dividing the total sales figure by the number of sales at that point in time. This figure will fluctuate as more sales come in, adding both to the total amount and the number of sales. Since additional business tends to grow, as the new customers build confidence in you, this figure should probably rise over time.

The *cost per sale* is computed by dividing the cost of the ad as already calculated by the total number of sales and shows you what you paid in promotional expenses to obtain each order. This figure can be compared to profit per sale, as they accumulate, to measure how successful the campaign has been.

The *percent of leads closed* shows how many of the leads have been closed out in some manner. Some may become customers, others may be dead leads, etc.

Leads that have not been closed out are still being followed up, so the total of percent of leads closed and percent of leads requiring follow-up should be 100%.

The number of leads that have not become customers yet, but are still considering your offer, should be indicated in the follow-up column. These may include prospects whose funds will become available when a CD matures next month, etc.

Income from sales (year-to-date) is the cumulative commissions (payout) on tickets written (sales made) resulting from these leads.

The *profit/loss figure* is the difference between your income from the program and its cost. At some point this should turn positive, although that will seldom be the case in the first few weeks of the program.

The *return on investment* is the profit (or loss) divided by the cost of the program.

Analysis

You might ask if it is really necessary for you to track all these numbers. Consider what this information can tell you and how you could use it to improve your future programs. Reviewing a single record sheet can indicate how quickly leads have come in, if that program was profitable, and if anything further is likely to develop from those leads.

Profitability can be determined by taking your commission dollars and comparing them to your costs. Perhaps not in the first few weeks, but certainly over time, net commissions earned must exceed costs or you do not want to repeat that ad or mailing program.

The follow-up column is an indication of the possibility of more business from the campaign. From this it is easy to determine if you should be working on pending leads or considering a new program.

The real value of this record keeping is the ability to make comparisons between ads, response vehicles, and mediums. You should be able to determine, over time, the *lowest cost lead source* and the *largest profit potential source*. Record keeping is the best way to monitor your results and ensure that you do not make the same mistakes over and over again. You will also be able to repeat the successful programs because you will have identified them.

A few parameters to help you establish how well your campaign has performed are shown in Table 13-1. These figures are typical industry averages based on field experience. They are not guarantees of any particular result and should be used only as a guide and for comparison purposes.

Table 13-1. Useful Statistics for Evaluating Marketing Results.

Measure	Financial Industry Average
Cost per lead	$ 20
Percentage of leads turning to sales	7%
Cost per sale	285
Average initial sale	10,000
Average first order commission	125
Percentage to be "followed up"*	50%
Percent "could not reach"	20%
Percent "no interest" (at some point in the contact cycle)	50 – 60%
Typical follow-up business after first order (one year period)	
Average number of orders	3 – 4
Average additional commissions	400 – 650
Average profit per account opened from leads**	240 – 490

*The followed up figure is an initial estimate. Eventually, some follow-ups turn into sales, some end in no interest, so the figures may total to slightly more than 100%.

**Average first order commission	$125
Average additional business	+ 400 – 650
Subtotal	525 – 775
Average cost of a sale	– 285
TOTAL PROFIT	240 – 490 (one year time horizon)

WHAT TO DO WITH LEADS THAT ARE GIVEN TO YOU

A lead may be given to you by your employer, or by an investment packaging firm hoping to curry favor with you and induce you to sell their products. Most securities salespeople feel these types of leads are not worth much effort and, unfortunately, that is often correct.

In many cases, however, leads generated for you by others can be quite valuable. To determine how useful these types of leads might be, you should consider several factors. This will help you organize your time and efforts.

First, determine how old the leads are. If they are fresh—less than a few weeks old—they are probably worthwhile. If you are handed leads that are more than a month old, you could be wasting your time following up on them. That is not to say that these leads should be tossed in the waste basket. But your priorities should be directed elsewhere. You might send these dated leads a short form letter to determine if they are still interested. That is an inexpensive way to keep a potentially valuable lead alive without spending too much time on the whole group. Obviously, if any of them reply again they should be considered a hot lead.

Second, check if the inquiries have already been fulfilled. If a package such as a prospectus and sales literature were sent, the leads are worth more to you. They are better leads because you have less work to do (the fulfillment has been done) and because you can try selling the prospects immediately rather than sending them literature and waiting for them to review it. You might call or send a note inquiring if they have additional questions.

For leads not yet fulfilled, you should send something, especially if the lead is recent.

Third, count the leads you were given. If you received just a few, and your fellow salespeople received a limited number, they are probably worthwhile. If an outside wholesale representative brings you a bundle of 50 leads and drops off similar packages at the other desks in your office, chances are these are worthless. Remember, quality leads usually cost around $20 each to produce, so if these were decent leads you would have just been given $1000 worth of inquiries. That is not too likely.

Fourth, review your previous experience with this source of leads. If they are provided by an outside firm, what has been your record of selling their products? If the leads were generated by your own firm's programs, are they the type of inquiry you would normally service?

For example, if the offer was for annuities, do you want to sell these particular instruments? Perhaps the problems with certain annuity products has caused you to avoid marketing them and your firm has just done a big promotional mailing featuring an annuity program. If you do not want to work the leads, perhaps you could trade those given to you with another salesperson who does want that type of lead, and in return you could get other leads that suited your needs better.

Beyond these general considerations, you should keep certain practicalities in mind. If you do not work the leads given to you, you may not be given any more from that source. This may, or may not, matter to you. But it should enter into your evaluation.

Tip: Keep in mind that a lead, no matter how old and cold it may be, is usually a better prospect than a random name selected for a cold-call.

Once you have determined that the lead is worth working, you will want to follow up these leads by using pretty much the same procedures and techniques outlined in the previous chapter. Treat a lead that has been given to you the same way as one you have generated. Just be sure you know to what promotion the party responded and what they wanted or have already been given. You will look foolish if someone inquired about a real estate partnership and you send them information about trust accounts.

If your firm uses an outside or internal service to track and follow up leads, you can assume that leads they give you are of higher quality since they are not interested in wasting money on unproductive leads and would use the information these systems provide to improve the performance of its promotional activities.

AUTOMATED SYSTEMS

While you can certainly maintain records of your promotional programs using the form shown earlier in this chapter, computer systems are available to help you do this more efficiently.

USING FULFILLMENT HOUSES

Some systems are run by outside service bureaus. They handle the receipt of leads, fulfillment of literature and they keep the records, sending you reports periodically. You can, therefore, concentrate on selling.

These services usually charge a per lead fee, or some fixed monthly rate based on expected lead volume. The service bureaus are often list brokers and can, thus, arrange a direct-mail program as well as the tracking and follow-up of leads generated.

The decision to use an outside vendor must be based on several considerations:

- The convenience of having someone else stuff envelopes for fulfillment and perhaps answer your telephone inquiries as well.
- The value of the record keeping and processing portion of the service.
- The relinquishment of some control by letting someone else handle your leads.
- The costs for the service.

Convenience

It certainly would be nice to have someone stuff all the mailers, answer inquiries, and send out fulfillment materials, etc. This is especially true as marketing programs grow in complexity and volume. It is one thing to fold and mail 100 letters, subsequently fulfilling two or three inquiries. It is quite another to assemble a package of information for 5000 and fulfill 100 or 200 leads.

These outside services sometimes can even accept your telephone inquiries, creating leads and fulfilling them for you. While some legal restrictions may apply concerning what a telephone operator may do for an investment inquiry, this approach can boost your productivity. An outside service bureau can make your marketing job so much simpler and permit you to concentrate on selling.

Value

Most fulfillment houses not only do the mundane physical labor of mailings and fulfillment, but they also provide sophisticated computer programs which can generate personalized letters, lead follow-up and reminders, data collection, and useful reports that present in summary fashion what is going on with your marketing program. A typical system is shown in Fig. 13-2.

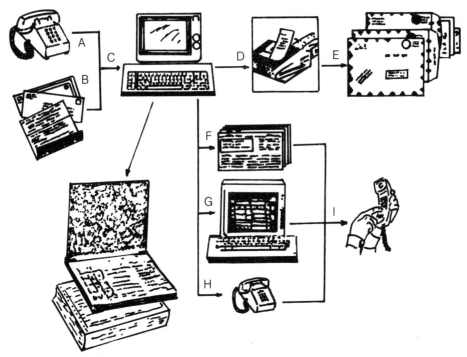

Fig. 13-2. Typical lead fulfillment service flowchart.

Here is a 10-point summary of what usually happens in one of these systems. Keep in mind that not all services offer every one of these features, nor may you require them all.

A. Telephone leads ring directly into the service bureau's operators. The callers generally ask for an extension number which identifies you as the advertiser, and the caller may not ever realize that they have not actually reached your firm.

   These bureaus may offer an 800 number as a convenience to you. Their operators take down the appropriate information, usually according to a script you provide, and these become regular leads.

B. Coupons and other written leads are sent directly to the service bureau, primarily by using a post office box called Customer Service Center. The prospects will probably be unaware that you are not receiving and handling the leads yourself.

C. The lead service inputs the lead information from coupons, letters, phone calls, etc., into their computers for analysis and storage.

D. The computers produce addressing materials such as labels, custom letters, etc. These are used to send your fulfillment information to the prospect.

   You can flag certain criteria or specific prospects for special treatment. For example, those that are already your customers could receive a certain insert, etc. Or pests, those who constantly inquire but never buy, could be deleted from the lead cycle.

E. The service bureau packages literature, as you have instructed, for fulfillment, addresses the envelopes, and sends them out to the prospects.

The computers can be programmed to verify certain information, such as checking that the ZIP code is in the state indicated and that your ad number A-4 was indeed on annuities and that is what the prospect wanted.

F. Lead information is printed on special forms and sent to you or whomever might be designated by you. The forms provide all of the data the original lead contained plus additional facts such as whether that prospect has inquired previously, if they are a customer, etc. Sometimes the forms provide for feedback as to the results of the lead. That additional data helps in analyzing the performance of advertising and direct-mail programs.

In addition, the system might detect that the phone number the prospect gave did not have an area code and may be able to add it. It might even verify that the prospect is already a customer of the firm, serviced by another salesman. This could eliminate some problems later on.

G. Sometimes lead information is transmitted via a computer system directly to the appropriate office or salesperson instead of being sent on a lead form. These are often interactive systems and you may be able to update the status of the lead "on-line." The chief advantage of this system is the speed with which information is moved and updated.

H. In some circumstances, the service bureau will telephone you, or the appropriate person, with a hot lead. This provides fast action on leads that require speedy responses if the system is not "on-line."

I. You would then call the prospect reported to you by lead form, computer system, or hot-lead phone call. You could then report the status of the lead, mainly if a sale occurred, if a follow-up will be required, or if it is a dead lead.

J. Periodically, the service bureau generates reports summarizing the marketing activities. These reports typically show how many leads were generated, how many turned into sales, etc. Much sophisticated analysis can be provided, often in graphic form.

A service bureau can generate a lot of data. Most will send you weekly, or perhaps even daily summaries of activity. Additional, more comprehensive reports will usually be run monthly.

The daily or weekly reports will most likely list leads and specific information about inquiries. The monthly reports will typically present summary data on marketing performance, costs, sales, etc.

In a typical service bureau marketing report, ads that were run during the past year and the status of each are indicated. Such information as cost per lead, cost per sale, number of sales, etc., are commonly provided.

The medium report shows similar information as the marketing report, but is in summary format. In this report you will see the performance of a particular medium as a group rather than each and every marketing activity in various media. There will usually be a number of other reports provided as well. Some of these will have to do with lead listings, follow-up listings, etc.

Control

One of the sacrifices that must be made when using an outside vendor is the relinquishment of a great deal of control. You tell the service bureau what you want and hope they will do it. Judgment about what to send in unclear situations, or how to solve problems, is left to the vendor in most cases.

You might have been able to interpret a note on a reply card, "I've got to roll over my CD next week," as a true sales opportunity. The service bureau's keypunch operator might miss that note entirely, entering the fact that the prospect checked off "Interested In Tax-Free Income" on your reply card. So you might not find out about the opportunity until it was too late.

And there is also the matter of trust. You are trusting the outside vendor with your sales leads. While it is unlikely that they will sell your leads to another financial services salesperson, if they do not run a tight ship they might lose some leads. Or they may accidentally send out the wrong information. Reputation will be important here.

Cost

The cost per lead for fulfillment services is relatively nominal, probably not much more than you might spend anyway because the service bureau can achieve great economies of scale. In comparison with what you might pay to generate a lead, this additional expense will appear slight. Typical charges per lead would be in the $.50 to $2 range, depending on exactly what was done for you, volume, etc.

The cost, when calculated from an overall point of view, is quite another matter. While a $1 per lead fee is minor, service bureaus typically specify a minimum quantity or monthly charge. This requirement might be 1000 or 5000 or even 10,000 *leads* (not prospects) per year. Most firms could easily meet this threshold, but few individual salespeople could even come close. As a result, you may not be able to utilize a service bureau to process your leads.

It may be worth asking anyway. If you use a vendor to do your mailings, they may be willing to forgo the minimums. Or your own firm may already have such a service in place.

If the company for which you work does have a fulfillment service, you may be able to utilize it to track leads you generate from your own programs. Of course, others would be able to monitor your results as well, but you would get the advantages of a sophisticated fulfillment system without having to generate huge volumes of leads.

IN-HOUSE COMPUTER PROGRAMS

Alternatively, there are a number of software programs available that do much the same analysis and record keeping that is offered by outside vendors. These programs operate on a personal computer or your firm's mainframe. These are typically software packages you can purchase. There are currently more than a dozen such programs available that can help you track and follow up your leads. These vary greatly in quality and effectiveness. More of these programs are becoming available and your choices should improve with time.

The typical system you run on your own computer has several segments. One part captures the lead data in a file for future use. Another part generates a label or letter for fulfillment purposes. A third part tabulates the number of leads, results, etc., for analytical purposes. And a fourth part acts as a tickler file reminding you to follow up or take other action.

Sometimes these programs are combined with systems that help you with the initial mailing—sorting names in ZIP-code sequence, for example—to cut down on postage costs.

One of the primary advantages of the in-house software programs is that you control your leads and all the information that comes from them. No one else handles your leads or maintains your files. While there has been no report of problems with service bureaus losing leads in large numbers, or worse, it is a possibility and you might feel more comfortable keeping the system in-house.

Another advantage of these software packages is that they are generally less costly than service bureaus, but you must handle the data input and fulfillment yourself, so some of your selling time will be diverted into that work.

Many of the new programs also incorporate prospecting systems, allowing you to generate initial mailing lists as well as track and follow up leads. The costs of these programs can range from around $500 up to the tens of thousands of dollars for huge systems designed for your firm's mainframe.

The data manager portion of many popular computer programs can also be used to track and follow up leads. The inquiries can be entered into the data manager file, labels generated, and reports produced indicating subsequent events that have taken place with the leads. While you may need some proficiency in setting up this type of system, it might prove more flexible—and probably significantly cheaper—than a prepackaged system.

Whether a computerized system is run internally or by an outside vendor, they primarily provide the analysis and data you need to judge how effective your promotional campaigns have been. Facts such as the cost per lead, cost per sale, etc., from each marketing effort are reported to you. Files of your lists and your responses are also maintained. This can make repeat mailings much simpler by having the system produce labels, letters, etc.

Another feature of many of these systems is the ability to recognize previous inquiries by the same prospect. That information often will not only make you look efficient in the eyes of the potential customer, it can help you cut down wasted time on unproductive prospects who ask for a lot of information but do not make purchases.

If you are considering using a computer to handle part of your marketing program, you should familiarize yourself with both internal systems and service bureau packages prior to making a decision.

If you do not employ some sort of automated system to monitor leads, use the suggested record-keeping forms available in Appendix C at the back of this book to manage your leads in that situation.

14

The Learning Process

LIKE MANY BUSINESS practices, advertising, direct mail, and promotion are more of an art form than a precise science. No one can tell you that if you do steps A, B, and C, you will get precisely a 2.7% response rate and 19 sales. There are, however, certain basic techniques that have been developed and tested over many years which will help you to improve the results you can expect to achieve in your marketing efforts.

Most every possible combination of copy, color, size, frequency, etc., has been tried for thousands of products and services. Certain patterns have been found that demonstrate there are effective methods of marketing in almost all circumstances. However, so much depends upon what is being offered, to whom, and by whom, that these concepts must be tested periodically in new situations.

That is why keeping records and experimenting with different programs is so important. It is the only way you will be able to gather information about various methods, evaluate what worked, and interpret why it worked. This should allow you to repeat your successes and avoid less effective approaches. Direct mail may work best for you. Perhaps leads from coupon advertising will produce more sales than telephone inquiries. Or possibly promoting one type of financial product will yield more sales volume than other products. Apply these experiences to your future programs and improve the results of those programs.

DATABASES

One of the primary benefits of marketing programs, in addition to making sales, is the creation of a great deal of information. These facts and figures, used properly, can provide a wealth of other advantages.

First, the data can reveal which marketing programs have been effective. This will be useful in selecting future promotional activities.

By analyzing the actual results of programs, a history can be compiled showing how each ad performed, how each media worked, and even how popular certain products and services have been. This information can enable us to target those activities that have paid off in the past and avoid making the same mistakes again.

Second, the information provides a prospect and client profile, helping you direct your efforts toward appropriate target audiences.

In addition to studying which types of marketing worked best, you can also examine the audience you believe holds the most promise of sales. The data can reveal that you were right, or wrong, about how appropriate a certain product might have been for a particular type of prospect. The facts can also guide us in structuring a marketing program for that particular group.

Third, you will know more about which products and services are most popular. Understanding what sells and why can be key to optimal time allocation in sales efforts, i.e., spending less time on less productive products.

Fourth, the data on file about your prospects will permit you to see if they have inquired previously and, if they did, on what. This can make you look right on top of things from the prospect's perspective. You can also determine their interests and needs better when you prepare for a sales call.

Identifying previous inquiries can increase your effectiveness as you are able to weed out the "deadbeats" that inquire about every product and never buy anything.

The prospect data can also permit you to check on a particular potential customer to see their status and if any special action should be taken, such as a follow-up call. This information can enable you to establish a ranking system for hot leads versus leads of lower priority.

To effectively utilize all the data marketing programs can generate, good records must be kept. This can be accomplished by using the forms presented throughout this book, or by utilizing a computerized system.

APPLICATIONS

The information gathered from marketing programs can be used to enhance future results. Assume that you have made three mailings, run two ads, and have done one tele-marketing program over the last nine months. Your records indicate the results shown in the two reports illustrated in Fig. 14-1.

By examining these tables, we can quickly see which activities were profitable and which were not. It does appear that this salesperson's success rate has been improving, generally, over time. It can also be noted that mailings seem to work best for them in terms of net profit (although telemarketing produced the largest percentage return). Mailings were also the most risky, producing the greatest range of loss and gain.

While the programs were not terribly profitable overall, they did bring in 31 new accounts at a profit of $441. It is reasonable to expect many of these accounts will produce large volumes of business in the ensuing years, and good profits as a result.

Clearly there has been a learning curve with direct mail. Mailing number one, done in February, achieved a 1.9% response rate (quite acceptable), a cost per lead of $30 (rather high) and a cost per sale of $437 (also high). The higher cost of the leads and sales contributed to a net loss on the mailing.

MARKETING REPORT

AD CODE	DATE RUN OR MAILED	PRODUCT/ SERVICE	LEADS YTD	COST	CIRC. OR LIST SIZE 000's	RE-SPONSE RATE %	COST PER LEAD	SALES #	$ 00's	AVE. SALE	COST PER SALE	% LEADS CLOSED	FOLLOW-UP #	%	INCOME FROM SALES YTD	PROFIT/ (LOSS)	RETURN ON INV. % YTD-ROI
M-1	2/9	IRA's	29	875	2	1.93	30.17	2	39.50	19.75	437.50	6.90	3	10	514	-361.50	-41.31
M-2	4/28	Tax Free	53	1272	3	2.12	24.00	4	95.70	23.93	318.00	7.55	10	19	1531	259.20	20.38
M-3	5/18	Airlines	72	1443	3	2.40	20.04	6	164.65	27.44	240.50	8.33	17	24	1811	368.15	25.51
A-1	5/18	Airlines	45	1120	150	0.03	24.89	5	73.40	14.68	224.00	11.11	17	38	1211	91.10	8.13
A-2	8/8	Annuity	175	3707	350	0.05	21.18	12	299.90	24.99	308.92	6.86	75	43	3599	-108.20	-2.92
T-1	10/16-10/27	Asian	18	350 Est.	.1	18.00	19.44	2	37.35	18.68	175.00	11.11	7	39	542	191.58	54.74
			392	8767	NM	NM	22.36	31	711	22.92	282.81	7.91	129	33	9207	440.32	5.02

MEDIUM REPORT

MEDIUM	LEADS YTD	COST	COST PER LEAD	SALES #	$ (000's)	AVE. SALE	COST PER SALE	% LEADS CLOSED	FOLLOW-UP #	%	INCOME FROM SALES YTD	PROFIT/ (LOSS)	% ON INV. YTD-ROI
Direct Mail	154	3590	23.31	12	299.85	24.99	299.17	7.79	30	19	3856	266	7.41
Advertising	220	4827	21.94	17	373.30	21.96	283.94	7.73	92	42	4810	-17	-0.35
Telemarketing	18	350	19.44	2	37.35	18.68	175.00	11.11	7	39	542	192	54.86
TOTALS	392	8767	22.36	31	710.50	22.92	282.81	7.91	129	33	9208	441	5.03

Fig. 14-1. Marketing and medium reports.

The second mailing, done in April, got a better response rate of 2.1% and its leads cost $24 each while its sales cost $318 apiece, more in line with industry averages.

Finally, mailing number three, done as part of a campaign with ad number one, received a 2.4% response, costing just $20 per lead and $240 per sale. As a result, it was very profitable.

This person apparently did not learn much from the first ad they ran. So they lost money on ad number two. This might have been a result of ad number one having been strengthened by the accompanying direct-mail activity, making it look good. Or, it may have been just plain bad luck on ad number two. In any event, either the ad, media, or product offered in the second ad was not as effective as it should have been. The advertiser will certainly want to change one of those variables before running that ad again.

The problem in analyzing the telemarketing program's performance is that there is so little data to review. The handful of leads and a couple of sales could be luck, or skill and timing. This salesperson might have received one or two fewer leads, raising the per lead cost to about $22 from $19. Or he might have had one less sale (leaving just one). That would have made his cost per sale $350 (rather high instead of low). But since his cost for telemarketing was less than $400 and he spent about half a day on it, spread over a two week period, plus some minor expenses, it was a very low risk proposition that paid off in a profit and two accounts.

The profitability of a program is partly dependent upon the success of the campaign to bring in leads and sales at a reasonably low price, and partly dependent upon how much those new customers actually buy, now and in the future. This is why it is important to look at profitability and return on investment as well as cost per sale and cost per lead.

A given sale might cost you much more than average, but if you can sell the prospect a lot of products or services, it can still be a profitable sale. Since each case will tend to be random, making it nearly impossible to predict the actual sales that will result, looking at results over time will help to establish the average and likely levels you may achieve. Using that information you can then rationalize, or decide against, specific future marketing activities.

Looking back at the Marketing Report, we see there is a large percentage of follow-up in each category. Typically, more than 50% of leads will require some follow-up for a variety of reasons. They might not have been reached, or could not talk at the time. Others may request that you again contact them at some future date (in many cases just to get rid of you).

Over time, this follow-up group will shrink as some become customers and others become dead leads. Generally, the older the marketing campaign, the smaller percentage of follow-up should appear. Graphically it would look like Fig. 14-2 for the average promotion.

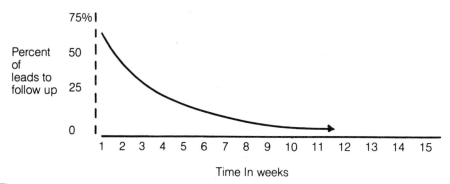

Fig. 14-2. Typical lead follow-up percentage over time.

The figure approaches zero, but probably never quite gets to zero because there seems to be one or two leads in every promotion that we continue to hope will turn into sales in the long run.

The follow-up category is a measure of potential additional new sales and accounts. Clearly, if about 50% of the leads require additional work and sales efforts, some portion are very likely to ultimately become customers. So the higher the follow-up number, the more we can expect additional new customers will be added to those who have already purchased. This is different from leads that became customers and then bought more later. That is follow-on business which adds important sales volume, but not new accounts.

The Medium Report provides essentially the same data as the Marketing Report, but in summary form. The information is condensed into the three primary mediums: advertising, direct mail, and telemarketing. This is useful for comparing broad marketing approaches.

While the data is based on only a limited sample of programs, we can see that telemarketing was the most economical method of generating both leads and sales (lowest cost per lead and cost per sale). Advertising came out the next cheapest cost per sale, but not cost per lead, and was actually unprofitable as a group. Since the follow-up percentage is still quite high in the case of advertising, there is a reasonable possibility that it will gain enough sales to change this ranking. Over time you should get a clearer idea of just how well each of these mediums have worked for you.

TESTING

Another important benefit of careful data collection is the potential to test new ideas or approaches. By running exactly the same ad in two different publications, you might be able to determine which will work best for you in the future. Or you could run the same ad in the same magazine a second time, but add a toll-free number and see what effect that might have on response rates and sales.

While many marketing principles *usually* work, only through testing can you determine what is right for a particular situation.

Some of the less expensive concepts presented in this book are geared for individual financial services salespeople. More elaborate programs are best used when a group of people are marketing together, or an entire firm runs a campaign. You should partake only in programs with which you are comfortable. Do not allow your fellow employees to talk you into putting up a $2500 share of a big promotional effort unless you are sure it is worthwhile and you do not have other ideas about how that money should be spent.

Start out small. Your greatest number of mistakes are likely to come earlier in your marketing career than later. By limiting the size of your initial programs, you will minimize the cost of any early failures. Keeping costs down with less expensive initial efforts may mean your results will not be nearly as impressive as if you ran bigger campaigns. It is, therefore, important that you not get discouraged early on. Direct mail and advertising do work. They can make more money for you. Used correctly, they are powerful allies and should improve your results over time. Used incorrectly, they can drain your resources.

So now you are ready to tackle your direct mail and advertising programs. Keep the following points in mind as you put together your campaign.

- There are many factors that affect the results of a promotional effort. Timing, the current investment climate, the specific products or services offered, as well as the design of your materials and the planning of your campaign all will have tremendous impact on your results. Consider the campaign as a whole and do not

204 The Learning Process

focus entirely on one particular aspect such as the attractive paper you will use in your direct-mail program while forgetting that mailing it on December 20th is a bad idea!

Be sensitive to events or conditions that may be discouraging to the prospects. For example, sending out a direct-mail campaign on the merits of the stock market the day after a 500-point drop in the Dow Average probably would not win you any support. Although you might consider alternative pitches for the circumstances, under these conditions it may be best to just wait for calmer times.

- Be sure to keep detailed records on your response rates, cost per lead, and cost per sale, etc. Only then can you fully assess the success or failure of your entire campaign or specific parts of that program. For instance, you may find a phone number-reply mechanism generates far more inquiries than a coupon, or vice versa. Apply these lessons to your future campaigns.

- Marketing concepts are constantly in flux. Improvements in technology as well as new approaches provide a changing and varied environment for marketers. To run an effective campaign not only involves learning from the past, but also keeping up with the present and future.

You should watch trends in financial advertising. Send for your competitors' literature—not only to see what they are offering, but also how they are offering it. Select the best parts to test for yourself. That is how you will be able to separate the new and effective approaches from the mere variations on an old theme.

If you apply the concepts presented in this book and use good common sense, you should be able to reap the benefits of a valuable marketing program. In time, your costs of programs should fall and your success rates should rise. Good Luck!

Appendices

..... [< L. *a*

..., to call attention; rei

ad·ver·tise, **ad·ver·tize** (ad
[-TISED, -TISING; -TIZED, -TIZ:
VERT], to describe or praise pu:
to promote sales. *v.i.* 1. t
attention to things for sale. 2
by public notice. —ad′ver·ti
tiz′er, *n.* —ad′ver·tis′ing, ad′v
ad·ver·tise·ment, **ad·ver·tize**
vĕr-tīz′mənt, əd-vūr′tiz-), *n.* a ɲ
usually paid for, as of things foi
ad·vice (əd-vis′), *n.* [< L. *ad-*,
to look], 1. opinion given as to
counsel. 2. *usually pl.* informatic
ad·vis·a·ble (əd-viz′ə-b'l), *adj.* t
mended; prudent. —ad·vis′a·bil:
ad·vise (əd-viz′), *v.t.* [-VISED
give advi.......

Appendix A
Glossary

THE FOLLOWING DEFINITIONS will be useful to you as you become involved in marketing and promotional activities. You may not encounter each and every term listed here, but many will come up in your discussions with printers, ad agencies, list brokers, newspapers, mailing houses, etc.

It is suggested that you review this glossary now so the terms will be somewhat familiar to you. The majority of these listings are discussed in greater detail in the text of this book. A few are mentioned here only, just in case you may need to know what they mean.

In a few isolated cases, words that have a particular meaning in the financial service industry have an entirely different implication in the marketing and promotional fields.

ACR—Address Correction Request. A postal service that can, for a fee, report forwarding addresses and errors in the addressing of your mailing. This can reduce the undeliverable count and get you the correct address information. See NCOA.

ad-a-card—A tear-off perforated coupon attached to ads. Typically found in newspaper supplements.

ad code—A method of identifying the sources of leads. Usually an alphanumeric symbol on coupons, mailers, and other response vehicles that tells the advertiser which promotional program generated that particular reply.

advance deposit account—An account set up at the post office from which postage is deducted for specific mailings.

advertising—The promotion of a product or service via print mediums such as newspapers, magazines, etc., or broadcast forms like radio and TV.

advertising agency—A service firm which can provide various aspects of advertising and direct-mail generation and execution. These firms contribute primarily a creative element, but their technical skills and efficiency can be important as well.

ANI—Automated Number Identification. Telephone system that tells the recipient of a call and the phone number of the person calling.

agate line—A basic unit of newspaper space which equals one column wide by one-fourteenth of an inch in height. Thus, there are 14 agate lines per column inch.

affidavit—Notarized record of commercial announcements aired by a radio or television station. A good way to check when and if your ad was run if you did not hear or see it.

affiliate—A station which carries the programming of a national network.

AM—Amplitude Modulation is the variation of the intensity of electromagnetic waves to transmit audio. The AM radio stations operate on frequencies between 540 and 1600 Kilohertz.

ARB—Arbitron. A rating service using daily information to determine audience size and composition of local television and radio stations.

audience—The number of people typically viewing, listening, or reading a particular medium.

audience accumulation—Total audience to a given campaign will build over time. Accumulated audience is the sum of different audiences exposed one or more times to a given ad.

audience composition—The demographic makeup of a medium: where the audience lives, how much money they typically make, etc.

Auxiliary Service Facility—a bulk-mail processing station of a Bulk Mail Center.

availability—A specific time period offered for sale by a radio or television station.

average frequency—The number of times the average household or individual member of an audience is exposed to a specific advertising schedule.

average sale—The typical sales value generated from a lead becoming a customer. Sales volume will accumulate as the lead matures into an account, but the average sale resulting from a marketing program will most likely not change greatly.

back of book—The selection of a magazine following the main editorial section. Refers to ad position.

billboard—a) A large posted outdoor sign advertising products or services. These are usually rented for a specified time period. b) An announcement about 5 seconds in length identifying an advertiser at the beginning, end, or in the breaks of a broadcast, i.e., ''—brought to you by . . .''

bingo cards—Response vehicles in the form of a postage-paid reply card offered by many magazines. Resembling a bingo game card, the reader circles or checks a number corresponding to a particular ad, mails it to the publisher and the magazine forwards a label or list of those interested to that advertiser.

bleed—An advertisement in which all or part of the graphic material runs to the margins of the page. For example, a reverse-out of black background with white printing might ''bleed'' the black to the edge of the page. A premium of 15% over the basic rate is usually charged, partly because a bleed requires special handling.

bonus spot—A free announcement added to a schedule. This may be done as compensation for difficulties with previous spots or as an incentive to advertisers.

broadcast advertising—Ads run on radio or television stations. Cable TV, though not truly broadcast, is still considered a broadcast medium.

bulk business mail—This rate includes third-class mail and those parcels weighing less than 16 ounces. This form of mailing is often used to mail catalogs and circulars.

Bulk Mail Center—A special postal facility for the processing and distribution of third-class and second-class mail in bulk form as well as fourth-class mail.

bulk rate postage—A special discounted postal rate that applies to qualifying mailings based upon quantity, weight, and certain sorting. The Postal Service rewards mailers for doing some of the sorting work for them. Bulk mailings often take longer to deliver than first class.

buyer—Agent who purchases media time for an advertiser and charges a fee for this service.

campaign—The entire marketing effort conducted within a predetermined timeframe, usually with one set of objectives.

cancellation date—The last date to delete previously ordered media activity with little or no penalty.

card packs—A form of group mailings. A collection of identically sized cards offering a wide variety of products and services mailed in a single package. Cost to reach each prospect is very low.

carrier route presort third-class mail—Third-class mail sorted by carrier routes is discounted from the basic bulk third-class rates. Quantities and weight restrictions do apply.

cash discount—A discount allowed by print media, usually 2% of net, to encourage prompt payment—typically within 10 days or so.

center spread—The two facing pages at the center of a magazine. Center spread is desirable because the pages are continuous with little or no interruption in the gutter (binding). Ads on these pages are more expensive than most other double pages.

Cheshire labels—Computer-generated labels on a continuous form. Mailing lists are usually delivered this way unless another form is specified. The basic label has no adhesive and requires a special machine to be affixed.

circulation—The average number of copies of newspapers and magazines distributed per issue. Includes both subscriptions and single-copy sales at newsstands, etc.

classified advertising—Print ads charged by the word, usually positioned in the classified section. These ads typically include no illustrations, coupons, etc.

closing date—The final date for contracting to run an ad in a particular issue of a newspaper or magazine.

clutter—High levels of advertising or a large number of small ads which tend to reduce the effectiveness of any given ad as it is possibly lost in the crowd of other ads.

column inch—The basic measurement for determining costs and layout dimensions in print advertising. A column inch is one column wide (a newspaper may have six or so columns on a page) by one inch high. Essentially a measure of area taken up by the ad.

combination advertising—The use of several ads or mailings at or near the same time so as to increase impact.

combination rate—A discount offered to encourage the purchase of advertising on one or more stations (or in two or more newspapers or magazines) with a common ownership.

compiled list—A mailing list developed from other lists and/or direct-mail respondents. Compiling a list from different sources can create a more powerful marketing tool.

compliance department—The legal representatives of your firm who must approve the copy and offer of any promotional efforts. They usually pass judgment on your meeting all legal requirements so you do not get into trouble subsequently.

confirmation—Agreement from a station that arrangements have been made for a specifically ordered schedule.

consumer magazine—A magazine which appeals to a general readership as opposed to a trade readership.

continuity—The maintenance of uninterrupted media schedules.

controlled circulation—Distribution of a publication restricted to special groups, usually people engaged in a common occupation.

conversion rate—A percentage measure of the inquiries actually becoming customers. For example, if a program produces 84 inquiries and 9 ultimately buy something, the conversion rate is 10.7%.

cooperative advertising—Joint advertising run by several individuals or local offices. Costs and leads are shared.

copy—The actual text of an ad or direct-mail piece. Copy usually goes through several rewrites before being finalized and should have compliance department approval.

corporate discount—A reduction of advertising costs computed on the basis of total advertising expenses from one source. Essentially a volume discount. If your firm uses a particular publication or other medium for its ads, you may qualify for a discount on your own program.

cost efficiency—A measure of media effectiveness. A comparison of potential audience to the cost of placement expressed as a cost per thousand (CPM). This may be cost per thousand individuals or possibly per thousand households. Obviously, the lower the cost per thousand the more efficient, but not necessarily better. That would depend on the type of audience and actual sales rates.

cost per lead—The cost of the campaign excluding nonrecurring expenses such as artwork, divided by the number of leads obtained. As more leads trickle in over time the cost per lead from that source should decline. If you know exactly how many times the campaign will be run, you could amortize the onetime production costs over the number of leads and get a more precise cost per lead figure.

cost per sale—The same calculation for costs as used in cost per lead, divided by the number of sales rather than lead quantity. Since not all leads will turn into sales, cost per sale will always be higher than cost per lead, usually much higher.

coupon—Response vehicle commonly used in print advertising. A coupon is typically an area of an ad to be filled out by the prospect with their name and address and selected additional information and then returned to the advertiser for fulfillment and follow-up. Coupons are most often used to request specific information or materials.

coverage—Advertising vehicle's reach shown as a percentage of total potential audience. Potential audience may be defined as a geographic or demographic target. For example, if your target is Seattle's approximately 500,000 residents and you use a local paper with circulation of 300,000, your coverage would be 60%.

CPM—Cost Per Thousand. The basic measure of media efficiency. Cost per thousand represents the promotional costs of reaching an audience of 1000 (individuals or households). See cost efficiency.

credit—A missed spot for which billing is to be adjusted rather than made up in broadcast time.

cutoffs—Points in time after which a spot cannot be aired. Usually affects late night broadcasts.

databases—The compilation of information about prospects, leads, sales, etc., that result from marketing programs. From a database you can obtain a wealth of information such as the characteristics of who is buying, what is selling and which programs are most effective.

dayparts—Periods of the day differentiated by audience composition and/or broadcast origination.

dead lead—A respondent to a campaign who has subsequently indicated no further interest or could not be reached within a reasonable period of time. Dead leads can form a valuable file for future direct-mail programs.

demographic edition—A special edition of a magazine targeted for a specific demographic group.

demographics—Characteristics of an individual or group of individuals such as their age, income, education, investment experience, etc., that are used as a basis for targeting a marketing audience.

direct mail—The solicitation of an offer using the mails to deliver the message. Direct mail consists of a package including information about the offer and a response vehicle. The response may also rely on the mails, or other means such as the telephone.

display advertising—Print ads charged by size and position. Graphics are usually part of these ads.

double spotting—In broadcast, running one spot announcement directly after another. This is different from a spot twice as long. In double spotting, two advertisements are run which normally could be broadcast separately.

downscale—A word to describe a person's status at the lower end of the socioeconomic scale.

duplication—The exposure of part of one vehicle's audience to a second advertising vehicle. Mailing to an area also covered by your radio ad would be an example of duplication. Some of the recipients of the mailing will have heard the radio ad and this process can increase impact and effectiveness.

earned rate—The actual rate for print space taking into account volume and frequency discounts. This is the rate that should be used for actual cost calculations.

editorial environment—The standard editorial content, tone, and philosophy of a medium. If a medium is ''pro'' business and carries business news, that is advantageous to advertisers in the financial services business.

endorsement—An additional fee that is paid to the post office for the service of returning undeliverable bulk rate mail.

estimate—A summary of anticipated media costs.

exposure—a) The perception of an advertisement or a commercial by an individual. This measures a prospect actually seeing your ad as opposed to audience size or reach, where the possibility of exposure is counted. b) The number of people in the audience who see the ad.

fixed position—The guaranteed location of an ad in a particular publication such as the inside front cover, or a specific time and day on a broadcast station.

faced—All pieces of mail arranged so that addresses and stamps or permits face the same way.

first-class mail—This includes letters and postcards sent by regular mail.

flats—Mail which exceeds the required dimensions for letter-size (11 1/2" long by 6 1/8" high by 1/4" thick). The maximum dimensions for flats are 15" long by 12" high by 3/4" thick. Flats are mailed at rates typically higher than for letter-sized mail.

flat rate—An advertising rate not on a sliding discount scale.

flighting—Scheduling patterns of activity separated by relative inactivity. A campaign may generate leads which are then worked while no advertising is done.

FM—Frequency Modulation is the variation of oscillation patterns of electromagnetic signal to transmit audio. Usually superior fidelity and less interference than AM radio. FM stations operate on frequencies between 88.1 and 107.9 Megahertz and typically do not have as great a range as AM stations.

four color—Black and three colors (blue, yellow and red) which are combined to produce full-color print advertising. This is usually quite expensive and generally unnecessary for financial advertising.

free standing insert—A preprinted ad of one or more pages which is inserted unbound into newspapers, especially Sunday editions. Also known as a Free Standing Stuffer. These are the items that usually fall out of the paper when you are carrying it home.

frequency—Repetition of exposure to an advertisement. This can lead to greater impact.

frequency discount—Reduced rates offered for multiple usage of a given vehicle.

frequency distribution—A breakdown of the number of times various audience subgroups are exposed to a particular ad.

fringe time—Television time periods adjacent to prime time in which most of the programming is originated locally and more ad spots are available.

fulfillment package—The information sent to respondents of an ad, direct-mail piece, or telemarketing program. This includes specific information promised or requested and would probably contain a prospectus on an offer.

gatefold—A special space unit in magazines which appears to be the size of one full page, but when unfolded reveals an ad of 1 1/2 to 2 pages in size. This is most often used in the Sunday supplement of your local paper to advertise department store sales, etc.

gross impressions—The total number of exposures to an advertisement or commercial.

group mailing—The teaming of several parties wishing to make a direct-mail campaign so as to minimize costs and maximize efficiency. The team effort often qualifies for discounts and economies of scale and can produce superior results at lower costs. See *card pack* and *cooperative advertising*.

gutter—The inside margins of facing pages in a publication at the binding.

headline—The main attention grabbing banner usually found at the top of an ad. This line should persuade a prospect to read the rest of the ad copy, so it is critical to have an effective headline.

horizontal rotation—The distribution of broadcast spots on different days of the week at the same time of day.

impact—The extent to which an audience is affected by advertising, measured by awareness, consumer attitudes, and actual sales.

impression—One exposure to one advertisement in one household or to one individual.

independent—A local station not affiliated with a national network (radio or TV).

inquiry—A response to direct mail or advertising campaign. An inquiry is a lead and a prospect. But all prospects are not inquiries until they have responded to your offer. Inquiries (leads) have given specific signals that they may be interested by responding. Prospects would seem to be interested, but have not actually indicated an interest. Wealthy individuals would all be prospects for a tax advantaged investment, but only those replying to an advertisement would be inquiries.

investment spending—Increased advertising expenditures with the expectation of increased sales and profits.

label—Usually a self-adhesive piece of paper containing addressing information for outgoing mail. Some labels such as Cheshire labels are not self-adhesive and require special machines to be affixed.

lead—Same as inquiry.

lead follow-up—The sales calls and additional efforts that must be made after a lead is received to try and convert it into a sale.

line rate—Cost per agate line; the basic unit used to compute costs for newspaper space. This is the basis for the rates quoted for column inches. Many publications have standard sized ads on which they also base their charges. These standard sizes are common to many publications and can be used in various media without size modification, saving repetitive design work and costs.

list—A collection of prospects having certain characteristics in common such as geographic location, education, investment objectives, income, etc. A list usually includes a name, address, sometimes a phone number, and occasionally a title such as Dr., Mrs., or Vice President, etc. Lists are often sorted by certain criteria such as by ZIP code, alphabetical position or job title.

list broker—A firm specializing in the rental of a large variety of lists. List brokers can guide direct-mail users in selecting appropriate lists to use and assist in the actual mailings. The list rental fee covers a onetime use of a list. Most other services would be charged additionally.

list cleaning—Over time lists accumulate undeliverable names—some people move, marry, or change their name for other reasons. To reduce the undeliverable content, names that have been returned from a mailing as not having been deliverable are removed from the list. Those with a new and different address have that information updated. This process is known as list cleaning.

list correction service—The Postal Service offers, for a fee, to delete missing or incorrect addresses and to inform you of new addresses based on forwarding information in their files.

list manager—The firm, often also a list broker, that obtained a mailing list from the party who developed it. A firm marketing suitcases might employ a list manager to rent their list to noncompetitive marketers so additional revenues can be generated. Managers usually handle only larger lists of 50,000 to 100,000 names.

list rental—The process of contracting to rent a specific mailing list from a list broker or manager for a given fee. The rental is a onetime agreement and another fee must be paid to use it again.

listening area—The geographic coverage of a radio station's signal.

mailing house—A firm providing direct-mail assistance. Services usually include stuffing materials into envelopes, addressing, affixing postage and mailing. Many mailing houses are list brokers, or are affiliated with brokers, and therefore they can provide virtually an entire direct-mail program from list selection to postal delivery.

makegood—The replacement of a spot missed due to a preemption or faulty transmission.

marketing—The means by which potential customers are informed of the availability of products or services. Typically advertising, direct mail, and telephone sales (telemarketing).

media—The various types of means used to communicate advertising messages. These include television and radio, magazines, newspapers, or direct-mail programs, etc. Media are the broad categories; medium is the individual vehicle.

media kit—A package of information about a particular advertising media. Usually includes a rate card, sample of the publication, description of audience and size, list of advertisers, etc. Available free upon request.

media planning—The process of analyzing media and marketing options and designing a schedule to meet specific advertising objectives.

media service—An organization capable of the full range of media functions. These services are hired for a fixed fee or percentage of the advertising budget.

medium—Any specific vehicle used to deliver an advertising message. A particular type of media.

metered mail—Postage printed on mail by a special meter that must be approved by the Postal Service. Metered mail must be mailed within the jurisdiction of the post office shown in the meter stamp.

minimum frequency—Minimum number of exposures thought necessary for an advertisement to be effective. This varies considerably from ad to ad and medium to medium, but three exposures is generally the least to get some effectiveness.

minimum size requirement—The smallest dimensions allowable for a package to be mailable. With few exceptions, the minimum size would be: 5″ long by 3 1/2″ high by .007″ thick. If a package is more than 1/4″ thick, these size requirements do not apply.

NCOA—National Change of Address Service. A separate service similar to the Postal Service's ACR (Address Correction Request), which can reduce undeliverables and inform you of the prospect's new address.

network—A group of television or radio stations associated for the purpose of airing programs simultaneously.

news release—A notice sent by you, or your PR agency, to various mediums about something deemed noteworthy. The objective is that they will include the information in their publication or broadcast. Potential free publicity.

opacity—The ability of paper to take ink on one side without showing through on the other side. This is especially important if you are printing on both sides of a page. If the message bleeds through the other side, it will make reading the other side more difficult.

open rate—The highest rate charged for a magazine or newspaper ad. Does not include earned volume or frequency discounts.

orbit—A scheduling arrangement in which a station will rotate an advertisement among different program vehicles.

OTO—One Time Only. A broadcast spot which is ordered in a particular time period for a particular day or week and which is not scheduled to be run in the same time period in subsequent days or weeks.

outdoor—Display advertising (billboards, posters) located out-of-doors along highways, on rooftops and walls, at bus stops, etc. Not recommended for most financial services advertising.

package—a) Group of television or radio programs and commercial spots offered at a discount by a network or station. b) The fulfillment materials sent out in response to an inquiry (fulfillment package).

panels—The unit of outdoor advertising. Cost is based on how many panels are used as well as where they are located and how long the contract to use them will remain in effect.

pass along reader—An individual who reads a publication that was purchased by someone else. An example would be a copy of an industry magazine read by the office manager and passed along to several other employees. Also called secondary readers.

penetration—The degree to which a medium or vehicle has achieved coverage of a particular target audience.

periodicals—Publications issued relatively infrequently, perhaps bimonthly or quarterly. These are usually targeted at specialized audiences and advertising space can be quite expensive.

personalization—The imprinting of particular information in a direct-mail piece that relates to a specific prospect. A personally addressed letter referring to the prospect's daughter as Amy, would be an example.

pop-up coupon—A separate tear-off coupon stitched into the binding of a magazine.

position—The location of a print ad on a page within a print vehicle. Or the position of a broadcast commercial relative to a program adjacent to or within the show.

postage meter—A machine used to print postage on envelopes and cards, or on tape for affixing to other packages.

postal permit—There are two types of postal permits: incoming and outgoing. Incoming permits are used by a mailer to permit respondents to mail back materials or information without affixing postage. An account at the post office funded by the mailer is charged for each incoming piece at a price somewhat higher than regular first-class rates. No charge is made for unreturned imprinted materials. Outgoing permit numbers eliminate the need to affix postage to each mailing piece the mailer is sending. A small charge for the permit number is made. The postage is charged at regular rates (first class, bulk, etc.) and the cost is deducted from the mailer's account.

precanceled stamps—Stamps already cancelled when they are purchased. These are typically used for mass mailings and save the post office a lot of work cancelling the letters later.

premium—An advertising premium is usually more valuable than a specialty item and is related to doing business with you. There are legal restrictions on "gifts of value" in the financial business, so be careful here. See *specialty*.

presort—A sorting of mail done prior to delivery to the post office so as to minimize postage costs. Examples would be a ZIP-code sorting to qualify for bulk-mailing rates or a state sorting to obtain a reduced first-class rate. Presorting might also be used to stagger a mailing by sending to one geographic area at a time.

print advertising—Advertising that appears in published material like newspapers, magazines, and periodicals.

product protection—A guarantee by a medium to separate ads or commercials of competitive services or products. A newspaper might agree not to run other securities related ads on the same page that your ad appears.

production costs—The fees charged to create and produce a mailing piece or an advertisement. These costs would include artwork, typesetting, announcer fees, recordings, etc. They are mostly of a onetime nature and are not part of the recurring cost of running the ad over and over.

proof—A preliminary run of a printed promotional piece. A printer will often print just a few copies before the full run is made so the customer can check the appearance. Any errors caught can be corrected fairly easily before commitment to full production is made. Sometimes proof is used to describe the camera-ready artwork given to a publication to print an ad.

prospect—Any individual identified as a potential customer by general characteristics or demographics. For example, wealthy investors would be prospects for tax-advantaged products. Prospects become leads (inquiries) when they respond to an offer and thus show specific interest in that offer.

psychographics—Characteristics of an individual (or group of individuals). These include life style, attitudes, personality, spending habits, etc.

rate card—A published listing of the advertising costs and mechanical requirements for a given medium. Usually part of a media kit.

rate protection—Guarantee given to an advertiser by a medium against rate increases in the medium for a specified period of time. This is typically done in return for certain assurances of minimum levels of advertising expenditures on the part of the advertiser.

reach—The total number of different homes or individuals exposed to an advertisement one or more times. Reach is usually measured over a certain time period and expressed as a percent of the total potential audience.

readers per copy—The average number of readers for each copy of a magazine or newspaper. This reflects not only those that subscribe or purchase the publication at a newsstand, but also those pass-along (secondary) readers.

readership—Total audience of a print vehicle.

regional edition—A portion of a national magazine's circulation that falls within a certain geographic territory (metropolitan area, state, or group of states) in which advertising can be purchased separately from the total circulation. A premium is usually charged for regional editions, i.e., advertisers pay a higher CPM.

remnant space—Unsold magazine advertising space, often in regional or geographic editions of national publications, sold at a discount. The publisher might have a quarter-page available in the Midwest issue only and press time is fast approaching. This space might be offered at a large discount, particularly since the advertiser has no choice on position or edition.

replies—The responses to a direct mail or advertising campaign. Replies could be in the form of coupons, letters, post cards, telephone messages, or even walk-in customers.

response curve—The graph showing the relative portion of all responses coming in over time. The curve will always approach 100% after enough time has passed, but rarely will it actually reach 100% since some leads can trickle in over months or years. The curves vary among mediums, but have a similar appearance.

response rate—The number of inquiries received as a percentage of the total audience universe. For direct mail, this would be the number of replies divided by the number mailed (less the undeliverable count) times 100%. For print advertising, the response rate equals the number of replies divided by the publication's readership, times 100%. For radio and TV, the response rate would be measured by the response quantity divided by the audience size times 100%.

response vehicle—The mechanism provided in a marketing program to enable the prospect to contact the advertiser. This might take the form of a postage-paid postal card, a coupon to be mailed back, an address to write to or visit, or a phone number to call.

retail rates—Rates for local retail advertisers that are built upon different discount structures from rates for national advertisers. If your firm advertises in a medium, you may qualify for lower rates than the retail rates in that particular medium.

return address—The address of the mailer showing from whom the item was sent. It should appear in the upper left-hand corner of the envelope, card, or package. A return address is important because it enables the post office to return undeliverable items and it helps the recipient identify who sent the item (usually a positive).

ROP—Run Of Press. A newspaper insertion for which a particular position is not requested. The cost is less for this type of ad.

ROS—Run Of Station. A commercial announcement for which a particular time period is not requested. The cost is less for this type of spot.

scatter—The scheduling strategy in which several different vehicles are bought within a time period to disperse the message flow and build reach.

secondary readers—See pass-along reader.

sectional center facility—An area defined by ZIP codes. The first three numbers of a ZIP code identify its sectional center. Used primarily in presorting and determination of postal charges.

seeded list—The inclusion of names on a list which are employed by (or connected with) either the list broker, list manager, or list owner. If the seeded names receive unexpected mailings, duplicate mailings, or non-approved mailings, they report these things to the appropriate parties and the unlawful user can find himself in a great deal of trouble.

sensitivity analysis—The mathematical calculation of how much more in sales, or additional responses, would be necessary to justify an incremental marketing expenditure. Part of a profitability analysis.

share of audience—The percentage of all viewing households which are tuned to a particular TV station, or in radio, the percentage of listeners tuned to a particular radio station. In a four-station market with each station roughly of equal popularity, shares would be approximately 25% each.

simulcast—To broadcast a program at the same time on a TV station and on a radio station, or two radio stations—usually one AM and one FM.

special—A single radio or TV show that replaces regularly scheduled programming. These are sometimes called spectaculars and attract added viewers or listeners. As a consequence, ads on these shows are usually more expensive.

specialty—An inexpensive gift or bonus item offered as an inducement to do business. These might include pens, key chains, paperweights, etc., imprinted with the giver's name and address. Or a specialty might be a special report or guide useful to the prospect. Specialty items are usually given away with no strings attached. See *premium*.

spill-in—The amount of viewing within one broadcast market to stations originating in a neighboring market. Reception of a television station from a neighboring state would be an example.

spill-out—Transmission of a TV or radio signal beyond its own market area.

split-run—The scheduling of two or more versions of an ad in different regional issues of the same newspaper or magazine. Usually used for ad-effectiveness testing.

spot—A single announcement or the period of time in which that announcement is scheduled. Typically 15, 30 or 60 seconds in duration.

spot TV—Television time offered by local stations as opposed to network TV.

spread—A single print ad positioned on two facing pages of a publication.

statement stuffers—Inclusion of a promotional piece with customers' statements or other regular mailing. In its most common form, a stuffer is simply a card with a brief offer and a portion to be detached and mailed back requesting more information. Sometimes the response vehicle is a statement to call the customer's salesperson if interested in the offer.

station break—Time period in which broadcast reverts from the network feed to the local station to announce call letters and broadcast local commercials.

strip—A television program that is aired on successive days during the same time period. Strip also refers to buying commercials each day of a telecast within this type of programming.

Sunday supplement—A local or nationally edited magazine included with the Sunday newspaper. Advertising in this item can be expensive and has not been shown to be particularly effective for financial advertising.

take-one mailers—Similar in format to statement stuffers, these promotional pieces are usually available in stands at conventions, hotel lobbies, taxi cabs, etc. Take-one mailers consist of an offer (usually explained in more detail by an accompanying sign) and a reply mechanism (usually a mailing card). These can be useful for financial services offers under the right circumstances.

target audience—The population segment identified as comprising the prime prospects for the product or service being marketed. Target audience is of critical importance in developing media strategies and directing advertising support.

third-class mail—(Bulk Business Mail) A postal class usually applied to circulars, printed matter, pamphlets, and merchandise weighing less than one pound.

toll-free telephone—An incoming telephone number using ''800'' instead of an area code. This means that the caller pays nothing to reach that number and the owner of the phone number pays all costs to receive the call. Toll-free numbers typically achieve better response rates from ads than do toll calls, especially if long distance calls are involved. WATS are special outgoing telephone lines and are entirely different from toll free.

tombstone ad—A type of financial advertisement indicating that a certain transaction has been completed and listing the parties involved. This was intended for informational purposes (often required by law) and little if any marketing benefits were expected.

trade magazine—Magazines edited and promoted specifically to reach members of occupational groups with advertising correspondingly directed at these groups. The *Registered Representative Magazine* would be an example of a securities industry trade magazine, and ads in that publication would appeal to stock brokers, financial analysts, etc.

UHF—Ultra High Frequency. Television broadcast on channels 14-83 (470-890 Megahertz).

undeliverables—That portion of a mailing that is returned by the post office because it could not be delivered. The reasons for not being deliverable include: 1) an old address that has not been updated, 2) an error in addressing, or 3) a change in name. Undeliverables exist in most all lists, but should not exceed roughly 5% of the entire list.

upscale—A term used to define individuals on the upper end of the socioeconomic scale (better educated, higher income).

vehicle—A particular advertising medium such as a magazine, TV program, or radio station.

vertical rotation—The distribution of broadcast spots at different times within the same day.

VHF—Very High Frequency. Television broadcasts on channels 2-13 (54 to 216 Mega-hertz).

waste circulation—Audience readership, viewers, or listeners outside a specific demographic or geographic target. For example, if you only sell securities in Illinois, an ad on a Chicago ratio station would have waste circulation among listeners in Wisconsin or Indiana. There will always be some waste circulation, just try to keep it to a minimal level. See *spill-out*.

WATS—Wide Area Telephone Service. An outgoing telephone line which permits a certain number of long distance phone calls with little or no additional cost over the basic monthly fee. A toll-free line is an incoming line; WATS are outgoing lines.

ZIP code—Zone Improvement Program. The five digits assigned by the post office to help identify a location for delivery. Each community has a unique ZIP code; sometimes larger communities will have many ZIP codes to designate each area.

ZIP + 4 code—A nine-digit ZIP code consisting of the basic five-digit ZIP code of the addressee plus a four-digit expanded code that identifies a sector (two digits)—a geographic portion of the ZIP code, as well as a segment (two digits)—a specific block, apartment building, firm, etc.

Appendix B

Summary of Handy Formulas and Worksheets

FORMULAS

Agate Line = 1/14 inch (14 agate lines = 1 inch)

Available Column Inches = Budget for each ad/Rate per column inch

Column Inches = Number of columns wide × length of ad in inches

Conversion Rate = (Number of sales/Number of leads) × 100%

Cost Per Lead = Variable costs of program/Total number of leads received

Cost Per Sale = Variable cost of program/Total number of sales

Cost Per Sale > *Cost Per Lead*

CPM = (Cost of Ad/Audience Size) × 1000

Lead Quantity Leveling Formula—Use this formula to estimate the allocations to obtain similar lead counts from two programs. The two percentages must total to 100%. If more than two mediums are used, each portion could be leveled using this formula and the three (or more) percentages would still have to total 100%.

Percentage of budget to Medium 1/Cost of average lead from medium 1 = Percentage of budget to medium 2/Cost of average lead from medium 2

Penetration = (Circulation or audience size/Target Audience Size) × 100%

Pica = 12 points or 1/6 inch (A measure of type size)

Point = One seventy-second of an inch (A measure of type size)

Production Costs = Artwork costs + typesetting costs + announcer fees + recording costs + all other nonrecurring charges

Response Rate = Number of inquiries/audience size or mailing list size*
                *Less undeliverables

WORKSHEETS

Budget Analysis Worksheet

Use this worksheet for a preliminary test of how reasonable your advertising or direct-mail plans may be in light of the funds available.

Step 1. Determine how many *sales* or new accounts you want.
    # of SALES = DOLLAR VOLUME/AVERAGE SALES PER ACCOUNT
Two of the three figures here will be assumptions you must make based on subjective estimates. You probably have a pretty good idea what your average sale of a given type of product has been in the past.

Step 2. Determine the number of *leads* you require.
    # of LEADS = # of SALES/CLOSING RATE
The closing rate will vary, but a reasonable initial assumption, until you gain further experience, would be 7%.

Step 3. Calculate the size of audience needed
    AUDIENCE SIZE = # of LEADS/RESPONSE RATE
The response rate can also vary considerably and will be much lower for most advertising than direct mail. As a start, estimate one-fiftieth (.02) of 1% for advertising and 2% for direct mail.

Step 4. Figure your budget per audience contact cost.
    BUDGET EACH = TOTAL BUDGET/AUDIENCE SIZE
The result should be in the $.01 to $.10 range for advertising and $.30 to $1 range for direct mail. While your results may differ somewhat and these figures are only guidelines, if you calculate costs much lower it is unlikely you will achieve them. Higher costs probably mean you cannot make any money on the program.

Step 5. Determine potential profitability of the program.
    PROFIT = (DOLLAR VOLUME × NET PAYOUT RATE) – BUDGET
Payout depends upon what is sold, etc., but 1% is a good initial estimate.

Sensitivity Analysis Worlksheets

These formulas can help you analyze whether an extra expenditure, or a cutback in costs, is justified.

Step 1: Additional Sales required =
    [Additional Cost per piece × Number of pieces] /
    Net payout rate percentage

Step 2: Additional Sales required per new customer =
    Additional Sales required (from Step 1) /
    Number of sales

Fig. B-1. Sensitivity analysis worksheet.

Print Media:

Step 1: Media ad budget*/Number of ads
      = Approx. budget for each ad
Step 2: Budget for each ad (from Step 1)/Rate per column inch**
      = Est. column inches used for each ad
NOTES: * After allocation for preparation, etc.
          **Use applicable rates for the number of ads
            you plan to run (frequency discounts).

Broadcast Media

Step 1: Radio Ad Budget*/Number of Ads
      = Approx. budget for each ad
Step 2: Budget for each ad (Step 1)/Advertising rate per spot**
      = Possible ad length in seconds

NOTES: * Less production costs
        ** 15 or 30 second spots

Fig. B-2. Ad copy versus budget worksheet.

	Rating									
Criteria:	Worst 1	2	3	4	5	6	7	8	9	Best 10
Wealth or Earning Power										
Business Title or job										
(Retired)										
Education										
Geographic Location										
Home Value										
Income Level										
Net Worth										
Previous Investments										
Level of Investments										
Type of Investments										
Years Investing										
Buying Habits										
Car										
Boat										
Plane										
Private Club										

Fig. B-3. Media rating worksheet.

Media	Unadjusted Ranking	CPM For That Media	Adjusted Ranking
Media 1	A	v	A/v
Media 2	B	w	B/w
Media 3	C	x	C/x
Media 4	D	y	D/y
Media 5	E	z	E/z
.	.	.	.
.	.	.	.
.	.	.	.

Fig. B-4. Results of rating analysis.

Appendix C
Ready-To-Use Forms

THE FORMS IN this section have been prepared to facilitate your record keeping of marketing programs. Feel free to photocopy and use them for your own personal promotional activities.

Mailing List General Record #_____

Quantity To Be
Mailed _____

List Used _____

List Source _____

Target audience or territory _____

Contents of mailing (describe) _____

Who did mailing _____ Reply Card Code _____

Costs: Labor. . . . . $ _____

        Materials . . . .   _____

        Postage. . . . .   _____

      Total Costs . . . . $ _____

Date Mailed	Quantity Mailed	Comments
_____	_____	_____
_____	_____	_____
_____	_____	_____
_____	_____	_____
_____	_____	_____
_____	_____	_____
_____	_____	_____
_____	_____	_____
_____	_____	_____
_____	_____	_____
_____	_____	_____

Mailing completed
on _____

Total
Mailed _____

Fig. C-1. Mailing list general record.

```
                     Mailing List Name File

Date Mailed _____        Lead Status

List Source _____        [ ] Dead Lead
                                            [ ] Undeliverable
Materials Sent _____        [ ] New Customer

                                           ┌──────────────────────┐
Reply Received? [ ] Yes    [ ] No          │ [ ] Follow-up on      │
                                           │     _____    │
Reply Date _____       └──────────────────────┘

Name _____

Firm (if applicable) _____

Address _____

City _____ State _____ Zip _____

Phone (_____)_____

Comments _____

_____
```

Fig. C-2. Mailing list name file.

```
                   Telephone Response Record

Responses from _____     Call taken by _____

Date _____ Time _____   Station or Ad code _____

Name _____

Address _____

City _____ State _____ Zip _____

Phone number (If given) (_____)_____

Materials to send them _____

Notes _____

_____

_____
```

Fig. C-3. Telephone response record.

VENDOR MAILING INSTRUCTIONS FORM

Date: _____

From: _____   To: _____

_____   _____

_____   _____

_____   _____

PHONE: (_____)_____

MAILING DATE _____   MAILING CODE _____

[ ] TIME   [ ] Mail Early OK   [ ] Mail Late OK
    CRITICAL   [ ] Do Not Mail Early   [ ] Do Not Mail Late

WORK TO BE PERFORMED: [ ] ASSEMBLING _____ (# of items)

[ ] SUBASSEMBLY [ ] Folding letters
    REQUIRED: [ ] Affixing labels to insert on reply card
                   [ ] Stapling or other operations? _____

[ ] INSERTING INTO ENVELOPE TYPE # _____

[ ] ENVELOPE CLOSURE: [ ] Self adhesive   [ ] Clasp
                      [ ] Moisture activated

[ ] ADDRESSING BY: [ ] Customer supplied labels
                   [ ] Vendor generated and supplied labels
                   [ ] Personalized letter
                   [ ] Typed address

[ ] POSTAGE FORMAT: [ ] Customer permit number imprinted
                    [ ] Metered postage, bill customer
                    [ ] Affix stamps, bill customer

[ ] POSTAGE RATES: [ ] Regular First Class_____
                   [ ] First Class presort_____
                   [ ] Bulk rate, specify which rate. _____

[ ] DELIVERY TO POST OFFICE: [ ] Vendor responsibility
                             [ ] Customer responsibility

[ ] TOTAL QUANTITY TO BE MAILED: _____

SUPPLIES: QUANTITY   DESCRIBE (Item #, etc.)

[ ] Brochure _____

[ ] Preprinted letter _____

[ ] Reply card _____

[ ] Other _____

[ ] MATERIALS SHORTAGE: [ ] Do not mail   [ ] Mail all finished

[ ] RETURN UNUSED MATERIALS [ ] Yes   [ ] No

NOTES: _____
_____

Fig. C-4. Vendor mailing instructions form.

Appendix D

Postal Services, Rates, and Regulations

THIS APPENDIX IS intended as a guide to many of the rules and regulations that will affect your marketing programs. These facts will have the greatest impact upon direct-mail marketing, but they are also relevant to other promotional activities where mailing might be an ancillary part—as in mailing a fulfillment package.

The information contained in this section is current to the time of publication. Since postal rates and regulations have been in flux in recent years, it is recommended that you check with your local post office before embarking upon any mailing programs.

The post office has a division, The Mailing Requirements Department, that can advise you on regulations and charges. The *National ZIP Code Directory* lists these offices. Or you can call the Postal Answer Line in most major cities. This is a computerized system which plays messages on specific postal topics of interest by pressing certain codes on your telephone. Your local post office has the number for your area.

METHODS OF MAIL DELIVERY

Express Mail. This is the fastest mail delivery system. Delivery is generally guaranteed for the next day. Letters and packages can qualify for Express Mail. The minimum charge is $8.75 for up to eight ounces and rises with weight.

First-Class Mail. The most common form of mailing for small users of direct mail is first-class regular mail. All first-class mail is given the fastest transportation available. This method requires no minimum number, no sorting and no special handling. The cost to mail a letter first class is currently $.25 for up to one ounce (about the weight of an envelope and three pieces of typing paper), and $.20 for each additional ounce. If you use the ZIP + 4 (nine-digit ZIP codes) you can mail for $.241 without doing any sorting. Not much of a savings, unless you are doing a very large volume.

First-class letters must measure between 5 and 11.5 inches long, between 3.5 and 6.125 inches wide, and between .007 and 1/4 inch thick. In addition, the length must be between 1.3 and 2.5 times the height. If your letters are larger than these dimensions you will be charged a surcharge for nonstandard mail. The current surcharge for nonstandard mail is $.05 each. Mail smaller than these dimensions, with a few special exceptions, cannot be mailed.

If your envelopes are nonstandard, it is suggested that you imprint "First Class" on them to ensure they get proper handling. You might also use the special large white envelopes (flats) with green striped borders to signify first-class mail.

A first-class post card will cost $.15 each to mail at current rates. The size requirements (except thickness) are the same as for a letter.

Priority Mail. If, for some reason, your package weighs more than 12 ounces, and you wish to send it first class, it should be sent Priority Mail. The maximum weight for Priority Mail is 70 pounds and the parcel cannot measure more than 100 inches in length and girth (distance around the narrowest part) combined. The minimum charge for priority mail is $2.40 and rises with weight and delivery zone (distance).

Presorted First-Class Mail. A minimum of 500 pieces of first-class mail sorted in ZIP code sequence can qualify for a special discount rate. The post office will grant you a discount of $.04 per letter (reducing the typical cost to $.21 each). If you sort by carrier route, the charge drops to $.195 for the first ounce. In the case of post cards, the presorted rate is $.13 each and the carrier route sort brings the charge down to $.115.

All of these costs can be further reduced by about a half cent each by using ZIP + 4 nine-digit ZIP codes. You can find out your ZIP + 4 code by calling the post office at 1-800-228-8777. You could also check the Postal Answer Line.

There are several other requirements as well. Each piece cannot exceed 12 ounces. The mail must be sorted as follows:

- Ten or more pieces to the same five-digit ZIP code are grouped.
- At least 50 pieces of the balance must be grouped to the same first three digits of the ZIP code (sectional code).
- The balance of the mailing counts toward the 500 minimum and must be sorted according to certain requirements, but does not qualify for the lower mailing rate.

In addition, the mailer must pay an annual fee and pay postage by meter, permit, or precanceled stamps. Each piece must indicate "Presorted First Class" on the envelope. A Statement of Mailing special form (3602) must be submitted and the mail must be delivered to the post office where the permit is issued, with some exceptions.

If you will not qualify for the 500-piece minimum, or do not want to bother with all of these procedures, there may still be ways to utilize the discount if you can pool your mailing with others. An outside vendor that provides presorting services can often add your mailings to others and thereby qualify your mailing for presorted rates. They will charge you a portion of the savings for this service, but you would still come out ahead.

Business Reply Mail. Business Reply Mail is a form of postage in which the recipient, not the sender, pays the postage. This enables a prospect to return a postage-paid card and have you bear the cost of the mail.

There are several ways to pay for this service. If you do not make an advance deposit, you would be charged $.40 for each reply (one ounce or less). Since you pay nothing for any prepaid mailers not returned, and response rates typically run only a few percent, this should not amount to much additional cost.

However, if you expect large volumes of replies, you can cut your per piece charge down to as low as $.05. To be entitled to this rate you would need to do the following:

- Set up an advance deposit account.
- Pay an accounting fee of $260.
- Barcode your reply cards (for postal sorting purposes).

You can quickly see that saving $.35 on each reply only makes sense on quantities over about 750 responses. At a 2% response rate, you would need to be mailing approximately 37,000 pieces. So unless you plan a huge campaign, or series of mailings, the $.40 per reply deal is probably the best.

You can also qualify for an $.08 per piece rate if you do not bar code, but the deposit, etc., are the same. You would need to be an even larger direct mailer to benefit from that deal because the savings are less and the accounting fee is the same.

While it may not be a factor for most financial services sales people working in the U.S., do keep in mind that Business Reply mail is valid only in the United States.

Second-Class Mail. Second-class mail is generally used by newspapers and other periodicals published at least four times a year and which are not primarily advertising. Unless you qualify, this rate is not appropriate for most marketing programs. The minimum basic rate per piece is currently $.032.

Third-Class Mail. This is primarily used for advertising and direct mail. Items that can be mailed third class include catalogs, newsletters, circulars, etc. There is no maximum size for third-class mail, however, it is considered non-standard if it weighs less than two ounces and exceeds the size of a regular letter (6.125" high by 11.5" long by 1/4" thick, or has a length which is less than 1.3 times the height or more than 2.5 times the height) and a surcharge of $.05 would apply.

It can also be mailed if it is between .007" and 1/4" in thickness and it is rectangular in shape, at least 3 1/2 inches high, and at least 5 inches long.

The speed with which third-class mail is delivered generally depends upon how far it is going. If it is a local mailing, it might get to its destination as quickly, or perhaps only a day or so later, than first-class mail. But if it is going across the country, it could take a week or more beyond the time that first-class mail might take!

There are four relevant rate schedules for third-class mail:

(1) Single Piece Rate—for mail not qualifying as regular bulk. As little as one piece can be mailed this way, but you will not save anything since the rates are the same as for first class in the lower-weight categories. The letter must have "Third Class" on its front between the postage and the addressee. As you approach the 16-ounce weight limit

the cost becomes significantly less than for first class, provided the piece meets the size restrictions.

Currently the range for single pieces is $.25 to $1.50. This could be quite useful for sending a heavy prospectus a short distance, where little time would be sacrificed by using a slower method. You could also possibly use the book rate for this purpose.

(2) Basic Regular Bulk Rate—Bulk mail in quantities of at least 200 pieces of 50 pounds. These can be presorted by carrier route or by ZIP code. The basic rate is $.167, which is reduced to $.132 for (3) *ZIP sorting* and to $.101 for (4) *carrier sorting*. These charges can be cut further by about half a cent if ZIP + 4 nine-digit coding is used.

Special Bulk Rate—A category for Not-For-Profit groups and political committees.

Bulk mail requires that your mailing be a general notice rather than a personal message directed at one particular individual. So you cannot use it to mail handwritten notes to your current clients. However, the definition suits direct-mail programs very well since a general message to the prospects is exactly what you will be doing. Bulk mail can also be used for sending catalogs, brochures, etc.

The requirements for bulk mailing limit the weight of the mailing piece to one pound, which should be very adequate unless you are sending a huge limited-partnership offering circular. Since it would be inadvisable to send that item in your initial mailing, the weight limitation should not create any problems.

There is an annual fee for bulk third-class mail as well as a onetime assignment fee (to get you your permit number). The annual fee allows you to mail bulk rate for a year at a particular post office (the one where you sign up for the permit). This type of bulk mailing must be brought to the post office and deposited with the appropriate individual in charge of bulk mail. Do not drop it in a mail box. The current annual and onetime setup fees are $60 each, but since rates have been changing fairly often recently, you may want to verify that with your local post office.

All pieces must be identical. Since your packages probably will not weigh more than one ounce, it is unlikely that you will qualify for the 50-pound minimum and you should assume you will need 200 pieces. (200 pieces at one ounce each totals only 12.5 pounds.)

Keep in mind that bulk mail is slower to be delivered than first-class mail, so if time is essential you may want to pay the premium required to mail first class.

You can further reduce your mailing costs in some cases by bar coding the envelopes. This helps the post office sort your mail more rapidly, so it also may get faster delivery. While bar coding might save you another half cent per piece, it really makes your package look like a bulk mailing. If image is important, and you are trying to make your letter look like it was written just for the prospect, bar coding would be a bad idea.

You can pay postage for bulk mailings using a preprinted imprint which indicates your bulk permit number and from which post office it was sent. There are quite a few rules about the type of imprint used as well as where and how large this must appear on your envelope, so do be careful.

You could also run the envelopes through your postage meter at the applicable rate. The meter must indicate that it is a bulk rate when it prints out. You do not need to date the meter impression if it is printed right on the envelope (a big advantage if you meter the mail some time before actually mailing it). But if you use a roll of special tape in the meter and affix the postage that way, a date showing month and year is required (no day).

Tip: Remember that the post office now requires fluorescent ink on all letter-size metered mail. If you do not use fluorescent ink you could lose your meter permit.

Using a postage meter enables you to include a bit of "advertising" in the imprint. You might put a small company logo in the imprint, or perhaps a slogan about the types of investments you market. Since the metered letters do not go through the postal cancellation process, your letters will probably come through looking better (less damage) and perhaps will be delivered a bit faster. But you do have to contend with the metered mail look as compared to the appearance of stamps.

You can get a substantial refund for metered postage affixed but not actually used. If, for example, you run 50 extra envelopes through the meter and then discover that you have run out of names on your list, the post office will give you 90% or more of the value back, if you make the claim within one year of the date on the imprint.

Precanceled stamps are also available for bulk rates (just as stamps are available for regular postage), but the bulk stamps are fairly clearly indicated to be bulk mail. While there is no extra fee to use bulk stamps, you will need postal authorization. Since these are precanceled stamps, fairly tight controls are used to ensure that used stamps are not reused. Your return address must be on this type of mailing.

If you use precanceled stamps for bulk mail, you can mail at a post office other than your own, but certain extra rules and steps apply. It will probably be far easier for you to just mail them at the post office where your return address is located. Figure D-1 illustrates various forms of bulk postage payment.

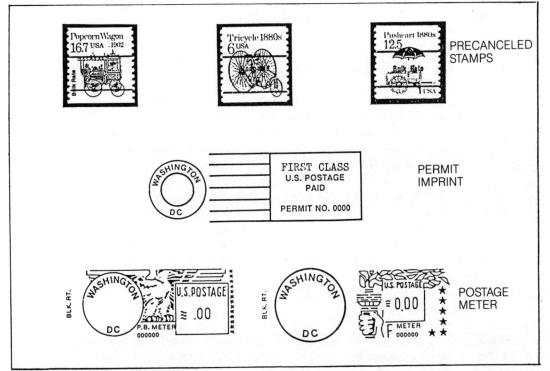

Fig. D-1. Forms of bulk rate postage.

PS Form 3602, July 1988   **FOR ZONE RATED MAIL USE FORM 3605**   **Side A**

U.S. Postal Service **STATEMENT OF MAILING WITH** **PERMIT IMPRINTS**	**MAILER:** Complete all items by typewriter, pen or indelible pencil. Prepare in duplicate if receipt is desired. Check for instructions from your postmaster regarding box labeled ''RCA Offices.''		Permit No.
Post Office of Mailing	Date	Receipt No.	Fed. Agency Subcode	Mailing Statement Sequence No.

Check applicable box	1st Class	1st Class	
☐ *International*	☐ *ZIP+4 Nonpresort* ☐ *ZIP+4 Presort* ☐ *DMM 365 Mailing* ☐ *DMM 366 Mailing*	☐ *ZIP+4 Barcoded* ☐ *Carrier Route* ☐ *Presort First-Class* ☐ *Single Piece*	☐ *Other (Specify)*

Processing Category *(See DMM 128)*

☐ *Letters*   ☐ *Irregular Parcels*

☐ *Flats*   ☐ *Outside Parcels*

☐ *Machinable Parcels*

Weight of a single piece			Mailing Identification Code:		
__ . __ __ __ __ __ lbs.					
TOTAL IN MAILING			**NUMBER OF**		
Pieces	Pounds	Sacks	Trays	Pallets	Other Containers

Name and Address of Permit Holder *(Include ZIP Code)*   Telephone No.

POSTAGE COMPUTATION

Piece Rates			No. Qual. Pieces	Rate Per Piece $	Postage
	1.	ZIP+4 Barcoded	No. Qual. Pieces	Rate Per Piece $	Postage
	2.	ZIP+4 Presort	No. Qual. Pieces	Rate Per Piece $	Postage
	3.	Presort First Class	No. Qual. Pieces	Rate Per Piece $	Postage
	4.	ZIP+4 Nonpresort	No. Qual. Pieces	Rate Per Piece $	Postage
	5.	Carrier Route	No. Qual. Pieces	Rate Per Piece $	Postage
	6.	Rate Category	No. of Pieces	Rate Per Piece $	Postage
	7.	SUBTOTAL (1 through 6) ▶			Postage

Name and Address of Individual or Organization for which mailing is prepared *(If other than permit holder)*

Name and Address of Mailing Agent *(If other than permit holder)*

8. Additional Postage Payment *(State reasons for additional postage payment under ''Comments'' below)*	No. of Pieces	Rate/Piece $	Postage
9. **TOTAL POSTAGE** *(7 plus 8)* where applicable ————————————▶			Total Postage $

The submission of a false, fictitious or fraudulent statement may result in imprisonment of up to 5 years and a fine of up to $10,000. (18 U.S.C. 1001) In addition, a civil penalty of up to $5,000 and an additional assessment of twice the amount falsely claimed may be imposed. (31 U.S.C. 3802)

I hereby certify that all information furnished on this form is accurate and truthful, and that this material presented qualifies for the rates of postage claimed.

Signature of Permit Holder or Agent *(Both principal and agent are liable for any postage deficiency incurred)*   Telephone No.

I CERTIFY that this mailing has been inspected to verify that it qualifies for the rate of postage being paid, and that it is properly prepared (and presorted where required) and that the statement of mailing has been verified and the necessary fee has been paid.

Signature of Weigher   Time

Round Stamp Required

Comments:

PS Form 3602, July 1988   **FINANCIAL DOCUMENT — FORWARD TO FINANCE OFFICE**

Fig. D-2. Zone rated mail use form.

PS Form 3602, July 1988   **FOR ZONE RATED MAIL USE FORM 3605**   Side B

_ U.S. Postal Service **STATEMENT OF MAILING WITH PERMIT IMPRINTS**	**MAILER:** Complete all items by typewriter, pen or indelible pencil. Prepare in duplicate if receipt is desired. Check for instructions from your postmaster regarding box labeled "RCA Offices."		Permit No.	
Post Office of Mailing	Date	Receipt No.	Fed. Agency Subcode	Mailing Statement Sequence No.

Check applicable box	3rd Class	4th Class
☐ *International*	☐ *Carrier Route* ☐ *Basic ZIP+4* ☐ *5-Digit ZIP+4* ☐ *ZIP+4 Barcoded* ☐ *5-Digit* ☐ *Basic* ☐ *Single Piece*	☐ *Library Rate* ☐ *Special 4th Class Single Piece* ☐ *Presort Special 4th Class*

Processing Category *(See DMM 128)*		Weight of a single piece			Mailing Identification Code:	
☐ *Letters*	☐ *Irregular Parcels*	__ . __ __ __ lbs.				
☐ *Flats*	☐ *Outside Parcels*	**TOTAL IN MAILING**		**NUMBER OF**		
☐ *Machinable Parcels*		Pieces	Pounds	Sacks	Trays	Pallets	Other Containers

Name and Address of Permit Holder *(Include ZIP Code)*	Telephone No.			POSTAGE COMPUTATION			
		Pound Rate	1. Pound Rate Postage Charge	No. Pounds	Rate/Pound $	Postage	
			2. ZIP+4 Barcoded	No. Qual. Pieces	Rate Per Piece $	Postage	
			3. 5-digit ZIP+4	No. Qual. Pieces	Rate Per Piece $	Postage	
☐ Check if nonprofit under DMM 623*			4. Basic ZIP+4	No. Qual. Pieces	Rate Per Piece $	Postage	
Name and Address of Individual or Organization for which mailing is prepared *(If other than permit holder)*		Piece Rates	5. Carrier Route	No. Qual. Pieces	Rate Per Piece $	Postage	
			6. 5-digit	No. Qual. Pieces	Rate Per Piece $	Postage	
			7. Basic	No. Qual. Pieces	Rate Per Piece $	Postage	
☐ Check if nonprofit under DMM 623*			8. Rate Category	No. of Pieces	Rate Per Piece $	Postage	
Name and Address of Mailing Agent *(If other than permit holder)*			9. **SUBTOTAL (1 through 8)** ▶			Postage	

10. Additional Postage Payment *(State reasons for additional postage payment on reverse side under "Comments")* ☐ See reverse side	No. of Pieces	Rate/Piece $	Postage

11. ☐ Check if applicable third-class bulk piece rate is affixed to each piece. *(Form 3602-PC required)*

12. **TOTAL POSTAGE** *(9 plus 10)* where applicable ————————————▶	Total Postage $

* The signature of a nonprofit mailer certifies that: (1) The mailing does not violate section 623.5 DMM; and (2) Only the mailer's matter is being mailed; and (3) This is not a cooperative mailing with other persons or organizations that are not entitled to special bulk mailing privileges; and (4) This mailing has not been undertaken by the mailer on behalf of or produced for another person or organization that is not entitled to special bulk mailing privileges.

The submission of a false, fictitious or fraudulent statement may result in imprisonment of up to 5 years and a fine of up to $10,000. (18 U.S.C. 1001) In addition, a civil penalty of up to $5,000 and an additional assessment of twice the amount falsely claimed may be imposed. (31 U.S.C. 3802)

I hereby certify that all information furnished on this form is accurate and truthful, and that this material presented qualifies for the rates of postage claimed.

Signature of Permit Holder or Agent *(Both principal and agent are liable for any postage deficiency incurred)*		Telephone No.	
			Round Stamp (Required)
	Time	A.M. P.M.	

PS Form 3602, July 1988   *U.S. Government Printing Office: 1988-219-694   **FINANCIAL DOCUMENT — FORWARD TO FINANCE OFFICE**

Fig. D-2. Continued.

Fig. D-3. Typical bulk rate sack label.

For each bulk mailing you must submit a statement of mailing on Form 3602, available at the post office. The particular type of statement will depend upon the type of bulk imprint you are using. Figure D-2 is one form of a Statement of Mailing.

The post office will also expect you to package your bulk mailing according to specific rules. All addresses must face the same way, each bundle should not be thicker than four inches, and the bundles should be held together with rubber bands. If you do not follow these instructions the post office may charge you more than the minimum bulk rate.

The basic presort rate applies if there are 10 or more pieces to the same 5-digit ZIP code (the additional four ZIP + 4 numbers do not have to be the same). These should be packaged together and the top letter marked with a special sticker indicating "D." After combining all the five-digit ZIP codes you possibly can, package additional letters according to their first three digits (same first three digits). Packages containing three-digit matches should be coded with a special sticker on the top letter indicating "3."

For those letters that do not fit the five- or three-digit packaging, sort by state. For each 10 or more pieces to the same state, package and affix a label indicating "S" on the top letter.

Finally, for those pieces that did not get into any of the previous packages, odd letters of less than 10 per state, bundle those so there are at least two states represented. These are coded with an "MS" sticker. Any pieces that somehow did not qualify for any of these categories, less than 10 pieces for a single state, for example, get additional packaging—check with the post office.

The packages, in turn, are sacked by type of packages and labeled according to their destination. Typically, a sack will require at least 125 pieces or 15 pounds. A sack cannot weigh more than 70 pounds. Again the weight will probably not be a factor for you.

A label on the sack should indicate where the mail is going, what it contains, and from where it was mailed. Figure D-3 illustrates a typical bulk mail sack label.

Fourth-Class (Parcel Post) Mail. Parcel post is used for packages which do not include any first-class letters and which weigh at least one pound. The weight limit is usually 40 pounds and 84 inches in length and girth combined.

Rates are determined by weight and distance sent. The current range begins at $1.63 for local delivery of two pounds or less.

Bulk Rate Fourth-Class Mail. Items qualifying for fourth-class mail can be sent under special bulk rates if the mailing consists of 300 or more pieces, all of identical weight. Pieces must be sorted by parcel post zone (distance). Note that fourth-class bulk rate requires 300 pieces while third-class bulk rate has a basic threshold of only 200 pieces.

Bound Printed Matter Fourth-Class Mail. Advertising and promotional materials may be sent at a special rate. These items must contain imprinted sheets and may not be personal in nature. The mailers must indicate "Bound Printed Matter" on or at the mailing permit.

Special Fourth-Class Mail. For books of at least 24 pages, 22 of which are printed, consisting entirely of reading matter, this rate applies. If you need to send a prospectus, only, to a large number of clients, this might be useful. The statement "Special Fourth-Class Rate" must be on the address side of each package. The delivery process will be fairly slow on these, perhaps as long as bulk mail.

Special Fourth-Class Presort Mail. If you sort a fourth-class mailing by ZIP codes and meet minimum quantity requirements, you can qualify for this rate. One level of discount requires at least 500 pieces, another requires 2000 identical pieces.

Appendix E
Recommended Reading

IF YOU ARE interested in further information about marketing, there are many publications and other books on the subject and related matters. This appendix lists some reading materials that financial services salespeople might find useful in developing their knowledge of marketing.

There are many organizations that are involved with and support marketing activities, the Direct Mail Marketing Association being a prominent one. You may want to join some of these groups to further your marketing knowledge and skills.

Books and Manuals on Marketing and Related Matters

Mass, Jane. *Better Brochures, Catalogs & Mailing Pieces*. St. Martin's Press: 1981.
DMMA Direct Marketing Manual.
Direct Mail/Marketing Association, New York, NY.
DMMA Fact Book On Direct Response Marketing.
Direct Mail/Marketing Association, New York, NY.
U.S. Postal Service. *Domestic Mail Manual*. U.S. Government Printing Office, Wash. DC.
Fundamentals of Direct Mail Marketing
American Management Associations, New York, NY.
Ross, Maxwell. *How to Work With Mailing Lists*. New York: Direct Mail/Marketing Association.
Ross, Maxwell. *How to Write Successful Direct Mail Letter Copy*. New York: Direct Mail/ Marketing Association.
The Law and Direct Marketing. New York, NY: Direct Mail/Marketing Association.
U.S. Postal Service. *Mailer's Guide*. Wash. DC: U.S. Government Printing Office.

Mailer's Guide to Postal Regulations. Chicago, IL: Crain Books.

U.S. Postal Service. *National ZIP Code Directory*. Wash. DC: U.S. Government Printing Office, (Annual).

Veck, John D. and Maguire, John T. *Planning & Creating Better Direct Mail*. McGraw-Hill, 1961.

Stone, Bob. *Successful Direct Marketing Methods*. Chicago, Il: Crain Books, 1986.

Novich, Martin. *Success On The Line*. New York: AMACOM Division of American Management Association, 1989.

Magazines and Newsletters on Marketing and Related Matters

ATCMU Newsletter
Associated Third Class Mail Users
Advertising Age
Crain Communications
Direct Mail List Rates & Data
Standard Rate & Data Service, Inc.
Direct Marketing Magazine
Hoke Communications, Inc.
DMMA Direct Marketing Journal
Direct Mail/Marketing Association
Memo To Mailers
U.S. Postal Service
Zip Magazine
North American Publishing Company

Index